forged in fire

ESSAYS BY IDAHO WRITERS

Mary Clearman Blew
Phil Druker

EDITORS

Library of Congress Cataloging-in-Publication Data

Forged in fire : essays by Idaho writers / edited by Mary Clearman Blew and Phil Druker.
    p.   cm.
  ISBN 0-8061-3678-2 (pbk. : alk. paper)
    1. American literature—Idaho—History and criticism. 2. Authors, American—
Homes and haunts—Idaho. 3. Idaho—Intellectual life. 4. American essays—Idaho.
5. Idaho—In literature. 6. Fire in literature. 7. Authorship. I. Blew, Mary Clearman,
1939— II. Druker, Phil.

PS283.I2F87 2005
814'.608036—dc22

                                                                    2004063796

A book sponsored by the Idaho Humanities Council

The following essays originally appeared in the following publications: "The Ashes of
August" by Kim Barnes (*Georgia Review,* Summer 2000); "What I Know of Fire" by
Robert Coker Johnson (*Gettysburg Review,* Winter 1995); "Rendering Gold by Fire
with a Master" by Steve Koehler (*Idaho Connections,* Internet version, Spring 2002);
and parts of "Jumping from the Frying Pan" by Holly A. Akenson have appeared at
various times in the *Lewiston Morning Tribune.*

Cover and interior design by A. E. Grey
Cover photo courtesy of Fotosearch

1   2   3   4   5   6   7   8   9   10

FOR RICK ARDINGER AND THE
IDAHO HUMANITIES COUNCIL

with thanks for their continuing support

Contents

FORGED IN FIRE

Introduction

Mary Clearman Blew

After the publication of *Written on Water: Essays on Idaho Rivers* by the University of Idaho Press, I was pleased with the book's success but had no thought of compiling another anthology. One afternoon in the spring of 2002, however, I was working in my campus office when Phil Druker, whose office is just down the hall from mine, stuck his head in to tell me that he had happened to bump into his old friend Ivar Nelson, director of the press.

"I jokingly said to Ivar, 'So you've brought out an anthology on water. What's next? Anthologies on earth, air, and fire?' And I'm afraid Ivar took me seriously, because he said, 'That's a great idea!'"

I laughed and shook my head. The more Phil and I talked, however, the more intrigued we became with the idea of a collection of essays on fire. To our friends, we must have seemed a bit obsessed that spring, because whenever we got together, we'd be reminding each other about historical fires—the terrible Big Burn in north Idaho in 1910, for example, in which at least eighty-five people died, or the 1949 Mann Gulch fire in Montana, which was memorialized by Norman Maclean in his classic *Young Men and Fire.* We knew of two prize-winning essays about fire in Idaho—Kim Barnes' "The Ashes

of August," and Robert Coker Johnson's "What I Know of Fire"—
which could form the core of an anthology, and surely we could
find more.

When we advertised for submissions, Phil and I both were surprised
at the quantity and quality of the work that poured in.
Screening these essays was our first major task, as we searched for
literary quality and for variety. We were heartened to find
that, along with work by writers we knew well, we had received
many fine pieces by beginning writers. Given that we live in
a state such as Idaho, whose hotshot crews are renowned, and
where wildfires light the ridges and thicken the skies with smoke
nearly every summer, it is natural that many of the essays
described firsthand experience on the fire lines. We soon found
that, for example, we could have assembled an entire anthology
on firefighting.

The nature of fire, however, touches a much wider range of
experience than firefighting alone, and while, after
lengthy deliberation, we selected wonderful essays like Jenny
Emery Davidson's "Holding the Line," Robert McCarl's
"Black Butte Jump," and Lori Messenger's "Ignition," which draw
upon direct experience with shovels and pulaskis and parachutes
and dirt and sweltering heat, we also sought essays that
illuminated other ways in which fire affects our lives. As Horace
Axtell notes, "fire is so dangerous sometimes. You got to be
careful how you use it. You got to respect it. Accidents happen so
quick," as illustrated in Robert Coker Johnson's account of the
trash fire that put a three year old in a hospital burn unit for
months and months, or by Karen Seashore's haunting memory of a
tragic house fire in "All Wild Orange."

To choose to live in the midst of Idaho's scenic beauty is to
choose to live with risk, as Kim Barnes shows in "The Ashes of
August." How much risk is acceptable, asks Lois Melina as
she remembers, in "Wild Places," taking her children camping
during fire season. In "Waiting," Diane Josephy Peavey
describes the tension that all ranchers experience as they wait for

lightning strikes and try to protect their livestock. Writing about another kind of risk, Peter Chilson compares a western fire season with African seasons of dust storms and revolution. In "Jumping from the Frying Pan," Holly Akenson dramatically recreates the fine line between living through wildfire and dying in it.

But fire is not only a threat; it is also a condition for life. How to keep a family warm during a Boise winter? In "Trash Burner," Susan Glave recalls the stolen Presto-Logs her mother burned. In "Warmed Twice," William Johnson meditates on the old wood-burning stove that provided a heart, or *focus*, for his family. Claire Davis writes of how shared memories of fire link her and her sister. For Paula Coomer in "The Good Red Road," building a campfire is at once an assertion of independence and a longing for the past.

Fire can have unexpected virtues. DiAnne Iverglynne, in "Reading the Glow," explains how she connects herself with countless generations of potters when she fires a primitive kiln on the banks of the Snake River. William Studebaker remembers the fire at the town dump in Salmon, Idaho, and Steve Koehler recalls the comic, insightful semester he spent smelting gold by an antique method in a University of Idaho lab. For Jeff Jones, a boy's fascination with firecrackers becomes a way to measure his maturing and understanding. Finally, Phil Druker provides a funny essay about his own mishaps with fire and with the woman he remembers as "Strawberry Blonde."

Earth, air, water, and fire: the four ancient elements which the Greeks believed made up the total of creation. It is little wonder that fire continues to grip our imaginations. Fire warms us, frightens us, entertains us—and Phil and I hope that these essays will warm, frighten, and entertain other readers as much as they have us.

Postcript

The closing of a press is always a cause for grief, and the closing of the University of Idaho Press, a few days after the proofs for *Forged in Fire* were submitted, was particularly saddening for the anthology's editors and contributors. We thank John Drayton, director of the University of Oklahoma Press, Chuck Rankin, editor-in-chief, and the acquisitions editor, Karen Wieder, for recognizing the qualities of *Forged in Fire* and bringing it to completion. We also thank the former director of the University of Idaho Press, Ivar Nelson, for his faith in the anthology, and especially we are grateful to former managing director Candace Akins for her editorial work and to former designer Amy Grey, whose hours of unpaid labor, truly above and beyond the call of duty, brought the proofs for *Forged in Fire* to completion.

Jumping from the Frying Pan

Holly A. Akenson

My husband, Jim, and I stood on the rock platform of the old
fire lookout with our student interns, taking in the big view
of the surrounding Frank Church–River of No Return Wilderness.
In all directions, mountain peaks punctured the sky. On this
blue-sky August day in the year 2000, we counted six mushroom
clouds of smoke rising from forest fires.

To the west was the Burgdorf Fire that would eventually grow to
80,000 acres. To the northwest rose the Flossie Fire, another
80,000-acre blaze that threatened a guard station. The smoke
column rising to the north was the Three Bears Fire, a 12,000-acre
fire on the breaks of the Salmon River. Forest Service river
rangers warned rafting parties to watch out for burning logs that
rolled down the steep canyon slopes into the river. To the east
loomed the Clear Creek Fire in the Bighorn Crags. The Clear
Creek Fire cut off access to and from the wilderness from the east
and would eventually encompass 150,000 acres. To the south were
the Pistol Creek Fire and the Stibnite Fire.

As we were about to leave, we noticed small tendrils of smoke
spiraling up from Diamond Point, twenty miles up Big Creek
from our home at Taylor Ranch. The previous week, the fire was
five acres; now it was 1,400 acres, but still small compared to

other fires in the area. We photographed "our" fire before making the 4,000-foot descent from the old lookout to our wilderness home.

Jim and I have been managers and scientists at the University of Idaho's Taylor Ranch Wilderness Research Station for fourteen years, training students, studying wildlife, developing programs, and upgrading facilities. Taylor Ranch is a place where research is conducted and students go to learn, but even as recently as 1996 we had no electricity and no telephone—only a few solar panels, propane lights, and a backcountry radio for communication. Now, we have a micro hydroelectric system to provide power for lights, a computer, and a satellite phone. But we still use mules for riding the wilderness trails; packing research equipment; and working in harness to mow hay and transport supplies, once even to pull an airplane out of a snowbank. Previously a guest ranch, facilities include five log cabins, two frame cabins, and five outbuildings. The sixty-five-acre property is surrounded by wilderness.

Taylor Ranch is the most remote year-round residence in the lower forty-eight states. Cessna 206s operated by experienced backcountry pilots provide our primary access with a thirty-minute flight from Cascade, McCall, Salmon, or Challis. The airplane approach in the narrow Big Creek canyon can be exhilarating or nauseating, depending on one's frame of mind. The airstrip is primitive, a ribbon of grass along Big Creek that also serves as mule pasture and hayfield. For those adverse to aerial adventures, the thirty-two-mile hike from the Big Creek Trailhead makes a better alternative.

Winter and spring are quiet times in the Idaho backcountry. We savor the beauty of the wilderness landscape and abundant wildlife, and find our lives entwined with the rhythms of the natural world. This is the time of year when Jim and I do our research on wolves and cougars, working from tent camps as we track the carnivores. During the summer, however, Taylor Ranch has a constant flow of students, research crews, and visitors coming and going weekly. We enjoy the busy season, teaching college students about wildlife and wilderness skills and interacting with visitors.

With the summer of 2000 winding down, and the wildfires growing, we cancelled several groups of visitors due to smoke filling the canyons and fires closing wilderness access. We called in planes from Salmon to fly out a hiking group when the trail was blocked by fire. We hosted the Root Ranch crew and twenty-three horses and mules overnight when they trailed out their stock fifty-two miles to safety at their base station at the Flying B Ranch; then we put up the Idaho Wilderness Company outfitters and their stock a few nights later as they headed out of the wilderness.

On the night of August 10, we watched a spectacular dry lightning display. During that storm a strike on Rush Point started a single tree on fire, five miles from Taylor Ranch. The next day, Jim and I decided to test the Taylor Ranch fire equipment. The students helped us lay out fire hoses, practice with the fire pump, and set up sprinklers around all of the cabins.

Wildfire was not something Jim and I were unfamiliar with. Before coming to Taylor Ranch we both worked for the Forest Service. We had been trained in firefighting and had each worked on a few large fires. Several fires had burned near Taylor Ranch since we had been living here, and we had coordinated fire activities with the Forest Service. In 1988 the 100,000-acre Golden Fire had roared up the ridge across from Taylor Ranch. When we saw the huge mushroom cloud of the Golden Fire building above the ridgetop, we had called the Forest Service on the backcountry radio. The ranger tried to convince us that the fire was six miles away—they had checked it that morning by spotter plane. A few minutes later we saw flames on the ridge and made a second call to the ranger. With sudden urgency in his voice, the ranger offered to send in a helicopter immediately to evacuate us. We were not ready to leave

Taylor Ranch, so a crew of smokejumpers was scheduled to arrive in the morning to help us. That night we locked the horses and mules in the corral in case we needed to make a quick departure. We wrote up a list of valuables to pack on the mules if we had to ride upstream to escape the fire. The next morning the smokejumpers flew over but could not jump as the wind was too strong and gusty. Finally they were able to arrive by airplane. For two weeks the firefighters worked out of Taylor Ranch, at first setting backfires, later monitoring the fire. The steep grassy slope down to Taylor Ranch acted as a firebreak and the Golden Fire never came closer, but we had learned about fire behavior firsthand.

Smoke settled in the drainage like fog on August 12, delaying the plane that was to fly the students out on the last day of their summer at Taylor Ranch. Finally, in the afternoon the wind blew the smoke out of the canyon and our backcountry pilot, Ray Arnold, was able to the fly the students out past the fire.
By evening we could see the fire from Taylor Ranch; it was moving downhill and toward us. We watched large flames engulf the ridgeline four miles upwind from us. Earlier, we had spotted a borate bomber airplane circling the fire and thought the Forest Service was dropping fire retardant on the leading edge to keep the fire from spreading toward Taylor Ranch, but when Jim called our ranger, Fred Dauber, he said the retardant was being dumped on an abandoned lookout. Jim told Fred that we needed firefighters at Taylor Ranch immediately, but the ranger said it was too late in the day to mobilize a crew. Later Fred confessed to us that the Forest Service fire model predictions indicated he had three days to get firefighters to Taylor Ranch.

We couldn't take our eyes from the flames. With the strong prevailing winds out of the west, it was clear that the fire would soon hit Taylor Ranch. At 7:30 P.M. we radioed Arnold Aviation. "Can you make a flight into Taylor Ranch right away? We need to fly out a load of valuables before the fire gets here."

Carol Arnold diverted Ray from another flight and he arrived fifteen minutes later. During those fifteen minutes, Jim and I decided what was most important to save; piled files, cameras, and photo albums in boxes; mantied guns, archery, and camping equipment in canvas as though we were going on a camping trip; and hauled saddles to the airplane. We stopped bringing gear to the plane when no room was left inside. As Ray flew off at dusk with 1,000 pounds of university and personal belongings, I wondered aloud whether I should have kept the video camera to document what would happen next. Still, it was a relief to know that some of our possessions were safe.

August 13 started out quietly. The smoke hung so close that we could not even see the barn, a hundred yards away. The ranger told us he planned to have twelve smokejumpers parachute to Taylor Ranch, but with the thick layer of smoke obscuring the terrain, the jumpers had to wait on standby in McCall.

Jim and I were full of nervous energy. We couldn't tell what the fire was doing, but felt we had to keep busy. I got out the pruners and the orchard saw and vigorously nipped every lilac, wild rose, and mountain ash shrub from around our log cabin, and dragged the branches to the orchard so there would be no fuel ladder to bring the forest fire to our house. Jim used the chainsaw to cut a firebreak through the riparian shrubs along the airstrip. The heavy smoke-laden air was oppressive, both physically and emotionally, and we found breathing difficult while working so hard.

At 2:45 the wind picked up and the smoke cleared. Now we could see a huge mushroom cloud boiling up on the north side of Rush Point. A wall of flames flared up on a ridgeline just a mile and a half west of us. We made a hasty call to the Forest Service. They were already trying to get the smokejumpers in, but just as in 1988, the fire was creating winds that were too strong and gusty for jumping. The smokejumper plane circled overhead, then returned to its base in McCall so the firefighters could transfer into a helicopter for a second trip. Jim's last words to the fire boss were, "The fire is moving fast; we may not be able to wait for the jumpers."

With the dull roar of the fire as background noise, Jim and I discussed our situation and weighed our options. Should we stay put and fight the fire, or should we leave with our mules? Was the pasture a safe place to hunker down under our hand-me-down fire shelters? Should we turn the mules out on the grassy slopes where there was not a lot of fuel? Should we submerge ourselves and our golden retriever, Mica, in Big Creek and lead the mules into the stream? Would there be enough oxygen to breathe when the fire came over us? Would we burn to death? We knew that the consequences of underestimating the risks of this fire could be fatal.

We decided we had to leave.

Going to work quickly, we saddled our four mules and one horse; riding saddles on our two most reliable mules, packsaddles for the other three animals. While Jim brought the canvas pannier bags and manty tarps to pack our loads, I gathered the few belongings we would take: the laptop computer, our daily journal, the ground-to-air radio, camera, wallets, and jackets. I couldn't forget the Civil War vintage canteen from the 1879 Sheepeater Indian Campaign on Big Creek. Plus, I still needed to round up sleeping bags, a camp stove, and food. I opened the trap door to the dirt-floored basement and went down the hewn log staircase to select the food we would take.

Suddenly Jim's voice interrupted my thoughts. "Come on! We have to go NOW!" he shouted. Startled, I grabbed a box of crackers and bounded up the stairs.

Once outside I saw why Jim was so excited. The air crackled with the sound of a freight train roaring right for us. The sky overhead and to the west was shrouded in black smoke. I stuffed our supplies into the pannier bags while Jim ran to the backcountry radio and tried to reach Arnold Aviation. No one answered.

Finally he raised Yellowpine Bar on the Main Salmon River. "The fire is here!" he said breathlessly. "We are leaving with our stock and headed for the Flying B. Please let everyone know."

Jim took a hasty look around the cabin. There was Yap, our decrepit eighteen-year-old cat, curled up on a rug and sleeping blissfully. He decided to leave him where he was; Yap probably couldn't escape the fire even if he was outside. We grabbed the pannier bags and hooked the loads on to Rocky's packsaddle. The canvas tarps were still laid out in the yard unused; we didn't have time to pack the other animals. We leaped into our saddles and turned the mules.

"Wait, should we turn on the fire pump?" I asked. Jim jumped down from Daisy, raced back to the cabin, and pulled the starter rope on the pump. He anchored the nozzle to spray water directly on our cabin.

We called to Mica to come and rode toward the Big Creek trail. Jim and I looked back at our cabin. A wisp of smoke curled just fifty yards above the cabin; another one twisted up along the airstrip. I pulled my camera from the saddlebag and took a few last pictures of our home. When I snapped the photos, I inadvertently dropped my pack mule's lead rope. I jumped down from the saddle and rushed to grab the rope, but sensing my excitement, Penny trotted away and began grazing. I yelled at her when I couldn't catch her; the roar of the fire and wind and the sight of flames racing up the hillsides fueled my sense of urgency. Mules are social animals and she would have followed us, but I was mad at myself for losing my temper. I took a deep breath, calmly walked up to Penny, and easily picked up her halter rope. We were off.

We craned our necks and turned in our saddles to look behind us as we rode from Taylor Ranch. We couldn't believe what we were seeing. The Diamond Point Fire had overtaken the fire that started on Rush Point, creating a tremendous fury. A wall of flames surged over the ridge above the airstrip. The leading edge of the fire was catching up to the spot fires we had seen above our cabin only minutes before. Flames suddenly appeared on Horse Mountain on the north side of Big Creek and raced up the steep rocky slope. As we watched in disbelief, fire materialized on the grassy basin of Cliff Creek above us, more than half a mile from the flaming Horse Mountain hillside. Instantly Cliff Creek became an angry orange and black bowl of fire. We were encircled in an arc of fire.

We rode past the automated weather station. The anemometer was spinning furiously as a stiff wind out of the east blew in our faces. "At least the wind has changed direction and will slow down the fire," I commented, and then realized the fire had created this wind as the searing heat in the rising mushroom cloud of smoke caused fresh air to be sucked into the base of the fire.

Just before we rode around the bend in the trail, we took a long, last look at the orange inferno engulfing our home. We devised an emergency plan as we rode: if the fire caught us we would ride the mules into one of the deep holes in Big Creek and submerge ourselves and Mica. If we had time we would unbridle and disconnect the lead ropes on the horse and the mules and let them fend for themselves. We continued to glance back, but the fire was no longer on our heels.

At Dunce Creek, four miles downstream, we heard a helicopter behind us. We were grateful, depressed, scared all at once. I pulled the ground-to-air radio from my saddlebag and tried to contact the helicopter but received no reply. Chunks of ash fell from the sky like giant snowflakes.

At 5:30 we crossed the bridge over the Middle Fork of the Salmon River and had to decide whether to spend the night at Waterfall Creek or continue on. The twenty-two-mile trip to the Flying B, our nearest neighbors, takes seven hours, and we had been riding two hours so far. Jim and I both had a lot of adrenaline in our systems and couldn't imagine just sitting around waiting for dark. It was easier to keep traveling, so we continued on.

The Middle Fork trail, like the Big Creek trail, was a narrow rocky path carved into the steep slopes and rock slides of the river canyon. Groups of rafters drifted down the current below us, looking relaxed and peaceful as they waved to us, an absolute contrast to the events we had just been through.

At nightfall we were hailed by a rafting party camped at Wilson Creek. Although eager to keep moving, we stopped to chat. Before we realized it, our story of the fire came bubbling out of us as we sat in our saddles with a throng of vacationers gathered around, their eyes wide open in amazement. Former Idaho governor Cecil Andrus was one of the guests. Andrus had coordinated a National Guard project using helicopters and an engineering battalion to transport and assemble a log cabin laboratory at Taylor Ranch ten years before. We told him we thought all the buildings had burned. Brian, the head river guide, invited us to stay with their group. We wavered. With concerned looks on their faces, the guests pleaded with us to have some dinner and spend the night. We agreed, and immediately the tension from our day of fire drained away. It was okay to stop running now; we could relax.

Smoke was thick in the Middle Fork canyon when we arose and hobbled the mules to graze. The early risers gathered to say good-bye and offer us spare clothing. Embarrassed by our need, we smiled and declined their offers.

On the trail again, we saw two riders approaching. At a wide spot we moved our mules off the trail to allow the riders to pass, but it was Mike and Scott, from the Flying B, who had come to meet us. They told us that many of our backcountry friends had called on their radios to express concern and had left their radios on late into the night in hopes of hearing that we were safe. After they heard we were evacuating, the Flying B crew had stayed up until 1 A.M., waiting for us to arrive. Ranch foreman Rick Dorony had slept in the tack shed so he could help us unsaddle our mules in the middle of the night. We felt honored by the compassion of our backcountry community.

Mike said that six cabins had been reported burned at Taylor Ranch. We were devastated. We certainly must have lost all five of the historic log cabins. We had lost the facilities, lost our home and belongings, and essentially lost the ability to do our jobs managing the University of Idaho's wilderness research station. Tears welled in my eyes, and I cried as we rode the trail along the river to the Flying B. What would we do with our lives now? At the Flying B, we called Arnold Aviation on the backcountry radio to spread the word that we were safe. We were elated to learn that only three buildings had burned, and none were the historic cabins. So we still had jobs and a life in the wilderness.

Later, we learned that the helicopter we had heard above Dunce Creek had been on its way to Taylor Ranch with five smokejumpers. The wall of flames had already swept over the ranch, leaving a thick layer of smoke that cut visibility for the helicopter pilot, but somehow he managed to land and off-load the smokejumpers and their gear. Both the cookhouse and bunkhouse had been on fire; the propane tank on the cookhouse was shooting a ten-foot flame out of the relief valve. It was too late to salvage those cabins, but the jumpers knew they could limit the damage to other buildings. One of them gassed up the fire pump we had left running and hosed down the blaze within feet of our cabin and full woodshed. The firefighters quickly doused flames at the tack shed and lit a backburn to remove flammable vegetation around the log laboratory.

We settled in at the Flying B guest ranch but planned to head home with the mules as soon as we could. Our plans to return to Taylor Ranch didn't work out, however, because the Diamond Point Fire was burning along the Big Creek trail below Taylor Ranch. Furthermore, all four trails out of the wilderness from the Flying B were closed or threatened by fire. The Flying B crew loaned us clothes to wear while we washed ours, and we continued to wait.

During the afternoon of August 14, a smoke cloud blossomed in the V of sky up Brush Creek to the west. Several new lightning fires had started nine miles from the Flying B on the divide between Big Creek and the Middle Fork. After our experience at Taylor Ranch, we urged Rick to get started on fire prevention. Rick didn't need much urging, so eight of us began cutting brush from around cabins.

On the morning of the 15th, the air was thick with smoke once again. The Forest Service wilderness staff made an unprecedented decision to close the Middle Fork of the Salmon River to recreational activities. Flying B guests and rafting parties flew out of the wilderness. By afternoon two large mushroom clouds from the Short Creek and Shellrock Fires billowed to the north and west. Our crew continued cutting brush and connected fire hoses to hydrants.

The next two mornings Jim and I saddled the mules and prepared to return home, but each day we made a phone call over the backcountry radio to the Forest Service and found out that night infrared photos showed active fire along the trail between the Flying B and the Taylor Ranch. In the afternoon the fires flared up and grew, and smoke in the canyon limited flying access. So we were not going anywhere.

Each night at dinner the conversation turned to what the fires would do. Most of us believed that the fire would eventually burn down to the Flying B, but we were confident we would be able to control the damage with our brush removal and our fire hose setups. Hope, the storekeeper, was fearful about the fire. Meanwhile, the Shellrock Fire was moving closer every day. Two Forest Service firefighters who had flown in were oddly silent on emergency planning. Their role was structure protection, not safety for civilians, so Jim and I helped Rick develop plans for firefighting and emergency escape. Rick called a ranch meeting to explain the details, and everyone was assigned a firefighting duty and a safety zone to go to in an emergency.

Not everyone was happy with the plan. Vickie, the cook, wanted to run the backcountry radio in the lodge, rather than taking refuge in the alfalfa field by the airstrip with Hope and me, but Rick was adamant that Vickie and Hope would not be able to run to the river fast enough in an emergency. I was not happy about the plan, either, as I had expected to be involved with firefighting, but Vickie's challenge had tested Rick's leadership, and I didn't want to erode his respect in front of his employees.

Long before daylight on the 18th, Rick rode his horse toward the forest fire at the head of Brush Creek to find the missing Root Ranch horses and mules that had been turned out to graze a week before. He brought nine of the twelve back to the corral. Meanwhile general manager Bill Guth flew to the Flying B and offered to fly anyone out who did not want to stay. Even Hope said she wanted to stay to help prepare for the fire. Jim made arrangements for Chris McDaniel, one of our students, to fly in to help clear the trail to Taylor Ranch. Jim, Rick, and Chris packed our mules with Forest Service hoses, pumps, and equipment, then transported rafting gear to the Flying B airstrip when dense smoke blocked out the airplane approach to the public airstrip. Constant airplane flights shuttled the last of the rafters from the wilderness.

Ominous mushroom clouds of smoke developed that afternoon: to the northwest was the Short Creek Fire; to the west was the Shellrock Fire. Our brush-clearing crew turned on the sprinklers and began hosing down cabins. The Middle Fork fire lookout radioed the Flying B to report that the Shellrock Fire was six miles from us and coming our way rapidly. He called it "a fire of biblical proportions."

The sky to the west turned orange; the time had come to initiate our firefighting plan. Our fire crew, made up of two Forest Service firefighters, ten Flying B and Root Ranch employees, and three of us from University of Idaho, took our positions. Some would use drip torches to set backfires. Others would man the fire hose stations or protect the hay barn. Vickie grabbed a few jugs of water and got her three dogs; Hope brought her dog; and I loaded up some tarps. We squeezed into the truck with the animals. I tried to drive slowly out to the field, but my heart was pounding.

The flames of the Short Creek Fire rippled and danced on the long ridgeline to the northwest. To the southwest, angry smoke clouds from the Shellrock Fire crowded the sky. I parked the truck in the center of the lush alfalfa field, facing the fires, and within ten minutes, we saw flames on the hillside just beyond the fence line. We jumped out of the truck. With dogs and gear, we moved as far from the truck as possible, twenty yards from the Middle Fork in case we needed to get to the river quickly. The fifty-five head of Flying B horses and mules shared the field with us. Alarmed by the flames, they galloped around the field. We jumped up and spooked them away from our area so we wouldn't be trampled, then watered down our tarps and huddled under them.

Suddenly fire engulfed the grassy hillsides all around us. A hot blast of wind from the south flattened us to the ground as the Short Creek and Shellrock Fires merged and roared up the east side of the Middle Fork. As the firestorm passed over us, the giant mushroom cloud of smoke blocked out the sun. It was afternoon but completely dark except for orange flames that glowed in all directions. Our silhouettes were backlit by fire, but we couldn't make out each other's faces. I fumbled with the ground-to-air radio to turn it on. We overheard two pilots. "I sure wouldn't want to be down there right now," said one.

I pushed the transmit button and shouted over the wind, "We ARE down here!"

"Is it hot down there? Can you breathe okay?" said a concerned voice.

"There's a strong wind, so we can breathe all right," I shouted back.

I felt mesmerized, watching the fires burning on the hillsides around us and blazing along the river, but as the sky began to lighten I looked toward the Flying B. A large orange aura emanated from the Flying B compound, shooting light high into the sky. Alarmed, I thought of Jim. Was he all right? Could anyone have survived the fire that created that radiating glow?

Then we heard the sound of the four-wheeler and saw Rick drive around the corner. I ran to meet him, searching his face for clues. He said that everyone was accounted for except one firefighter and that Jim had gone to look for him. I rode with Rick back to the buildings to help fight fire.

The devastation at the Flying B was incredible. I glanced around as we hurried through the compound to meet up with Jim. The firestorm wind had caused most of the damage. The propane shed had collapsed and wisps of smoke swirled from the still-smoldering firewood in the roofless woodshed. Branches and lawn furniture were strewn about the lodge lawn; electric wires and radio antennas lay on the ground. A roof had blown off an old log cabin, revealing the original sod roof that one of the early settlers had put on a hundred years ago. The hay barn was gone, and only a glowing pile of radiant heat remained of 3,600 bales of hay. Crumpled hunks of metal barn roofing glistened from the depths of the clear water of the Middle Fork and littered pastures up to half a mile away. I saw dead ravens, pelted from the trees by the firestorm wind. Many of the fire hoses had burned up. A Douglas fir tree had fallen on one cabin and smashed in the roof. The cabin we had been staying in had burned to the ground.

I spotted Jim spraying down the hydro shed and ran over and hugged him. I was so glad to see that he was all right and to be with him.

From Jim I learned what had happened after I had gone to the field. The sky overhead and to the west was dominated by boiling orange and black clouds as the fire swept down the slope toward the Flying B. The freight train sound roared in Jim's ears, even louder than on Big Creek. Jim realized he had not cut the fence along the river to allow the mules to escape, so he raced to the pasture. Cricket, our smartest mule, watched him cut through the strands of barbwire. Just as she stepped through the gap, the wind ripped a section of corrugated metal roofing loose from the barn. The screeching of metal on metal spooked the other mules and horse, and they galloped down the field away from the barn. Cricket spun and sprinted after them. Jim could hear them, but it was too dark to see them.

He turned, saw embers ignite the hay in the pole barn, and ran to help throw buckets of water on the stack, but it was futile. The barn was an inferno. Joanne dropped her bucket and ran for the river. Marian dashed from the radio in the lodge to the river.

Jim ran to the shop to leash Mica and Rick's dog and get them to the river. He turned the doorknob and pushed against the door— it wouldn't open. The fire-caused winds had created a negative pressure inside the shop. Rick and Scott arrived and helped force open the door with their shoulders. By now there was no way to get to the river, and as they ducked inside, the wind's intensity increased. Debris pelted the shop, sounding like a hurricane.

When the wind subsided, Jim, Rick, and Scott stepped outside to find that the woodshed, filled with fifteen cords of firewood, was on fire; all that remained of the roof was a tangled heap of metal on the ground. Nearby, the propane shed had collapsed and scattered twelve propane tanks like bowling pins. The men jumped into action, grabbing hoses, but another huge burst of wind roared down the hillside, and again they retreated to the shelter of the shop. When the wind died down, they ran back outside to hose down the woodshed fire and stomp out embers near the propane tanks.

The firestorm wind hit the suspension bridge that crossed the Middle Fork of the Salmon River, yanking it from the slots in the footing, straining its giant eyebolts, and whipping the bridge into the air like a sheet on a clothesline. Decking lumber was flung into the air. When the wind released its grip, the bridge slammed down, buckling its twelve-inch I beams into a W like an accordion. Joanne and Marian, who were under the bridge when it buckled, drifted down the river to safety, although their eyelids were burned by the scorching heat from shrubs ignited along the riverbank.

Chris was going to help one of the firefighters do a backburn, but as their drip torches touched the dry grass and flames sprang up, the wind shifted and blew the flames back on them. Sheer athletic ability and adrenaline powered them as they vaulted over two 6-foot fences. The firestorm wind propelled the men down the road in a cloud of gritty sand and blew them into a hawthorn shrub. Mountain mahogany trees, uprooted like tumbleweeds, were hurled against Chris and Mike, as lumber shards from the barn impaled the ground around them like darts.

Jim found the missing firefighter, Doug, still at his firefighting post, desperately trying to get the water pump cleared of debris. When the firestorm hit, Doug had jumped into the four-foot-deep reservoir we had created in the stream for the fire pump. He stayed submerged to protect himself from the searing heat, as flames consumed the trees and shrubs surrounding the little reservoir.

We had little time to talk as ground fires were still threatening the buildings. Everyone found tasks. Jim pulled an expanded five-gallon can of diesel fuel away from the burning hay. Others sprayed buildings with the remaining fire hoses that had not burned or ran the chainsaw and moved burning logs away from the buildings. I grabbed a fire extinguisher and put out a fire on the corner of a cabin roof. Twice I extinguished fires that burned along the rubber hose between the water pump and its fuel tank. Acrid smoke filled the air. Our eyes watered and we had trouble breathing, but we covered our mouths with handkerchiefs and for an hour and a half worked to save the remaining buildings.

I set up a portable backcountry radio and notified Bill Guth about the firestorm damage. In the evening a Forest Service helicopter landed and flew one of the firefighters out to have the second-degree burns on the backs of his ears treated. Rick had an eye injury but didn't want to fly out, so I located a patch and ointment in the first aid kit and doctored his eye. Jim checked on our stock and found they had escaped the flying debris from the barn by running through the fence. Penny was limping and had many lacerations on her chest from blasting through the barbwire. I treated her cuts, but she was still quivering eight hours after the event.

When we gathered for dinner we finally had time to listen to everyone's fire story. We talked late into the night, fueled by the adrenaline that was still surging in our blood. After hearing the harrowing stories, we asked ourselves again, "How could we all have survived?"

The firestorm had moved with amazing speed. It had swept over the Flying B less than an hour after we had heard that it was six miles away. The fire had been clocked at seven miles in twenty-two minutes; that's almost twenty miles an hour, but we had watched it move even faster than that, and estimated that the winds could have been a hundred miles an hour. We were all fortunate and blessed to be alive.

As Jim and I retired to our new cabin with Mica, I took a last look around before going inside. Thousands of little fires glowed on the hillsides in all directions. I wanted to remember forever what this wildfire looked like and felt like.

By morning our excitement had worn off. The heavy smoke layer matched the deep depression that settled over our crew. Our eyes were red and sore, and we were coughing from so much exposure to smoke. We wandered the smoky landscape, taking in the shadowy black remnants that had been living trees and shrubs just the day before, trying to comprehend what had happened around us.

Jim discovered a severely burned fawn lying in the ashes in agony. There was no way to save it, so Jim had to put her down with his pistol. We found dead animals, including a burned bear cub and numerous birds and squirrels, blown to the ground by the firestorm wind. George found a young saw-whet owl, alive, but listless. I knew if the owl could recover from the fire, then we too would be on our way to emotional recovery, and I was determined to rehabilitate it. Rick and I traded shifts, giving it water with a medicine dropper, but at noon when I went to check, it was dead. I had put too much faith in that owl pulling us out of our depression. Now we really felt hopeless.

We spent several days moving debris, piling windblown branches, collecting roofing and lumber scattered across the lawns and fields, clearing ash from the water lines, and sifting through the burned cabin debris looking for Jim's wallet. It was routine work, mindless, and we worked without joy or enthusiasm. Our nerves were shot and everyone was touchy. Squabbles broke out among the crew. We struggled to improve our outlook, but it was difficult when all around us were the ruins of the Flying B and a charred landscape. Mica injured her leg while swimming to retrieve a stick, so I scheduled a flight to take her to our veterinarian for surgery.

The Diamond Point Fire was no longer active along the Middle Fork and Big Creek trails—it had merged with the other fires and swept past by now. At first light we loaded the mules for the trip back to Taylor Ranch, and Jim and Chris forded the river with the stock. The trail was less hazardous than Jim expected, and even the fireproof foil wrap on the bridge didn't deter Jim's riding mule, Daisy. They reported that riding up Big Creek was ghostly; burned trees and logs still smoldered and flared on the other side of the creek. Heat radiated from a burning snag near the trail.

It was hard for me to say good-bye to our firefighting crew; we shared so many powerful memories. As I flew out of the smoke of the Middle Fork with Mica, I was surprised by the dazzling colors of the blue sky and green hillsides carpeted with living trees. It was a jolt from a new reality: everyone else does not live in a blackened, burned landscape. I had been living under that smoke cloud for too long.

After Mica's surgery, I was eager to return home. On the flight in, we flew for miles over the burned expanse. The 149,000-acre fire had burned a thirty-mile section of Big Creek before extending across the Middle Fork. All the areas we knew so well were burned. From the air, Taylor Ranch shined like a bright green oasis surrounded by monochrome patterns of blacks and grays.

For Jim, the first view of Taylor Ranch was not as bad as he had expected. The entrance gate was burned, but the log cabins still dotted the forested edge of the green pasture. A bear meandered past the hay barn. The cookhouse and bunkhouse were charred skeletons, but the tack shed was undamaged. Most amazing was the blackened landscape surrounding Taylor Ranch: forest, riparian shrubs, grasslands, and cliffs all had burned.

When Jim showed me the burned cabins, I was amazed by how close the fire had come to several of the cabins that did not burn. The forested slope behind our cabin was severely burned; the Douglas fir forest with its tangle of ninebark shrubs was transformed into a steep slope of rocks and charred black spires. Dense deciduous vegetation along the streams was converted to a naked expanse of ash. Gnarled remnants of shrubs jutted from the ground. Wind had carried the fire across the bunchgrass slopes, burning each and every bunchgrass clump down to its roots. The scorching heat of the windblown flames had even killed the sparse scattering of mountain mahogany trees growing on the cliffs. But we were particularly shocked when we hiked to Sagebrush Flat. Not a single sagebrush remained. The plants had been completely incinerated; red circles of ash from the intense heat were the only indications that plants had grown there at all. The flat looked like an asphalt parking lot.

The unburned oasis at Taylor Ranch attracted wildlife. Two does with twin fawns fed and bedded in our yard without concern. A snowshoe hare moved into the thicket by the house. A few days after arriving home, I spotted a loose pile of grass alongside the airstrip—a cougar's way of covering its kill. I walked over to investigate and was taken aback by the sight of two deer heads sticking out of the pile. I pulled the grass away and exposed the carcasses of a half-eaten doe and a fawn. When I returned to check for the cougar the next day, a female bear and two cubs were feeding on the deer. Within a couple weeks, Jim and I had radio collared several bears, and we continue to monitor those bears along with cougars, wolves, elk, and deer to see how they adapt to the fire-changed environment. We enjoyed our oasis, but whenever we hiked from Taylor Ranch we faced the bleak landscape the fire had left around our home. The burned river bottom was an eerie moonscape; it gave me a prickly feeling. My boots sank deep into the ash as I examined ancient miners' campsites and bighorn sheep skulls, previously hidden by vegetation.

Friends tried to comfort us by reassuring that fire is a natural process and healthy for the environment. Intellectually I agreed, but in my heart I couldn't help but focus on the destruction, and I was angry that my friends could so blithely suggest that this change to our environment was all positive. They didn't have to live in a blackened landscape like we did. I tried repeating the mantra, "Fire is good," as I explored the burn, but I just felt melancholy.

Now, whenever I travel away from the Big Creek canyon, the sight of rolling mountains carpeted in green still amazes me, and I wonder how my views on other things—politics, government, nature, and relationships with people—have been altered by my life in the wilderness.

I wonder, too, how the experience of the big fire of the summer of 2000 has changed me. Facing the danger was exhilarating and challenging, but being in a position of need—of food and clothing—was difficult. I feel a close kinship with the folks at the Flying B and recognize how much, even here in this vast wilderness, we count on our friends and neighbors.

I still work to reconcile my belief that fire is a beneficial part of the natural environment and my sense of loss when I gaze at the burned landscape. I find the altered landscape fascinating, but not beautiful. Instead, I have learned to focus on the elements that do contain beauty, such as the new shoots erupting from the earth, fed by the living roots of a burned tree, and the flowering plants I have never seen before, like the frilly-leaved "golden smoke." Where did it come from? Elk and deer are healthy and increasing in numbers, feeding on the flush of new vegetation. Lewis's woodpecker young, safe in their nests excavated in dead cottonwood trees, clamor for food. In this monochrome environment, colors become vibrant: the perky yellow balsamroot framing Taylor Ranch in the spring, the fragrant pearly blooms of syringa on the rocky hillsides in summer, the peach and red and yellow hues of hawthorn and Rocky Mountain maple and cottonwood growing along Big Creek in fall, and the clumps of enormous white snowberries in winter. Ash from the fire provides nourishment for all.

It Begins with Fire

Horace Axtell and Margo Aragon

Horace, a Nez Perce elder, spiritual leader, translator, and author, and I frequently collaborate on writing projects. We look forward to discussing Nez Perce culture and community with anyone who is interested. As in most native communities, there are topics that are more inaccessible than others. We didn't realize that fire would be one of them.

Fire is an important element among traditional believers of walásat *or* ipnúuncililpt, *also known as Seven Drums. Walásat is more a way of life than a religion, but its practitioners believe in a Creator, the Earth as Mother, and the power and sanctity of Nature.*

During our interview sessions, Horace and I found it difficult to find experiences about fire that were appropriate for the written page. That is not to say there aren't lots of memories of fire. There are plenty of old stories and contemporary experiences that include smoke and flame. However, there is a vast difference in Nimíipuu/Nez Perce culture between talking about a thing and writing about it. The results of one's written words may live far longer than the words were intended to live. The telling of an event, even if it occurred generations ago, can still invoke an essence so potent that it may alter contemporary practice. Writing about instances of where and when smoke and fire occur may make us responsible for what transpires after the words are read.

Deciding what not to write is as important as deciding what can be written. Horace and I realize that this concept greatly differs from contemporary American writing, but there is much about Nimíipuu/Nez Perce culture that differs from contemporary American living. For this reason, so much of what transpires with smoke and fire in the land of the Nimíipuu must remain unwritten. Perhaps this abbreviated essay is the ideal metaphor for an elemental act that occurs quickly, catches our attention, and yet, in spite of our best analysis, remains elusive. ——M.A.

'atamaal means the month of fire. It's the second month. I think that's the only month that has anything to do with fire. The rest of them have to do with weather and fish and a lot of things like that. I remember that I heard how they used fire to heat rocks, especially for the sweat house. The mud bath, they used to use for cleansing. Many times they had to heat rocks. They heated rocks for baking roots in the ground and also they baked meat. I remember eating bear meat that they baked in the ground along with different kinds of roots.

The kind of rocks they used was the rock you get on the hillside. They don't break up or pop. I guess people could get hurt trying to heat river rocks, 'cause they're the ones that explode. They pop pretty hard. I've seen them pop. Then when you dip them into cold water they don't break as quickly as any other kind of rock.

Back when people didn't have any tools, like an axe or a saw, Indians made their tipi poles. They didn't exactly cut down live trees. They always got the dead ones. When they grow in a thicket they sometimes get undernourished, I guess, and some of them just fall over, roots and all. So these are the ones they used to drag out of the woods. This is what I heard: they would measure their poles and then burn the ends off. After a tree's been burned, you can rub it on a rock to make it a little sharp. That's how they sharpened their poles so they'd stick in the ground better. They never tried to make poles out of green ones. They wouldn't burn. So they never really made tipi poles out of green wood. But nowadays we can do that.

My grand aunt, I used to watch her cook. Just on an open fire. You'd be surprised how the old people could make bread. The

word for that was *cepéletpiin 'ipaax*. The translation is like "picture."
Picture: *cepéletpet*. So we used to call it "picture bread." They made
them round, like a loaf, but only flatter. They put it in a frying
pan and leaned the frying pan by the fire and put a stick back
here to hold it so it would have an angle. Just leave it there. When
they got one side browned, they'd take the stick off and turn it
over, turn the bread over, and then do the other side. And keep
turning it like that and it come out just beautiful. My grandma
used to make those in the mountains. I used to really like that.
And then she could also make pies out there like that. Same way.
To cook it on the bottom, she'd hold the frying pan over so it
would get brown from the bottom, too.

Take sticks, kind of curvy sticks, and sharpen both ends. Poke one
end into the ground and put your meat or fish or whatever you're
cooking onto these sticks and just hold them by the fire. Keep
turning them. There's a few people who do that, yet. Especially for
eels. That's really a good way to cook them. 'Cause as the eel is
cooking, all that oil, it just kind of runs out on the ground. I've
tasted eels like that. They taste so good.

Also, I used to watch Grandmother smoke hides. Like the buckskin.
When they finish curing a buckskin, it comes out pure white. So
in order to make it a tan color, you have to smoke it. Have you ever
smelled buckskin? It smells so good. I'm so fortunate. I still got a
piece of that, yet. Smoked buckskin. I like the smell of that.

I used to watch Grandma also, when we got heating in the house with
fire, in the stove. There was another stove that she used to call a
cooking stove. A lot of the older people, yet, still remember some of
these things. The wood in a kitchen stove had to be made a little bit
smaller so it would burn better. They used that to heat up the
cooking stove and I remember having to split that kind of wood up
for that. And, of course, the heating stove could take a little bit bigger
pieces. But the wood had to be dried. You can't use wet wood and
expect it to burn. So that takes a lot of preparation. To get ready for
the winter, we had to make enough wood to last, just in case. If it got
colder you'd have to build a little hotter fire. I remember my grandma

was so . . . I don't know how to explain her. She could sleep and then all of a sudden we'd hear her get up and put a little more wood in the fire in the middle of the night when it was cold. And I could feel that heat in the morning when we got up. Grandma'd wake us up and already have a big fire going downstairs. She used to make us do different things to prepare, like chopping wood. She showed us how to do all that. Every night we'd take turns making what we call shavings. We'd take a butcher knife. She had a big knife, almost like a machete, not quite as long. I don't know where she got that, but we used to use that to make shavings with. We had to make a pile for the kitchen stove and a pile for the heating stove, because we never had papers like we do now. We used to use matches. Grandma used to get matches all the time. *tuhuuc.* That's what you call the old matches, *tuhuuc.* It's just what they called it. I guess most of the time you brush it on something to strike it. It's an action I guess. And it lights up.

That's why I say fire is so dangerous sometimes. You got to be careful how you use it. You got to respect it. Accidents happen so quick.

That's why I'm pretty cautious with fire. I always worry about it. And I know how bad a burn on your hand or someplace hurts. It hurts for a long time. I'm always careful with fire.

The word for Mother Earth is *pika wetes. Nuunim pika wetes,* our Mother Earth. And wind is *hatya. Hatya.* And *ala* is fire. Earth, wind, and fire. And *kuus.* To us, here, I think *kuus* is our leader. 'Cause without water, we don't live. Mother Earth is our caretaker. We get our nutrients, our food. We compare that with a mother who feeds us when we're babies, from her body. So Mother Earth feeds us in the same sense, all her life.

The important thing to remember is that we, as Nimíipuu, connect ourselves to Nature for our way of life. That takes in a lot of territory. Like all the animals around here. And the ones that give us food and the ones that live in the water that give us food. Mother Earth gives us food from the ground, the mountains, the streams. When Nature does something, it takes care of itself. It's just the way a person believes, I think.

The Ashes of August

Kim Barnes

Late summer light comes to Idaho's Clearwater Canyon in a
wash of color so sweet it's palatable: butterscotch and toffee,
caramel and honey. It is as though the high fields of wheat, the
darker ravines tangled with blackberry, sumac, and poison
ivy, the riverbanks bedded in basalt and shadowed by cottonwood
and locust—all have drawn from the arid soil the last threaded
rindles of moisture and spun them to gold. By four o'clock,
the thermometer outside my kitchen window will read 105°. In
another three hours, a hot whip of wind, and then those few
moments when the wheat beards and brittle leaves, even the river,
are gilded in alpenglow. Often my children call me to the window,
and even as we watch, the soft brilliance darkens to sepia. But
soon there will be the moon, illuminating the bridge that seems to
levitate above the pearlescent river. Some nights my family and I
spread our blankets on the deck and lie uncovered to trace the
stars, to witness the Perseids of August—the shower of meteors so
intense we exhaust ourselves pointing and counting, then fall
asleep while the sky above us sparks and flares.

Other nights there is no moon or stars, only clouds gathering in
the south and the air so close we labor to breathe. "Storm
coming," my daughter announces, and we wait for the stillness to
give way, for the wind we'll hear first as it pushes across the prairie

and down the draws, bringing with it the grit of harvest. Bolts etch the sky, hit the ridges all around us; the thunder cracks above our heads. Perhaps the crop-saving rain will come, or the hail, leaving our garden shredded and bruised. Sometimes, there is nothing but the lightning and thunder, the gale bending the yellow pines to impossible angles, one tree so old and seemingly wise to wind that we watch it as the miners once watched their caged canaries: should the pine ever break, we may do well to seek concrete shelter.

These are the times we huddle together on the couch, mesmerized and alarmed. We know that the storm will pass and that we will find ourselves to have again survived. We know, too, that somewhere around us, the lightning-struck forests have begun to burn; by morning, the canyon will be nearly unseeable, the sunset a smoky vermilion.

The West, Wallace Stegner so famously noted, is defined by its aridity, and this stretch of north Idaho canyon land where I live is no exception. The Clearwater River is the reason for the numerous settlements along its reach as well as those of its tributaries. Logging, mining, agriculture: all are dependent on the presence and ways of water. Fire, too, defines this land, and at no time more so than in the month of August, when the early rains of spring have given way to weeks of no measurable precipitation, when the sweet blossoms of syringa and chokecherry have shriveled and fallen, when wild plums hang blistered with ferment. We must go high into the mountains where the snowpack held longest to find huckleberries, our belt-strung buckets banging our legs, our mouths and fingers stained black, and we go prepared to defend ourselves against two things: the bears who share our fondness for fruit, and fire. Our bear defense is little more than loud conversation and an occasional glance toward the perimeters of our patch. For fire, we carry in our pickup a shovel and a water-worthy bucket. If called upon to do so, we could hope to dig a fire line, or drown a few flames if lucky enough to be near a creek or spring.

Born and raised within a fifty-mile radius of where I now live, I
have memories of late summer that are infused with fire. As a child
growing up in the logging camps of the Clearwater National Forest,
I knew August meant that my father would rise at two a.m. to work
the dew-damp hours before noon, when a machine-struck spark
could set the wilderness ablaze. But no one could mandate the
hours ruled by lightning, and with the lightning came the fires—as
many as fifty or sixty from one storm—and with the fires came the
pleas for volunteers to man the pulaskis, buckets, and bulldozers.
Often, the loggers were not asked so much as pressed into
service, ordered from their sites and sent to the front lines still
wearing their calked boots and pants cut short to avoid snags.

Like my father, my uncles had taken up the life of the
lumberjack. Our communal camp was a circle of small wooden
trailers, out of which each morning my cousins came, still in
their pajamas, rubbing the sleep from their eyes. I remember my
mother and aunts in those weeks of searing high-altitude
heat, how they rose with their husbands and made their biscuits
and pies so that the wood-fueled stove might cool before
dawn, then loaded a pillowcase with sandwiches, fried pies, jugs of
iced tea and Kool-Aid that would chill in the creek. Somewhere
just over the ridge the men battled to keep the fires at bay,
while my cousins and I explored the cool recesses of the stream
bed, searching for mussels whose halves spread out like angel
wings, prying the translucent periwinkles from their casings to be
stabbed onto hooks that would catch the trout we'd have for
supper. My sensory memories of those afternoons—the sun on
my shoulders, the icy water at my knees, the incense of pine
and camas, the image of my mother and aunts lounging with the
straps of their swimsuits pulled down, the brush of skin
against skin as my cousins sifted the water beside me in their
quest for gold—are forever linked with my awareness of the
smoke rising in columns only a few miles away and the drone of
planes overhead, belly-heavy with retardant, the smell of
something dangerous that caused us to lift our faces to the breeze
as it shifted. When the men returned they were red-eyed and
weary, smudged with pitch and ash, smelling like coals from the

furnace. I watched them drink tumbler after tumbler of iced tea, wondering at the dangers they faced, and thought that I might want to be like them and come home a fighter and a hero.

As a child raised in the woods, I gained my awareness and wariness of fire by way of the stories told by my elders as they sat around the table after dinner, picking their teeth with broom straw, pouring another cup of the stout coffee kept warm atop the cookstove. New fires brought stories of old ones, and so August was full of fire, both distant and near, burning the night horizon, burning the edges of my dreams.

There was the fire of 1910, the one most often remembered by those old enough to have witnessed its destruction, their stories retold by the generations who have sat and listened and seen with their own eyes the scars left across the land. That year, July had come and gone with only .05 inches of rain. Thunderstorms had started spot fires throughout the Clearwater National Forest; the Forest Service and its small force of men, working with little more than shovels and picks, could not hope to suppress so much flame. And then came August, "ominous, sinister, and threatening," according to Forest Service worker Clarence B. Swim's account of that summer in Cohen and Miller's, *The Big Burn.* "Dire catastrophe seemed to permeate the very atmosphere. Through the first weeks of August, the sun rose a coppery red ball and passed overhead . . . as if announcing impending disaster. The air felt close, oppressive, and explosive."

"Ten days of clear summer weather," the old-timers say, "and the forest will burn." No rains came, and the many small fires that crews had been battling for days grew stronger and joined and began a run that would last for weeks. It swept up and down and across the Clearwater drainages: the Lochsa, Warm Springs Creek, Kelly Creek, Hemlock Creek, Cayuse Creek—the Idaho sky was black with ash. One Forest Service veteran, Ralph S. Space, whose written history of the Clearwater Forest contains

lively anecdotal recollections, remembers smoke so thick that, as a
nine-year-old boy rising to another day of no rain, he could
look directly into the sun without hurting his eyes. The chickens,
he said, never left their roost.

On 21 August 1910, the wind began to blow, picking up velocity as
the sun crested, until the bull pine and white fir swayed and
snapped, and the dust rose up from the dirt roads and fields to
join the smoke in a dervish of soot and cinder. Men along the
fires' perimeters were told to run, get out, it was no use. Some
took to the creeks and rivers, pulling their hysterical horses along
with them. (One legend tells of a panicked horse breaking away
and racing the fire some fifty miles east to Superior, Montana—
and making it.) Others fled northward, subsisting on grouse whose
feathers were too burnt for them to fly.

As in any war, many who fought the fires came away scarred, some
bearing the marks like badges of courage while others, whose less-
than-brave actions in the face of disaster had earned them the
coward's stripes, hid themselves in the backrooms of saloons or
simply disappeared. One man, part of a group sent to fight the
blaze near Avery, Idaho, was so undone by the blistering heat and
hurricane roar of the approaching fire that he deserted, pulled his
pistol, and shot himself—the only casualty to beset his crew.

One of the heroes was a man named Edward Pulaski. When he
found himself and the forty-three men he led cut off from escape,
he ordered them into the nearby War Eagle mine, believing the
large tunnel their only hope for survival. As the heat rose and the
fire ate its way closer, several of the men panicked and threatened
to run. Pulaski drew his pistol and forced the men to lie belly
down, faces to the ground, where the coolest air would gather. He
hung blankets across the tunnel's entrance, dampening them with
what water he could, until he fainted. By the time the flames had
passed around them, sucking the oxygen from the cavern,
replacing it with a scorching, unbreathable wind, five were dead
from suffocation. Another man who had chosen to run before
Pulaski could stop him was found a short distance away: the rescue

party had stepped over him on the way in, thinking the blackened mass a burned log; only on their return trip did they recognize the charred body for what it was. Pulaski had stood strong in the face of events "such as sear the souls of lesser men," declared the Washington, DC, *Star*. He would go on to become even more famous for his invention bearing his name, the pulaski—a combination shovel, ax, and mattock that since has become standard equipment for fighters of wildfire.

Pulaski's story is just one of many that come from that time of unimaginable conflagration. For three days and nights the wind howled up the canyons and down the draws, taking the fire with it. The ash, caught by updraft and high current, traveled for thousands of miles before falling in places that most Idahoans had only heard of: in Saskatchewan, Denver, and New York, the air was thick with the detritus of western larch and hemlock; in San Francisco, ships dropped anchor outside the bay and waited for days, unable to sight land through the blue-gray smoke that had drifted south and descended upon the city. Norman Maclean wrote that in his home town of Missoula, "the street lights had to be turned on in the middle of the afternoon, and curled ashes brushed softly against the lamps as if snow were falling heavily in the heat of August." The "Big Blowup," they call it now, or the "Big Burn"—not one large fire, but 1,736 smaller ones that had come together across the Clearwater Region. By the time it was over, three million acres and many small towns across Idaho and Montana lay in ruins; at least eighty-five people, most of them firefighters, were dead.

The Big Blowup of 1910 was not the last August fire to rage across the Clearwater: 1914, 1919, 1929, 1934—major fires every five to ten years. The fire of 1919 is synonymous in my mind with the North Fork of the Clearwater, where I spent much of my childhood, for it is there, in the middle of the turquoise river, that a small rise of land bears the name Survivor Island. I remember how, aware of its legendary significance, I studied the island each time we passed along the dusty road, how the heart-flutter of danger and adventure filled my chest. What written history I can find records how two packers and their packstrings, two Nez Perce, and several wild animals had found safety from the fire by swimming to the island. But the story I remember has only three characters: an Indian grandfather, his grandson, and a black bear, all secure upon the island as the fire raged by, the winds it generated whipping the water into whitecaps. At some point, the story became embellished with a detail I still can't shake— how the child, emboldened by the success of their escape, wanted to kill the bear, and how the grandfather would not let him. Perhaps the elder understood the mythical ties he and his charge would forever have to that bear; perhaps he believed that nothing else should die in the face of the carnage that surrounded them.

With each year's August, I feel the familiar expectation that comes with the heat and powder-dry dust boiling up from behind the cars and logging trucks. Expectation, anticipation, sometimes fear of what lies just over the horizon—August is a month of waiting for storm, for fire, for rain, for the season to change and pull us away from our gardens, our open windows and doors, back to the contained warmth of the hearth and the bed that comforts us.

Yet some part of me loves the suspense of August, the hot breath of morning whispering the possibility of high drama, the calm and complacency of dog-day afternoons giving way to evening thunderheads brewing along the ridge. Something's afoot, something's about to happen, and I shiver with the sureness of it.

Years when I have lived in town, surrounded by asphalt, concrete, and brick, there was little to fear from the dance of electricity lighting the sky except the loss of electricity itself. Here in the country, on the south-facing slope of the Clearwater Canyon, what surrounds us is something as volatile and menacing as the tinder-dry forest: miles of waist-high grass and thistle the color and texture of straw. Just such desiccated vegetation fueled the flames that killed the men made famous by Norman Maclean's book *Young Men and Fire* (1992), the story of the tragic 1949 Mann Gulch blaze.

We have no rural fire district here; those of us who have chosen to call this small settlement home know that should a wildfire come our way, we have only our wits to protect us—that and every available gunnysack, shovel, hoe, and tractor the community can provide. All through the summer we watch from our windows as the sun leeches the green from the hills and the color from the sky, and the land takes on a pale translucence. Come August, we have counted the days since no rain, and we know that somewhere a storm is building, perhaps just to the south where the horizontal plane of the Camas Prairie intersects the vertical thrust of the Seven Devils—the mountains whose peaks rise jagged and white through the brown haze of harvest.

We check our flashlights, our candle supply; we fill our bathtubs with water. There will be wind, which will switch the sumac and send the sagebrush busting across the gravel roads; it will tear the limbs from the trees, drop them across the power lines in some part of the county so remote that the service crew will take hours, sometimes days, to locate and repair them. Then comes the lightning, blasting the tops from the tallest pines, striking the poles that carry our phone and electricity. The lights will flicker, then fail; the air conditioner will moan into silence. Pumps that pull the water from the springs will lapse into stillness; our toilets and faucets will gurgle and go dry. If we're lucky, what passes over us will be nothing more than the black raft of storm clouds, and the seconds we count between lightning and thunder will never fall below five. But there have been times when the bolt and jarring crack have come simultaneously, and we have known, then, that the lightning has touched somewhere near us, and that we must watch more carefully now and smell the air and be ready to fight or to run.

The summer of 1998, on just such an evening, we sat at the dinner table with my in-laws, who had arrived from Illinois for a weeklong visit. My husband, Bob, and I had each kept an eye on the clouds mushrooming behind Angel Ridge; to my Midwestern relatives, the oppressive humidity seemed nothing unusual, but to us, accustomed to zero percent air moisture, the too-still air signaled a weather change. When I stepped out on to the deck, I could hear the wind coming, huffing its way up the canyon like a steam engine. Within minutes, I was hit with a blast of hot air, then felt the cool come in behind it. The first reverberating boom made the hair stand up on the back of my neck, a response so atavistic I could barely resist the instinctual urge to take shelter. Instead, I raised my face to the wind, redolent with fennel and sage, locust and mullein, the arid incense of a summer's rich dust; along the edges of the breeze, I could smell the dampness of distant rain.

Back at the table, we drank our coffee and shared stories of the past year. I got up once to fill a few pitchers with water. The lightning moved closer—only a few seconds between the flash and thunder—and then a clap so loud and close we all jumped. Not really a clap, not even a boom, but a sharp, ripping roar. Bob and I looked at one another and headed for the porch, and then we could see it: to the west, a narrow column of smoke just beginning to rise. Even as we watched, the column grew thicker, and then we felt the wind gain momentum, pushing east toward us.

The county road, we knew, was our best hope, cutting between us and the fire, providing a fuel-free strip where the flames might falter. Earlier in the summer, Bob had cut, raked, and burned a fire-line around our house, decreasing the chances that fire could reach us, but what we couldn't shield ourselves against were the airborne cinders already beginning to descend.

"It's right behind the Bringman place," Bob said. "If we don't get it stopped, they'll be in trouble."

I had a vague acquaintance with Mr. and Mrs. Bringman, a retired couple who have worked the canyon land for decades. Their house and outbuildings sit a quarter-mile above and to the west of us, in the middle of what was then a good crop of ripe wheat. We had come to know them as we have come to know most of our neighbors: by our happenstance run-ins at the PO. Mr. Bringman is also known for his homemade wine. Local history holds that his land had once belonged to a man of some note who had imported grapevines from France and planted them in the sandy bluffs above the river. "Noble vines," Mr. Bringman pronounced, and we began saving our empty store-bought bottles so that, once a month, he could swing by on his four-wheeler to collect them and drop off a sample of the wine he had put up the past summer, which we dutifully shelved, though he insisted it was quite ready to drink now.

"You get on the phone," Bob said. "I'm going up there." Already the smoke and ash had darkened the sky to a deep shade of gray.

"Wear boots," I said. "Take a wet handkerchief and gloves."

While Bob gathered his gear, I picked up the phone and dialed. Mrs. Bringman's voice came on the line, high-pitched and quavering. "Tell your husband to get here as fast as he can," she said. "Call anyone you can. It's coming our way."

I hung up, then began a series of calls, knowing that for each call I made, two more would go out, word of the lightning strike spreading faster than the fire itself, fanning out across the ridges and high prairie for miles, until every family would be alerted. I knew that every wife and mother would dial the next number down the road, that each man and his oldest sons would don their hats and boots, grab their shovels and buckets and be out the door within minutes, all guided by the pillar of smoke that marked the point of danger as surely as a lighthouse beam.

I paused in my calling long enough to kiss Bob as he hurried out the door. I could see the charge in his eyes, the urgency and excitement, and I felt the regret and longing and resignation I had as a child when the men had gone into the wilderness, to the front where the stories were being made and the dramas played out.

"Remember how fast the fire can move," I said. I had a momentary image of my husband scrabbling across the canyon's steep pitch and felt my heart jerk with fear. "Do you have a lighter?" Bob nodded, remembering, as I remembered, the story of the ranger who survived the Mann Gulch fire.

"Be careful," I cautioned.

"I will," he said, and was gone.

In *Young Men and Fire*, Norman Maclean researches and
describes the 5 August 1949 blaze that caught and killed all but
three of the fifteen Forest Service smoke jumpers who had
parachuted into the Helena National Forest of Montana. They
had been on the ground for less than two hours and were working
their way down a hillside toward the fire—an error that would
cost them dearly, for a fire racing uphill can easily catch even the
fastest man. But what they had found was a simple class C fire, no
more than sixty acres. It was a "ground" fire, one the men
expected to mean hard work but little danger.

Yet there is always danger when a wildfire is present, and so the
crew knew that this one might "crown," as its charred path
suggested it had done already before moving back down into
undergrowth. The fire that has crowned is what creates the great
roar of sound so many survivors describe as the noise of a fast-
moving train descending upon them, so loud that communication
becomes impossible. A crown fire creates its own weather system:
the warmer air rises and the cooler air rushes down to replace it,
creating a "fire whirl," a moving convection that can fill the air
with burning pine cones and limbs, as though the forest itself has
exploded. This incendiary debris gives rise to spot fires that can
flare behind or in front of the fighters; crews find themselves
suddenly surrounded, ringed by fire that seems to have come from
nowhere, sprung up from the ground and converging.

With these conditions comes the possibility of the phenomenon
firefighters most fear: the "blowup." Blowups occur when fresh air
is drawn into the "fire triangle" of flammable material, high
temperature, and oxygen. Few have witnessed a true blowup and
lived to tell of it, but those who have speak with wonder of the fire's
speed. Maclean recounts the experience of fire expert Harry T.

Gisborne, perhaps the first to observe, survive, and describe a blowup. The 1929 fire Gisborne detailed occurred in Glacier National Park and burned ninety thousand acres with almost incomprehensible swiftness, demolishing "over two square miles in possibly two minutes, although probably in a minute flat."

The Mann Gulch smokejumpers were young and had dropped on to a terrain that may have seemed at the time less threatening than the densely wooded ridge in the distance. They were at a point where the tree-studded mountains broke open to grassy plains dried to amber. Perhaps they believed themselves safe amid the loose-rock slope and low-lying vegetation, but they were tragically mistaken. They had their tools—their shovels and pulaskis—but what they did not have was knowledge of the ways of this fire and of how, within an hour, it would cross the gulch and push them screaming up the steep hill, crest at the top, and die there with them. Bunchgrass, cheat grass, some immature pines mixed in with older growth—these were all that was needed to create the blowup that engulfed the men. Two of the three who survived did so by racing the fire to the ridge and winning; the third, the crew's foreman, saved himself by escape of another kind: instead of running, he stopped, struck a match, set fire to the grass at his feet, then stepped into the flames he had created. He lay face down on the still-smoking earth, covered his head with his hands, and waited for the main fire to catch and sweep over him. And it did.

A steeply pitched basalt-strewn slope covered with dry grass and scattered patches of timber—the very terrain into which Bob was headed. I prayed that he would have the foreman's presence of mind should the fire overtake him. I could see the flames themselves now, flaring twenty feet into the sky. I let the screen door swing shut, went back to the phone, and began another call.

The men came in their pickups and stock trucks and cars, on their four-wheelers and tractors—a steady parade passing by our house. Having exhausted my list of numbers, I gave up my station to stand with my children and in-laws where our gravel driveway met the gravel road. We tried to determine what we could of the fire's direction. We waved our support as our neighbors flew by— driving too fast, we thought, though we understood their urgency. On the slope just above us, the Goodes and Grimms and Andersons had set their sprinklers atop their roofs, dampening the embers and sparking ash that floated and fell around us like fireflies in the darkening sky. I'd instructed my ten-year-old daughter and eight-year-old son to stand ready with the hose, knowing that should the power lines go down, our electric pump that drew water from the spring below would be useless; our only defense against the fire would be whatever water remained in the storage tank. But if we used that water for prevention, we would have none left should the fire reach us.

As twilight deepened, the fire's glow grew more distinct along the western horizon, until the last rays of sunlight were indistinguishable from the orange-red aura melding sky to land. My mother-in-law, city raised and only half understanding her son's desire to live in such a wild place, did her best to rein in her fear; my father-in-law, nearing eighty, paced in frustration: he should be out there, offering what help he could. Had it not been for the fire's location along the breaks of the canyon, our ability to keep him clear of the battle would have proved much more difficult.

We all knew the immediate danger Bob and the other men faced— the fire—but there were other concerns I kept to myself. Just down the road from our house is a jut of land named Rattlesnake Point: we kill an average of two diamondbacks per year in our yard; the annual score we spy along the roads and paths outside our property we leave be. In times of fire, every living thing flees from what threatens it—cougar, deer, elk, rabbit, pheasant, field mouse, bear, and rattlesnakes, too, slithering ahead of the heat faster than most could imagine, sometimes smoking from their close brush with death. My hope was that, should Bob encounter a snake, it would be too intent on escape to strike at the legs of a man.

And then there was the terrain itself: fragile shelves of talus, slanted fields of scree. The land could give way beneath your feet, begin moving like a tipped mass of marbles. I have had it happen before, while hunting chukar, and found myself grabbing at the smallest outcroppings of sage and buckbrush, feeling them pull loose in my hands, the only thing below me a chute toward an outcropping of columnar basalt that would launch me into the canyon. I've always been lucky, able to catch a knob of stable rock or wedge my foot into the roots of a stunted hawthorn, but that memory of falling, of gathering momentum, of hurtling toward endless open space, has never left me. I knew that Bob was sure-footed and careful; I knew, too, that in the lapse of light, the ground's definition would fade.

The smoke thickened. We covered our faces with our hands, coughing, our eyes watering, unwilling to abandon our vigil, knowing how much more those closer to the fire were having to endure. I ordered the children back to the house, but they would not go. They wanted to be of some help, perhaps believing, as I did, that our standing guard might somehow keep the fire at bay. The glow had moved higher up the ridge; the flames leapt, receded, then leapt again. With the wind and lack of equipment, we had little hope that simple manpower could contain the fire. I estimated that a half-mile of pasture land separated us from the conflagration—that and the road—and I told myself we could hold our ground for a little while longer before loading the cars with what we most treasured: photographs, books, laptop computer, the children's most precious belongings. The possibility of losing our home and everything in it seemed very real to me, but I considered it with little emotion. What was uppermost in my mind was the safety of my loved ones: the family that gathered closer as the smoke increased, and my husband, somewhere just over the ridge, risking his life to save the nearby houses and barns, the crops and timber, perhaps even an entire small town should the fire run the ridge and drop over into the next draw. At that moment, I wasn't sure the saving was worth the risk. How could I weigh the loss of my husband against nothing more than property and economy? There was little chance that anyone other than the firefighters was in danger—by now, everyone in the county had been warned. Why not stand back, allow the fire to meet the river on one side, the linkage of creeks on the other? In the end, it would burn itself out.

But then I remembered the stories—the fire of 1910, the young men who had died so suddenly by thinking the distance between them and the fire enough—and I realized that this wasn't about the wheat field a mile down the road or the home of the family at the bottom of the draw. It was about fire. It was about crowning and whirls, convection and blowups. It was about August and a summer's long drought. It was about three million acres burned in a matter of days—the width and breadth of many whole states.

What I wished for, then, was the help of all the technology and knowledge such fires of the past had brought into being. The fire of 1910 showed everyone that crews of men scattered about the burning edges would never be enough, and then the Forest Service began its study and transformation of firefighting. But we do not live in a forest; we live on private land, too distant to warrant the protection of the city, too sparsely populated to afford the luxury of a volunteer fire department. That August of 1998, our situation was little different from the one facing the farmers and loggers and townspeople of 1910: our primitive tools had not changed, and at that moment, I began to realize that our chances of saving our home had not, either.

I moved down the driveway, preparing myself to announce that it was time to pack up, to position ourselves by the river where Bob might find us. But then came the roar of something overhead— the thrum and air-beat of a helicopter. I looked up to see what I had believed would not come to us: help from the outside world.

From beneath the helicopter hung a length of cable attached to a large vinyl-and-canvas bucket. The pilot did not head for the fire but for the river, where he hovered and dropped and filled the bucket with nearly one hundred gallons of water—a half ton hoisted up and swinging from the Bell Jet Ranger. As we watched, the helicopter leaned itself toward the fire's furthest point, the bale opened, and a sheet of water rained down.

My daughter and son let loose with whoops of excitement. My in-laws and I clapped and hugged, jubilant at this unexpected turn of events. Again and again, the pilot followed his path from river to fire, until the ribbon of flame along the horizon had dimmed to a faint glow; within an hour, we could no longer point to even the smallest flare.

We stood watch as night came on, unable to see the helicopter now but tracing its direction by the deep hum that drifted to us on the smoky breeze. Although we were safe, rescued by the graces of the Clearwater–Potlatch Timber Protective Association, who had sent the helicopter because they were fighting no fires of their own, we all knew our wait was not over: somewhere in the darkness was our father, son, and husband. The line of vehicles that had sped by us earlier now came in reverse—a slower-moving column whose lights passed over us as we held up our hands in a gesture of greeting and gratitude.

"Bob will be coming soon," I said. "Let's go make him some fresh iced tea."

We walked the few yards back to the house, turned on the porch light. Our jubilation had been replaced by a quiet fear that grew with each passing minute—fear that receded and then leapt up each time another pickup approached but did not slow and turn into our driveway.

"He should be back by now," my father-in-law said, pacing from the window to the door and back again. "Maybe I should go see if I can find him."

I knew that Bob and the other men would have driven off-road and into the fields, gaining what time they could against the fire. Even if we could locate our four-wheel-drive, there was no guarantee Bob would be near it. Without light, the diminishing fire behind him and the total blackness of rural night before him, he could walk for hours before finding his way back to where he had parked.

"I think we should wait," I said. "He'll stay as long as he's needed. Someone will come and get us if there's trouble." I listened to my own words, only half believing. What if Bob had gotten turned around, fallen into a ravine, been isolated and trapped by the fire? What if he were lying somewhere in the dark, injured, unable to save himself?

I thought again of the rough terrain—familiar to me from the many walks Bob and I had taken, the many hours we had spent exploring and visually mapping the area. The fire likely would have eaten its way across Bedrock Canyon, down to the river and up to the top of the ridge, creating acres and acres of charcoal earth, charcoal sky—like a black blizzard. How could we hope to find him?

We made the tea. We gathered and washed the dinner dishes. We distracted the children with books and puzzles until none of us could be distracted any longer. We gathered outside in the cooling air, still heavy with smoke that would hang in the canyon for days.

"Come on, Bob," I whispered to myself. "Come on." I thought of my mother and aunts then, waiting as I waited, fighting the growing panic with the mundane details of daily life. How many hours had they spent watching from the window above the sink, their hands submerged in soapy water, their fingers blindly tracing the knife's edge? How many Augusts had passed in a haze of worry and despair as the lightning came down and the flames rose up and the men disappeared into that place where no one could reach them?

But then, the lights at the top of the driveway, the held breath, the release as the engine idled and died.

I let my daughter and son reach him first, escort him into the house. He was covered with soot, his white T-shirt scorched, burned through in some places; his face was red, nearly blistered beneath the ashy smudges. We hovered around him, offering tea, voicing our concern and sympathy. I stepped up close, breathed in the familiar smell of everything burned—the dead grass and live trees, the cloth on his back, the singed hair.

"I'm so glad you're okay." I wanted to cry—out of relief that he was home, out of anger at the fire, out of frustration that I had found myself caught up in the same cycle that my mother had known so well. I knew that the stories Bob would tell of the fire would become part of our family's shared history, that we would recite and embellish the narrative with each passing summer, that we would always remember the way he shook his head when he told us: "There was no way we were going to be able to stop it. But then I heard the helicopter, directly overhead. I looked up just as the bottom of the bucket opened. I've never felt anything so good in my life."

The next day, we drove downriver to view where the fire had burned—an oily pool spread across the golden hillside. After the fire subsided, Bob had found himself disoriented and had wandered in the dark for an hour before coming across several other men. Together they were able to find their way back. "I can look up there now," he said, "and have no idea where I was."

Later, when I asked my son what he remembered about the fire, he answered quickly: "I remember that I couldn't breathe." My daughter recalled the ash falling and my concern that we would lose our water supply. And she reminded me of something I had forgotten: "What I remember most," she said, "is how badly I wanted to go and help fight the fire, and how you wouldn't let me."

Perhaps she will be the one to leave the phone and go to the place where stories are being made, the one who will not be left behind. One of the most respected smoke jumping crews in the country is composed entirely of women; of the fourteen Oregon-based firefighters who died in the Colorado fire of 1994, four were female. I shudder with the thought of my son or daughter choosing to try himself, herself, against such an adversary. I wonder if I would come to dread and despise the month I love so well, for I am strangely wedded to the tyrannical heat, the thunderstorms, even the fire—the absolutism, the undeniable presence of August in my life.

Instead of wading the ashes of August, I spend many late summer days wading the river. This is Nez Perce land, and the water's flux covers and uncovers the remnants of their ancient industry: arrowheads, spear points, blades of obsidian. I come to the Clearwater armed only with a hook and line, meaning to fool the fish with a tuft of feather, a swirl of bright thread. I step in to my waist and feel the strange dissonance of temperature—my feet numbing with cold, the crown of my head hot with sun. I stand for a moment, brace myself. I am all that is still, an island anchored by nothing more than the felt soles of my boots. I load my line, cast toward the calm above the current. I imagine the fish rising, its world a kaleidoscope of shattered light.

Through the cooling nights of fall, during the long nights of winter when ice rimes the eddies, I dream of August, the water at my hips, my line lacing the sun. I wake to the odor of woodsmoke—my husband firing the stove—but for a sleepy moment it is the warm wind that I smell, the burning of yellow pine and prairie grass and wheat stubble. I smell summer sage and mullein, the licorice spice of dog fennel. I smell the cool drift of fish scent off the river. I open my eyes, expecting early light, the windows still open to the morning breeze, but what I see instead is the darkness before sunrise, the frost that glistens each pane of glass, and I am bereft.

Tourist of Fire, Prisoner of Dust

Peter Chilson

At a gas station in Orovada, Nevada, firefighters in dirty uniform yellow shirts and green pants loiter around a school bus in the parking lot. It's early morning and they munch on donuts and jerky. A few feet away I hunch over a topographic map spread on the hood of a white federal government 4×4 pickup with a double cab. A man in a silver hard hat, his shirt smeared black and brown, stands beside me.

"Lightning fires," he says, pointing northwest and then tapping the place on the map with a pen. "All across the Double H, we've been at 'em all night."

I'm a little edgy and not sure why. The fires are far away on mountains that look rocky and bare. I ask what's burning.

"Grass, sage, pinion pine," he says, and looks from me to my pickup, a small rear-wheel drive Toyota with Idaho plates. "It's all up there. Fuel load's pretty dry."

Later, in my truck, a notebook and Nevada topographic atlas open in my lap, I circle the Double H Mountains, west of U.S. 95, a few miles south of the Oregon border. To calm my mind, I try to make notes, but have trouble clarifying thoughts. So I start a list. I write down the plants and the term "fuel load." I pause, flip a page in my notebook and write, "nervous for some reason." Smoke spreads across the sky.

It is July 17, summer of 2000. Fire season is upon the West—an onslaught that arrives every spring when weather launches a war of sorts. The afternoon before, 100 miles north, I'd parked off U.S. 95 in eastern Oregon's high desert to watch thunderstorms in a hard southerly wind. Through field glasses I could see egglike mammatus clouds boil on the southern horizon over Nevada. The sky, not quite black, shattered as lightning dropped in the east, then the west. Thunder stayed distant. The rain arrived in sheets.

That night, in a motel room in McDermitt, Nevada, the roof leaked water on the bed. Faint lightning bounced off the window drapes, as if it were trying to get in but could only throw dim light, not fire. Somewhere lightning struck with awful power.

"Lightning was the terror of the Forest Service," wrote Betty Goodwin Spencer, an Idaho journalist, in her history of the 1910 fires that burned the Northern Rockies. "One slender blue-white flash was followed by a rounded puff of smoke, an acrid smell, and flames." That was what I'd seen in Oregon, from a distance. At dawn I drove south from McDermitt past mountains that rose up brown and red to the west, beyond alfalfa fields. Clouds shrouded the ridges, the remains of the night's storm, I thought. But morning soon revealed columns of smoke rising from the slopes. What lightning left. The smoke led to the gas station where I found the firefighters and the man with the map.

Now smoke erases the Double H Mountains as if they never were, an image I realize connects me to a place in my past and part of what has shaken my nerves. I think of West Africa during a season when dust owns the land and war rages under dust's cover. The smoke here works like the fine dust of the harmattan, a Saharan wind that scrapes the desert, whipping up dust from October to March. The wind signals a season of war, when attacks by desert rebels are expected. This is an African parallel to fire season, the notion of cyclical climatic events that send people out to fight on two continents—dust storms in Africa and fire weather in the American West.

The man in the hard hat folds the map and shouts to his firefighters. "Come on, we're outta here."

In the margin of my map, I write, "Fire and Dust!"

Agadez, Niger, December 25, 1992. I stand in the road, bewildered. Soldiers at a checkpoint have removed my backpack from the bus I was riding. The vehicle continues on into the city, disappearing after a few meters in fine white dust that makes the surrounding world an impossibility.

I'm a freelance journalist traveling on a tourist visa across a land at war, a part of northeastern Niger that foreigners are forbidden to visit. The Tuaregs, Berber nomads who have lived for centuries off their camel herds and by raiding—each other, other tribes, and desert caravans—are fighting to claim pieces of the Sahara from Mauritania to Chad. They are only a few hundred fighters, maybe. No one really knows. The Tuaregs cloak their movements in dust. I took this trip to write about how the military keeps the road to Agadez open in this civil war. All day on the bus, and at frequent stops, I've been talking to officials, travelers, and drivers, and watching light tanks and pickup trucks full of soldiers roll up and down the road. I've got my story. Now I have other problems.

A soldier takes my passport, directs me to a hotel in the city, and tells me to report to the police in the morning. But where? I have no landscape to fix on, no sense of a city nearby. Standing beside my pack, I look at him blankly and wipe dust from my lips with my fingers.

Nothing is so frightening as a prolonged dust storm in proximity
to war. Landscape loses every identifying point, every familiar
edge and curve, as if dust could dissolve inanimate objects and
make them reappear, suddenly. In this place there is only me,
the asphalt, and these men waiting in a cool, dusty wind that turns
their green uniforms gray and my red beard white.

"You can't leave the city," a soldier says, holding up my passport.
The soldier, khaki turban wrapped around his head, thumbs the
pages. He wears sandals.

I want to say, "What city?" Instead, I ask in French (language of
the region's former colonizers), "Est-ce qu'il y a un problem?"—
"What's the problem?" Then I add, "Je suis touriste."

"You might be a mercenary," he says quietly, slipping my passport
in his breast pocket.

His calm unnerves me. A pistol in a leather holster hangs from his
belt. Folded neatly under the belt is the red beret of Niger's
Republican Guard, the unit responsible for protecting important
officials and government posts. A soldier stands beside him
pointing a machine gun at me. He wears boots and the green
beret of the Gendarmarie Nationale, the paramilitary police. I
wonder what to say. But to argue, even to appear to argue, I know,
would make things worse. In Niger, mercenaries are put to death.

"How do I get to town?"

"You walk." The soldier wearing the turban points down the road.
"It's not far."

I stopped in Orovada for coffee, on my way to see friends in
Arizona, but I've found remnant emotions of three days in a West
African city where I was briefly a prisoner. The past surfaces in a
twitch in my right eye as I look through binoculars at how wind

plays the smoke over the Double H Mountains. The feeling
distracts me, as do the firefighters who talk and laugh as they
gather at the door of the bus. Then, abruptly, I realize what else is
bothering me—fear, not of fire, but of the uniformed firefighters
who have become, in my mind, like soldiers blocking my way.
The fear passes. I watch them board the bus and smile to myself.
They're only firefighters.

After Africa, where I was always near civil war or some political
crisis, being a spectator to a war of nature in my own country
gives me the notion of control. Not that I wasn't a spectator in
Africa—I was—but things got too involved for my nerves. Fire
weather is a curiosity I can indulge with little risk, if I choose.

So, I'm enjoying this.

On impulse, I make a call on the gas station's pay phone and ask
information for the National Weather Service in Reno, the nearest
big city. I speak to a forecaster named Roger Lamoni and explain
that I'm a writer curious about storms over northern Nevada. I
expect annoyance from someone with no time for a science lesson,
but Lamoni answers with friendly passion. He says the storms
originated more than 2,000 miles northwest.

"That came from the Gulf of Alaska," he says, "a long ways."

Lamoni talks of "low pressure troughs," "high pressure ridges," and
"convective activity," as though the sky has gears and wheels. He
uses verbs like "sweeping," "spreading," and "converging," to
describe twenty-four hours of weather that produced what I saw in
Oregon. A moist low-pressure cold front moved southeast toward
the northwest coast and made landfall over northern California
and southern Oregon early that day. The system "pushed" east
over the Sierra Nevada Mountains and near Reno hit
desert, where heavier cool air forced lighter desert air up in the
atmosphere. The rising and falling rush of air condensed
enough moisture and stirred enough instability to produce dozens
of thunderstorms at close quarters. They swept north from the

Nevada trucking town of Winnemucca on Interstate 80 to northeast Oregon and southern Idaho. The storms fired lightning across Nevada but withheld moisture until they passed over Oregon, where lightning and rain fell at once.

"We're talking about a little moisture falling from very high levels," Lamoni says. I listen and watch smoke blur the sun. "Not much was hitting the ground, but there was a lot of lightning. And a lot of fire weather warnings. You happened to be where rain hit."

Lamoni explains something else. The rain that wet my field glasses on that Oregon roadside the previous afternoon was a mix of moisture sucked up from the northern Pacific waters of the Gulf of Alaska and from melting snow in the Sierra Nevada Mountains. The moisture came from a low pressure "trough," a giant oval of air that hangs over the Gulf of Alaska, southeast of the Aleutian Islands. The thing whirls counterclockwise and on radar resembles a white crab, absorbing moisture and "spinning off," as Lamoni puts it, small "disturbances"—little troughs—and "lobbing them" across the ocean and over the northwestern U.S. coast to rain on Seattle and Portland, to drop snow and rain on the Inland Northwest east of the Cascade Mountains, and to fire lightning all the way to the Northern Rockies and Montana's eastern plains all summer.

Numbers help tell the story. Each lightning strike is picked up by radio waves and recorded in some National Weather Service office. From 1940 to 1975, lightning started 220,000 fires across the West. Of the 27,000 fires that burned in the West in the summer of 2000, most were lightning starts. In fact, lightning causes 70 percent of the fires that burn across the West every summer. I mention all this by way of revealing the power of a storm that set a mountain range ablaze long before I felt the rain. This is about awe, that biblical way fire weather presents itself across the land like a sign from the Old Testament—"the son of Man coming in a cloud with great power and majesty."

So, as Roger Lamoni and I talk, Nevada is burning. Oregon is not.

I thank him and drive on south. (I learn later the Double H fires combined and burned 71,000 acres in three days.) I hear on my car radio that a lightning fire has closed Colorado's Mesa Verde National Park. Lightning fires rage in Idaho and Montana, forcing evacuations and raising new talk of the 1910 fires in the Northern Rockies. The so-called "Big Blow-Up"—which lightning started and rain finished off months later, after fire razed whole towns—killed eighty-five people and burned three million acres. This summer, across the West, wild fires will burn almost seven million acres.

But I'm a tourist of fire, unaware of policy and the science of fire behavior, of things like "burn indexes" and "dew points." In Africa, I was working and never had the luxury of being a "tourist," someone who travels for pleasure and with the freedom to move about without fear. Now it occurs to me how much I like that word, "tourist." I'm traveling for my own curiosity. From my pickup, moving south across Nevada, and then east through northern Arizona and eventually north back to Idaho, I see smoke occupy shrub steppe and forest. In towns like Show Low, Arizona, and McCall, Idaho, Forest Service air tankers and helicopters land day and night and exhausted firefighters walk the streets. But I rarely see flames, mostly just the weather of it all, dense white clouds where fire is intense, clouds that take possession of the land and pack it away, undercover.

The soldier in sandals and a turban, my passport in his pocket, partly dissolves in the haze as he walks to a small cinderblock guardhouse. The one with the machine gun nods to me and points the barrel down the road.

Twenty soldiers in red and green berets wander the checkpoint, a place marked by the guardhouse and a length of rope stretched between iron stakes across the road. Marked, too, by gun positions, empty pits three feet deep and protected by sandbags.

Three positions make half-moon formations on both sides of the road. Sand crawls up the sandbags in drifts, up the block walls of the guardhouse, and up my trouser cuffs. Wind gusts hit the gun pits, obscuring them in small sand-dust clouds as if the pits have just been captured.

I saw this from my seat when the bus pulled up at the checkpoint, and more as I got off. I can see now as I try not to look, try to appear like a tourist, as if I notice nothing. I can briefly see bloodstains, for example, on the clothes of a figure crouching in a gun pit a few feet away. This person, a man I think, is a lump in dirty gray robes. His head, wrapped in a turban, rests on his arms folded atop his knees tucked against his chest. The blood, still red and fresh, stains the cloth stretched over the knees. A rebel, maybe, or a traveler without proper papers. Someone in trouble.

Soldiers huddle in groups, talking and smoking. Three play cards on a straw mat. Some carry machine guns. These are black Africans, not lighter-skinned Berbers or Arabs.

They have not searched my pack. I hoist it to my shoulder, wondering if they will ask me to leave it behind. Suddenly, I no longer care about my story or the civil war. I'm worried about being in this city a long time, and about ending up like the bloodied man in the gun pit. I nod to the soldier and begin walking, my eyes on the asphalt. A little later I look back and see only dust, as if the checkpoint had been a dream.

I failed as a war correspondent. Not enough nerve. Africa taught me that. But nerve is not an issue now. I'm following the weather.

For the record, a weather report: In the early evening of July 8, a week before I left Idaho, a storm system blew inland from Northern California and moved northeast to Idaho and Montana. The storms were driven by another Gulf of Alaska "low," which, over the Sierra Nevada Mountains, picked up remnants of a monsoon storm from the Gulf of California, then moved inland to cast lightning into central Idaho's Payette National Forest. In the early morning hours on July 9, a lightning bolt struck a ridgetop of dry grasses and ponderosa pine near a road intersection called Burgdorf Junction, starting a fire that smoldered six days before aircraft spotted it. Meanwhile, federal fire bosses announced that fires across Idaho and Montana had already burned an area the size of the state of Maine.

On July 21, on Interstate 40, I pass Winslow, Arizona, around noon, watching heavy gray clouds form to the south. Monsoon moisture is surging north over the Arizona–Mexico border and late that afternoon casts lightning onto forests across northeastern Arizona, where there's been no rain in a month. In hours, forests are ablaze. Lightning slices the darkened sky as I drive down U.S. Highway 77 into the Apache Sitgreaves National Forest. In the morning, at the campground where I pitch my tent south of Slow Low, the sky is gone. There is only smoke that makes my eyes and nose burn. The pine trees around my campsite fade into the smoke, which denies me a view of the world beyond fifty feet. Radio reports confirm the fire is miles away, not a threat. Still, standing in my camp and watching the smoke, I experience the same momentary fear that visited me at the gas station in Nevada. The feeling leaves when I consciously think about it.

Except for my paranoia, none of this is unusual. The West burns every summer. Fire weather is born in May when spring's rising heat forces a seasonal reversal of the northerly wind over the Pacific waters of the Gulf of California, off Mexico's west coast, and the Atlantic waters of the Gulf of Mexico. The wind blows inland to the north until September. Over central and northern Mexico, afternoon storms rise on the fuel of solar heated air, gathering moisture in puffy cumulus clouds and moving north across Texas and Arizona to form thunder and lightning storms. Stronger systems spread over southern California, Utah, New Mexico, Colorado and at times into the skies over Nevada, eastern Oregon, and the Rocky Mountains of Idaho and Montana. The monsoon dominates Southwest summer weather and harasses northern regions, often lending energy to the moist low-pressure cold fronts born in the Gulf of Alaska. In turn the Alaskan fronts that define Pacific Northwest weather sometimes feed monsoon activity in the Southwest.

Two weather systems. A summer of fire.

"Sand," wrote the English scientist Ralph Bagnold, "collects," while dust "scatters." He called this "a problem of aerodynamics." Sand particles, mostly heavier grains of quartz, can't remain airborne long or fly more than a few feet above ground, so sand collects against whatever it hits. But dust, finer grains of quartz, rises into the air as high as 15,000 feet.

Bagnold, by specialty an engineer and by passion a geomorphologist (he studied the connection between geology and the shape of landscape) and lover of deserts is important to me for what he says about deserts. While traveling in West Africa in 1986, I read his book, *The Physics of Blown Sand and Desert Dunes*, which I found on a shelf in a hotel lobby in Gao, a city in Mali on the edge of the Sahara. Soon after his book came out in 1941, the German Army occupied Libya and Bagnold was called up by the British Army Signals corps and sent to Egypt, where he developed desert warfare tactics. His knowledge came in handy in a place where dust and sand interrupted the rhythm of a war that engulfed much of the northern Sahara.

The English have much to say about desert sand and dust, and they should. They've spent much of the last three centuries wandering two of the world's driest places—North Africa and the Arabian Peninsula. Another Englishman, James Lucas, a historian and veteran of the North Africa campaigns, has written about that peculiar desert battlefield reality—the notion that the very surface of the land rises up in strength to act as both enemy and ally. Desert winds, he wrote in his 1977 book, *Panzer Army Africa*, whipped dust into a

Gritty fog . . . as thick as soup . . . . The side which could
attack under cover of Khamsin [Arabic for the seasonal "hot
wind"] had the advantage of approaching almost totally
concealed from sight and sound.

So, with war on my mind, I walk down the road into Agadez,
where everything is a grainy shadow. African life normally spills
into village and city streets at night. People wander, sit outside
homes or at food and coffee tables, talking, arguing, flirting, doing
business, listening to music. In Africa, life is community.

But the city's sandy byways, lined by ancient mud brick homes, are
mostly empty. I pass men huddled around a hurricane lamp.
They clutch cloaks about their bodies and stare sullenly at me.
Agadez is a thousand years old, long a center for the Saharan
caravan trade. After Niger's independence in 1961, Agadez became
an attraction, a resting point for merchants and adventurers
crossing the Sahara to Algeria. Tourists stopped here for a meal
and a bed and to see the towering mosque that is the city's
oldest structure.

The last major Tuareg rebellion peaked in 1917, when rebel bands
under the leadership of a young Tuareg nobleman, Kaossen,
surrounded the French garrison here. The siege persisted for three
months, involving hundreds of Tuaregs from bands in the Air
Mountains to the northeast. They attacked in small groups, often
shielded by blowing dust. But the garrison held until a relief
column arrived. Every citizen and soldier in the city is aware of
this history.

A passerby directs me to the nearest hotel, whose name I've
forgotten. In the tiny lobby I find a boy who goes to find
"le directeur." After a while a large black man in a flowing blue
robe and white skullcap enters the room. He looks alarmed.

"Monsieur," he says, "what are you doing here? The Tuaregs are kidnapping tourists, you could be killed." In fact, rebels had made hostages of French tourists in Mali and Niger.

I shrug, feigning ignorance, trying to play the tourist. "I'm sorry," I say, "I'll get the first bus out."

The man shakes his head and sends the boy to prepare a room. He asks for 5000 CFA francs, about $15, for a room, including breakfast and dinner. "The police will want to see you in the morning." He studies me. "We haven't had a foreign guest here in a year."

I'm the only guest in a hotel of twenty rooms. The building was constructed with cement, unusual in such an old and poor city. Smooth mud stucco covers the walls and pointed minarets line the edges of the roof. In one corner facing east, the direction of the Moslem holy city of Mecca, a minaret rises several feet higher than the rest.

In the dining room I sit on a bench at a long wood table and eat a slab of tough meat, probably dog, with canned peas, gritty with sand. The man asks to join me. We share a large bottle of beer.

He talks of tragedy and loss. Weeks ago, he says, near Agadez, rebels shot to death a village chief who refused them supplies.

"They've destroyed me, you know, and this city." He looks at his feet while I eat. "The rebels come day or night. They take cars, they take camels. Sometimes they'll attack a patrol and kill a few soldiers. You can hardly call this war. It's banditry."

He is quiet. Then he says, "You're going to have trouble."

In my travels I pass in and out of smoke, stopping to watch it swell and spread in the atmosphere, or right over land. I spend half a day chasing thunderstorms across the Hopi Reservation in northern Arizona, hoping to witness a lightning strike. I don't, but I've come to understand something. What I've found in fire weather is a surrogate war. My kind of war, the sort of conflict where destruction is not intentional, the people who wear uniforms are not threatening, and technology is benevolent. Here's what I mean.

On August 4, weather and fire lead page one of the *Arizona Daily Star*. I see the paper while staying with friends in Tucson. "Across the West," the story says, "dry thunderstorms generated 75,000 lightning strikes that sparked more than 400 new forest fires in a single day." Among the regions hit were the mountains of central Idaho and Montana's Bitterroot Valley, where fires were already burning and "whole mountain ranges disappeared into hazy wood smoke." Forest Service chief Mike Dombeck, touring the fire lines, said, "We're really at the mercy of Mother Nature."

These storms also started fires across eastern Oregon and the Southwest, striking parts of Arizona, Nevada, Utah, New Mexico, and closing Colorado's Mesa Verde National Park for the second time.

All in one day.

During such events, statistics tumble into National Weather Service bureaus in Tucson, Phoenix, Salt Lake City, Boise, Denver, Albuquerque, and Reno, where banks of computers and radio equipment sit on white tables beneath fluorescent lights, and thunder cells show up on Doppler radar in bright red blotches, like laboratory blood smears. A meteorological metamorphosis. In these bureaus, weather passes through the tight prism of science, detected by electronic impulses that travel from golf ball shaped radar towers atop high mountains to computer screens that show swirling cloud masses in bright animation.

The radar signals strike atmospheric particles—dust, insects, birds, and rain. Most particles are too small to be noticed, but rain is so highly reflective it shows up clearly. The results flash in multiple colors—green for the weakest storm systems, and moving up the spectrum of threat to yellow and then red. Finally, there's purple, for the most intense storm, the kind that drops ten inches of rain in an hour. A double click of the cursor arrow on one storm blotch pulls up a thunderhead's "profile," showing moisture level, wind temperature, direction, and speed on colored bar graphs. A storm revealed like a cutaway slab of meat.

Radar doesn't pick up dust very well. Forecasters in West Africa rely on satellite photos and ground observation. Four times a day at the Agadez airport someone records details of visibility, wind speed and direction, and temperature, and reports the findings by radio to Niamey, Niger's capital, where the government radio broadcasts regular weather reports.

From where I'm sitting, on an old oil drum at the Agadez police commissariat early in the morning, dust is blowing the world to whiteness. The commandant will see me, I am told, but he's busy now. I wonder what has become of my passport between the checkpoint and here.

The commissariat is several square cement buildings in a courtyard surrounded by high cinder block walls lined by acacia trees. Dust coats everything in the compound. Three police Land Rovers with khaki canvas roofs are parked against one wall. At the compound gate, a woman wrapped in cotton cloth squats on a wood stool over a fire, cooking millet flour biscuits in peanut oil. She stands and brushes the dust off her wrap. Outside, in the street, armed gendarmes in green berets stand guard.

Across the compound, five gendarmes sit around a teapot set on a bed of coals in the sand. I buy hot biscuits and join the tea group, intent on making friends. In Africa, the key to waiting is to appear not to care. The soldiers give me a cinder block seat while they sit on the ground. I offer to make tea.

Hours later I'm still here. We sip strong, sweet green tea from shot glasses. The tea boils for a fifth round. I pick up the pot by the handle, using a cloth to protect my fingers, and raise it above my head, tipping the spout until a brown stream spills into a glass on a metal tray, splashing tea all over. The cooling process. I take the glass, hold it high, and pour the tea back into the pot. I hand the glass to a sergeant with a rifle across his lap.

We speak little, each man silently coping with cold and dust.

In late afternoon, a soldier steps out of the main building and shouts something in Hausa. "Kai, Anasara"—"Hey Christian man," a reference to me, the non-Moslem. The sergeant looks up. "The commandant will see you," he says. He follows me inside.

He shows me to a room where an officer in a green turban and French army greatcoat sits at a desk. The turban forms an oval around the man's narrow face. His lips are gray and cracked. The officer motions me to sit in a small metal chair. I see my passport among papers on his desk.

"What are you doing here?" He slips the passport out from the papers and drops it back on the desk. The document lands on dust, a gray film like fine ground glass. He bites his lower lip in the corners, where I see his lip has been bleeding.

"Well, I'm a tourist, and a poorly prepared one." I shift in my seat. "Agadez is a beautiful city. I wanted to visit."

He rubs his eyes. "No one questioned you before you got on the bus to come here?"

"No." A nervous twitch tugs at the corner of my right eye. My hands shake, so I fold them between my knees. The idea that my situation might worsen, that they might accuse me of spying or whatever, becomes more real in his presence. My body tightens and I am short of breath.

He sighs and says, "We can't fight a war if people don't do their jobs." He reads through the pages of my passport, which is full of tourist visas from across West Africa: Senegal, Ivory Coast, Burkina Faso, Nigeria. African governments rarely grant visas specifically for journalists. The stories we write are not often positive.

"You are traveling a lot," he says, his eyes on my passport.

I smile. "I'm a high-school teacher," I lie. "I've just taken time off to travel."

He closes the passport and looks at me, biting his lower lip in the corner. He opens a desk drawer and withdraws a stamp and inkpad. "Do you know the problems you could cause us if they kidnap or kill you?" He takes my passport and finds a blank page, pressing the stamp to the paper. Then he puts his signature across the stamped circular emblem. Later, I see that it says, "Commissariat de Police d'Agadez."

I relax, my shoulders slumping a little, though I hope he cannot detect the change. I tell him I'd like to come back when life is calmer, but the officer shows no reaction to my words. For a minute he makes notes on a sheet of paper.

Finally he says, "There is a government bus returning to the south tomorrow. This will show the checkpoint guards that you have seen me. They'll let you pass."

On my way out of the compound, I wave the passport at my tea companions and they wave back.

In the morning the sky is clear blue. The dust has blown off and the air has cooled. The wind hasn't let up, though, and dust will return. But for the first time in this desert I appreciate the sun. As the bus leaves the city, I stare out the window at a rocky landscape, alternating brown and red. No trees. Some prickly prosopis bushes. Little sand. Nowhere to hide.

A Land Cruiser pickup full of soldiers travels behind us. A soldier says we have nothing to fear now that the dust has cleared. I don't believe him, but we arrive safely in a city some 150 miles southeast.

I've seen fires in six Western states this summer, so smoke is a familiar presence. Now, I've decided that to understand fire weather more clearly, it's necessary to get closer to fire. I have to join the troops, so to speak.

This is why on the afternoon of August 18 I'm sitting in tall grass a quarter mile up the north slope of central Idaho's Salmon River Canyon. I've been issued a fire retardant yellow shirt and green pants, hard hat, goggles, gloves, high-calorie bag lunch, and an escort of experts—Mike Edmonston, thirty-eight, a pudgy, confessed "office man" who normally follows weather on Doppler radar in the Tallahassee, Florida, Weather Service office; and Sid Beckman, forty-two, a wiry Forest Service fire behavior analyst and ex-Hotshot firefighter. They're studying how the canyon winds move the fire, now advancing a half-mile a day.

Across the river, on the south slope, fire smolders west downriver through dry grasses and willow bushes, slowly progressing to a point where it will drop into Bear Creek, a drainage thick with ponderosa pine. The wind has shifted just as Edmonston, sitting to my left, said it would. Soft gusts are blowing east and hot up the canyon, and up the slopes. The wind moves at fifteen miles an hour in ninety-three-degree heat at 3:02 P.M., according to the anemometer in the hands of Beckman, squatting to my right. "I spend a lot of time on fires, doing this sort of thing," Beckman says, "looking for a place where I can get close and watch." For this kind of work, both men carry two-way radios.

Just twenty-four hours earlier Edmonston had pulled up satellite images on his laptop computer, revealing monsoon moisture moving north into southern Idaho. Hopes were high in fire camp that the system might bring rain to the mountains farther north.

But this morning the satellites had more news: The front drifted to the southeast so all rain bets are off. (It has barely rained in two months.) He broke the news at the 6:00 A.M. briefing, warning that afternoon wind gusts might intensify a fire that has burned 41,000 acres in the Payette National Forest, a blaze big enough to have a name—the Burgdorf Junction Fire.

Edmonston, bleary eyed and shivering in a ski parka and ball cap, made that report in chilly darkness on a plywood stage mounted with topographic maps and surrounded by brown aluminum frame tents. This is the fire operations center near Burgdorf Hot Springs, twenty-five miles north of McCall.

"I'm upgrading our alertness to a red flag fire warning," he said, meaning they could expect the fire to burn aggressively. "Our biggest worry is a hard wind shift in the afternoon."

The incident command team and crew bosses, some fifty men and women in yellow and green uniforms and steel toed boots, listened quietly. Beckman followed with a report on what crews could expect from the fire under those winds. Twice a day, at 6:00 A.M. and 9:00 P.M., during a two-week assignment, Edmonston and Beckman climb the stage to predict weather and fire for people from a dozen state and federal agencies. If they are wrong, if, say, unexpected winds fuel the fire and catch a crew by surprise, they have to face the same people hours later. This morning, news of two firefighters killed by lightning in Utah was posted on the camp bulletin board.

After the briefing, the pair decided to visit the canyon. But Edmonston had to check a few things first. Beckman smiled. "He's gotta do his voodoo," he said.

We walked to the "Situation Tent," furnished with worktables, wall maps, fax machines, a two-way radio, and telephones. A huge plywood map table stood in the center. Edmonston huddled with a laptop, like a crystal ball, checking satellite photos and weather data. Above his head, taped to a shelf, hung a note scrawled in black ink: "THE GOVERNOR WANTS TO KNOW RIGHT AWAY IF THERE IS A BIG FLAREUP!" Edmonston worked the phone, trading information with the Weather Service in Boise, and collecting temperature, humidity, fuel moisture, and wind data from electronic field instruments planted around the fire. I stood behind him with Beckman, who grinned.

"You sure you want to stick around?" he asked me. "Mike's gonna start mumbling incoherently. Then he kills chickens. It gets messy." Even Edmonston laughed.

Now, nine hours later, after a long drive into the canyon and a jet boat trip upriver, we've climbed to this position on the north slope. Across the river, we've lost sight of the fire which is slowly "backing down" a northwest-facing grassy slope into Bear Creek— a slope that rises 4,000 feet from the river to the canyon rim. The slope faces away from us, but we can see the smoke thicken as the fire crawls into thicker vegetation. To the east across the river something snaps, loud and sharp. I look upriver to already burnt ground and see a smoking snag fall in a cloud of ash.

"Amazing," Beckman says. "This is the offspring of a single lightning strike."

Lightning from a thunderstorm that came from the Gulf of Alaska to deliver it without rain. This is the strike that hit July 9, on a high ridge a few miles south of where we sit. To date, the Burgdorf Junction Fire has drawn 1,500 firefighters, including Army infantry and eight helicopters.

Edmonston sits with his knees drawn against his chest. "I want to see how the wind channels through this canyon when it gets this hot." All night and through the morning, he explains, cool air has been moving downriver with the fire. But now under a hot afternoon sun reinforced by heat radiating off canyon walls, the wind has reversed direction and the consequences are about to erupt as the warmer, more unstable air gathers momentum in up-slope gusts.

I make notes, glancing at the smoke. Beckman sits with his legs splayed out, listening to Edmonston. "It's the old witches' brew," Beckman adds. "You get winds going to different directions and a lot starts to happen."

The fire is moving faster down in the creek, which we know from the roar of flames we can't see and the billowing smoke we do see. The sound competes with the chopper hovering a few hundred feet overhead and which has been dumping river water on the fire all afternoon from a big rubber bucket. Edmonston taps my shoulder and points, but my eyes are already there. Flames like yellow and orange jack rabbits have jumped the drainage and are leaping in full view up the creek's east-facing slope, now working with the hot updraft, not against it. The fire feeds off it, creating its own winds that suck the flames upward. A pine tree explodes in ribbons of orange as I watch, not frightened, but obsessed. Fire demands that kind of attention.

So can dust and sand. Watching the flames raises memories of my fascination in Africa for the way a dune creeps like an ocean wave in slow motion, erasing roads and villages from the land. In summer, monsoon season in Niger, massive sand-dust clouds precede the rains, descending in high winds to make swift destruction of crops, like fire.

Fire races up the drainage and Beckman says, "Ohhh, look at that bad boy go. There's a Hotshot crew on that ridge. They're not happy right now."

I think of Norman Maclean's book, *Young Men and Fire*, the story of thirteen firefighters who died on a Montana mountainside in 1949 when a fire storm 2,000 degrees hot roared right through them. In 1994, the South Canyon Fire in Colorado killed fourteen firefighters. Lightning started both blazes and wind helped to make them killer infernos.

Beckman picks up his radio and alerts the crew on the ridge. The helicopter pilot, too, reports what he sees. The fire reaches the ridgetop, 4,000 feet above, in forty minutes, but the crew is safely out of the way.

Edmonston says, "I'm going to keep that red flag warning for tomorrow."

Just before Labor Day, the end of fire season begins the same way it started for me—under heavy wind and rain from a storm front out of the Gulf of Alaska. Weather forecasters in Boise call it an intense storm system that tracked into the Pacific Northwest and the Northern Rockies, bringing rain to lower elevations and snow higher up. Smaller storms follow and this time rain overwhelms lightning and the fires fade. Still, a month passes before the Northern Rockies' fires are extinguished or controlled. The Burgdorf Fire peaks at 66,000 acres before surrendering.

By then I'm home in northern Idaho, arranging notes from the summer alongside my journals from Africa, pondering fire amidst memories of dust. Notebooks sprawl across the floor, among photographs and maps. I find a loose page of writing in one of my Africa notebooks. A forgotten anecdote taken from a newspaper report in Niger.

In 1985, my notes say, three Land Rovers carrying the family of the Agadez region's military governor disappeared in a dust storm northeast of the city. His wife, children, and their escort of soldiers vanished. The convoy was found months later. The vehicles were partly buried in sand drifts with the bodies of the wife and children. The remains of the soldiers lay outside.

The Good Red Road

Paula Coomer

I think I am supposed to be afraid, sitting alone here on the banks of the Lostine River in the Blue Mountains of northeastern Oregon, a long way from any home, current or past. It might be one of perhaps five dozen evenings spent in this very spot during these last sixteen years: the mosquitoes losing spunk with sundown's chill temperatures; conifers smelling like sweet green hashish thanks to another day in a string of days marked by pre-season heat; and the Lostine, rushing between root-infested banks with early runoff, her skin sparkling, dusky, and fast. A river moving cold and deep—bad news for my philosopher self contemplating a wade to that silt-edged expanse of beach across the way and a look back to illuminate what it is I want from this place, to lend shape to the question bag I bring.

But I don't really need to wade ice water to gain this awareness because this campground is a ghost scene from my second marriage. A place of grilled trout, coyote impressions, K-Mart sleeping bags. A place of squeal-laced river baths and boxed wine in ceramic coffee cups. A place where my oldest son once tiptoed away at dawn, taking his pint-sized rod and reel and a nightcrawler to the water to catch a perfect Dolly Varden for breakfast, an act of such self-sufficiency as to make his father shake his hand and say, "Atta *boy!*" and me slip off to the outhouse to save the embarrassment of tears. Even his then three-year-old brother was impressed by his feat.

In two months, that daring fisherman will hit twenty-one. Three months more and the younger one will turn eighteen. I've not come here to wallow in some empty-nest lament, however. Ten years after my divorce, I'm ready to be done with the nightmare of single parenting, the visitations, the swapping custody, that exquisite sword known as child support. The constant whiplash of emotions daring me to commit either abuse or neglect, or my children to carry out some gory cat vendetta, their damaged psyches retaliating against the neighbor kids for god-knows-what, and for which I'd forever feel not only blame but the compulsion to scoop up the ashes.

Don't get me wrong. I'm glad we've all made it this far and that no one is left in a vegetative state, and I am sure I will look back on this year not as the end of an era but rather the beginning of something new. But as the boys leave for college—the oldest getting a late liftoff—I find myself angry at them, finally, for the injustices wrought against me and my own gentle youth. For suckering me into conceiving them because I loved the snowy blue eyes of their father. For baby diapers and bottles and tonsillectomies and ten days in the pediatric ICU, watching IV antibiotics scoot through a tube into the scalp of my youngest just six months after he was born.

"Thank goodness you brought him in when you did," the doctor said. "Many parents ignore symptoms until it is too late." Hearing that the infection was isolated to his left shoulder was supposed to be a relief. It might have chosen his spinal cord. Or his brain. But recounting those long nights spent waiting to see whether my baby was going to live or die doesn't make me less pissed at any of them right now for having left me. My heart feels dark and sinister, and I run around thinking, "That's it! To hell with them all! I never wanted a family, anyway, and now it's finally done and over, that's all."

Not to mention the fact that I spent eleven years in the pursuit and execution of a nursing career I didn't want, due in part to that detailed hospital visit, where I rocked my baby to sleep for a week-and-a-half of naps and nights, crooning as we looked out from within a fishbowl surrounded by emergent pediatric nightmares.

A friend recently sent a quotation from Ranier Maria Rilke, who said, "have patience with everything unresolved in your heart and try to love the questions themselves as if they were locked rooms or books written in a very foreign language." According to Rilke's formula, one day you wake up realizing you've "lived your way into the answers." But here in my Lostine River sanctuary, staring at a mug of ice cubes and tonic water and gin with its chewed-up lime floating atop—its wreck testimony to the Swiss Army knife I should have sharpened before leaving the house—I'm forced to live with the question of whether my brain is truly intact: for some reason, I ignored my intuition to bring firewood, forgot even to bring a bucket for dousing embers, not to mention the legally required camp shovel and ax. I seem to have left home with nothing much beyond the notion of surviving the sleeping part, giving little thought to provisions. I brought a carton of yogurt and a raw chicken breast in the Igloo, but this fire I kindled from bits and scraps of forest floor refuse has dwindled to a point no brighter than the very twilight I meant to fend off, certainly too spartan for cooking. So I'm forced to hike the newly graded dirt road to look for logs the U.S. Forest Service might have left. Sometimes, when windfall impedes automobile traffic, they chainsaw it into cordwood and leave it stacked along the ditch. Most of it is delivered to primitive campsites such as this one, so the requisition comes guilt-free—one of the privileges of knowing the habits of federal workers in the American West.

The American West. The other question to be raised at this point, I suppose, besides why a woman at forty-four turns to isolation as a way of disinheriting its potential dangers, is why this same woman left her biological family and homeplace for the American

West in the first place. You could say I was simply not intrigued, as a child of the 1960s and '70s, by what my people had settled for—hundreds of years of uncivilized, sequestered living in the mountains of Adair County, Kentucky. Even though Mom and Dad raised us in the hills of southern Indiana, I don't think they could see that they had traded one set of mountain people for another. And I couldn't understand why the lot of them—southern Kentucky or southern Indiana—still squatted in the same places, watching the old buckboards and rank-and-file storefronts silver and dry into dust, why nobody wanted to get free of tobacco barns and shiny, black, man-high mules and old round-nosed pickup trucks constantly in need of having a brake line bled or a tire patch kit picked up from town—which, of course, required walking miles of dirt road or catching and hitching one of the mules.

It is hard to see the moon from certain Oregon backroads in the middle of June. Especially if you're a thirty-five-year-old woman on a scavenger hunt, driving into the American night on I-84, the east–west interstate between Portland, Oregon, and Boise, Idaho. Driving from motel to motel with a man you barely know, looking for his wife, a lissome blonde police trainee, and your husband, a police corporal. There are forty-three motels pockmarking the 120-mile span of asphalt between La Grande, Oregon, and Kennewick, Washington: some heavy with the exhaust of eighteen-wheelers idling in the parking lot; some nondescript, with two or more layers of door-studded cement floors and iron balcony railings. Some crumbly stucco places with Mexican workers and heavy white women courting in open doorways. Some pleasantly shingled, with family rates and meager neon lights beckoning travelers. Some fairly elegant, after the New West fashion. We cruise each parking lot looking for his wife's silver Grand Am.

There is much to occupy our talk on this June night, but my passenger is interested in only two things: the news I have just

shared with him about a day in April when I discovered his
blonde wife with my gray-at-the-temples husband parked
at a game preserve overlook, where every manner of wildlife, from
nesting falcons to an autocratic bull elk and a handful of cows,
could be observed. That, and the new lace undergarments he'd just
given to his wife. "Goddamn black underwear," he keeps saying.
"Goddamn black lace French underwear, and she goes and
does this." As soon as we find their lovenest, he says he's going to
tear the place apart looking for them, to see if she's "used
them" with my husband.

We hit every burg and sidestreet, and it takes nine hours, but we
finally discover his wife's car parked at the Shilo Inn Resort in
Kennewick, Washington. By that time, it was 6:00 A.M., and we had
grilled the frightened desk clerk until he reached for the phone
and asserted that we should either register or leave. So we wait in
the parking lot next to her silver Grand Am and exchange the
rhetoric of limbo and cuckolds while daybreak crazies the shadows
of the central Washington desertscape and lifts the scent of
sagebrush with the evaporating dew. I explain my missing teeth,
pulled the previous week to uncrowd my mouth for the braces I
hoped would make me pretty enough to hold onto my husband.
He sheds brief tears. Says he cheated on her once, too, that he
deserves this. Neither of us wants what is taking place; we both
wish for the courage to blow the two into smithereens.

As it turned out, there was blood and death enough in our
discovery without our adding to the drama. The dominoes fell—a
dispatcher (her best friend) submitting to the duress and
admitting to her concurrent affair with another officer, whose wife
developed unrelenting diarrhea and vomiting and had to be
hospitalized for anorexia; a deputy sheriff whose wife attempted
suicide after his liaison with a jail matron came to light; and
another corporal's hanky-panky, which apparently drove his
father-in-law, already diagnosed with cancer, into taking a shotgun
to his own face. And then there was my usually blue-jeaned or

uniformed husband who began wearing muscle pants, neon shorts, and luau shirts. My thirst for Black Velvet and diet Coke became unquenchable.

And the tears of everybody's children—fifteen in all—who were dropped headfirst into the abyss of broken families with one single panic-filled stroke of some monster-god's plot-making. "I always hoped this would never happen to us," my oldest son said. So for weeks afterward, we as a family drove the truck and camper up to this very spot on the Lostine, Friday afternoons through Sundays, thrice stopping in a little town called Elgin on the way home, filing into the matinee to eat popcorn and watch *Dances with Wolves*, all the while acting as though nothing had happened.

My private response to the fracturing of my marriage was to fold up a glossy nursing magazine recruiting ad for the Indian Health Service and carry it around with me. I took it out several times a day to alternately sob and stare at the handsome white doctor's face and the shaman-like gaze of the Indian nurse in white uniform and starched nurses' cap, then to study the Indian prayer hanging on my cupboard. *Oh Great Spirit, whose voice I hear in the wind, I am small and meek, and need your courage and wisdom . . . .* I ran my finger over the pink-shadowed Indian reservations on the Rand McNally Road Atlas. Calculated the distance to Lapwai, Idaho. To the Nez Perce. Chief Joseph and his band of rebels. I had been at the Nez Perce museum at Spalding, camped at Ollikot in the Oregon Wallowas. I knew about the famous Nez Perce battle at Big Hole, Montana, and their failed flight toward freedom from the U.S. Army, was moved to emotion by stories of their stamina, their statuesque resolve. Surely I, too, could survive. The Nez Perce reservation was near enough for my two sons to see their father regularly, yet too far for those demon-blue eyes to charm me back into their grip. And, as fate or luck would have it, there was an opening for a public health nurse in Lapwai. The road seemed to fork two ways: I could pack my children and a few possessions, and head back toward the hellfire and brimstone of my Kentucky heritage, or once again bank my salvation on whatever remained undiscovered about the wilds of the American West and its propensity—at least in my mind—to challenge and grow all who heed the forces of its unseen call.

Before I drove to the U.S. Forest Service office just outside La Grande, where my soon-to-be ex-brother-in-law was superintendent of timber sales, to pick up an application for federal hire, I drove to Lapwai to examine the place for myself. Part of me wanted to remember that I was a white ex-flower-child lunatic raving about Indian rights with friends and family over an Easter Oregon desert night and a metal-ringed campfire. A very silent part of me understood that I was of Appalachian heritage, with an attachment of full-blood Cherokee ancestors. Luckily, during that first touring visit, my future office mate, a famous Nez Perce fancy dancer named Leroy Seth, took me aside and politely told me that *every* blue-eyed white person who hired on with the Nez Perce had a Cherokee grandmother.

I heeded Leroy's couched warning, but still thought perhaps I had been called to Idaho. That it was part of my destiny to work with the Nez Perce. Becoming a pioneer woman yet again, for better or worse, I headed into the unpredictable vicissitudes of western American life.

Fire is a wicked thing. Wicked as the foil-colored waters below my feet. My campfire and the river suck me in. The night is a black ghost, and I long for a distraction. Part of the Lostine's mystery, however, is that I might stand here naked at daybreak or cloaked between the gray atmospheres of dusk and feel alone but not lonesome or afraid. There's no bear, no coyote wail, not even a chipmunk. No tires mucking spring roads. I listen to the sound of that water, its rush more urgent than the syncopation of the Pacific, which is its goal. But I can't stand here much longer or the sound will pull me closer and I will not get to the task at hand.

Because as much as I want answers, in this twilight I do not want
to face what the fire will conjure for me.

Because the fire is going to tell me to stop mourning. It
will remind me how much I daydreamed of being alone during my
20s and 30s, when I was saddled with those two bird mouths
to feed and the bellowing, bellicose husband who made fun of my
feet and my teeth, required me to cater and kowtow to life
his way, and bade me ignore private longings and poetic
inclinations. My husband and sons were tantalizing human prisms
that shed glorious colored light, but in my darkening soul I
perceived them as sharp and dagger-like enough to kill me. On
bad days I dripped tears like some tree with its limbs cut off,
for the world passing its time without my part in it, for whatever
hippies still danced at Haight-Ashbury, whatever poets still
read at coffee shops in Greenwich Village. I thought a lot about
Sylvia Plath, bastion of my teenage library days, who was
lucky enough to have found literary purchase, then blew it all
in a stupid oven (How could she be so unoriginal? How many of
us owned electric just to keep ourselves from doing that?), a
mere symbol of hearth and responsibility. How better, I used to
worry, for the sake of the artist in us all, if she had hanged
herself. At least hanging takes courage. The oven was
just so . . . tempting.

But to end my life in my twenties, to walk away from the
world without waiting my turn, to give up my chance
at contributing to the pool of lust or knowledge or ignorance,
to leave Plath's brand of wicked legacy for my children was
worse than they deserved. And what sacrilege, to have generated
some of those thoughts while sitting on this very mountain
perch with my sons struggling against the tide of bedtime while
my husband's Club Cab Dodge pickup with fourteen-foot
camper waited nearby, and me oblivious and stirring embers
with the sharpened end of my marshmallow stick, feeling
nothing but the edges of pitch darkness leaning against my
roughened parts.

The problem between my husband and me came down to fire and water. In his classic study of the hero archetype, *Hero with a Thousand Faces*, Joseph Campbell talks about the sacred marriage of fire and water, in which the goal of male fire is to enter and make blessed the female water, the water in turn used to replenish and transform the people. The hero during his quest must at some point enter a period of great darkness, from which seemingly there is no escape, being reborn and transcending to new life through the waters of the womb. This transformation is repeated frequently in stories from western culture: Jonah in the belly of the whale, Dorothy in the dark forest, Jesus's death and entombment, and most recently, Neo after his introduction to the Matrix. At some point, through the joining of fire and water, the beast regurgitates, the wicked witch is killed, Jesus who once walked on water becomes alight with the flame of atonement. In Eskimo mythology, Raven—the trickster—finds himself in the belly of the whale (or water beast) and comes upon a beautiful virgin. Although he holds a pair of fire sticks, and needs only rub them together to ignite the flame that will bring about the death of the whale and render a feast for his people, it is lust and the virgin's subsequent deflowering that causes the whale to convulse the two through his spout. The virgin drowns in the expulsion. Raven survives, but then remembers his fire sticks and re-enters the whale, traveling inside the beast to a separate island before he ignites the fire that kills the whale. Raven's selfishness has left him to consume the feast by himself.

In the Catholic ritual of Holy Saturday, the day between Jesus' death and subsequent resurrection from the belly of Hell, a sacred candle is lit and carried by a processional while the priest chants, "As the heart panteth after the fountains of water, so my soul panteth after Thee, O God! When shall I come and appear before the face of God? My tears have been my bread day and night, while they say to me daily: Where is thy God?" At the baptistry, he blesses the water: "to the end that a heavenly offspring, conceived by sanctification, may emerge from the immaculate womb of the divine font, reborn new creatures: and that all, however distinguished either by sex in body, or by age in time, may be brought forth to the same infancy by grace, their spiritual mother." Then he makes the sign of the cross over the water, dips his hand and tosses water to the four directions, and breathes three times on the water in the form of the cross. As he submerges the candle and extinguishes its flame, he intones, "May the virtue of the Holy Ghost descend into all the water of this font," then repeats the movement and blessing twice more. Finally, the people are sprinkled with the blessed water.

I used to try to picture my husband's demise, creating mind-reels powerful enough to make tears well up. I saw myself standing over his coffin in a black hat and veil, western-cut dress, cowboy boots, looking beautiful enough that one of the other officers would step in to comfort me. Saw the American flag draped and seven cops standing in a row, pointing rifles skyward one-two-three times for a total of twenty-one shots. Practiced the emotions I'd feel, learning of him and my sons in a fatal car crash, the black cherry Dodge Caravan skidding along its top down I-84, burning a fire scar across my life that divided married from husband-less, making a void of the word motherhood. All of it rehearsal, I think now, for what was coming. Not that I wanted them dead, of course, only our dynamic changed. I wanted peace, not the volatile EKG of police officer charm and rage. At parties, other wives used to joke about what they'd do if their husbands were ever shot in the line of duty—radio in and tell them to drag the body to the post office. Police officer spouses got an extra hundred thousand dollars if an officer died defending federal property.

People asked me prior to my heading out on this camping trip, *why on earth* I wanted to come up here so early in the spring to such a lonely place. One well-meaning male friend even said, "You might as well hang out a shingle that says you don't need a man." Well, that is part of the trick. In the past ten years, I have learned to do everything alone, doing taxes, traveling in Europe and major U.S. cities, taking my sons backpacking in the Idaho Rockies. Nighttime alone in the mountains was the only thing left to face. And somehow prove that I am more than the sum of my experiences. That I still have untapped potential.

It will not be until the writing of this essay reaches its eleventh version that I will come to know the truth and say to a colleague almost a year after this trip: *I did not want to get divorced.* A marriage, like anything else, is at once full of salvation and iniquity, water and fire, but when children are born into it, there is no room, as long as no one is bloodying anyone, for quitting. People tell me that my leaving was about my own survival. About blazing a trail for my sons. About being a fire on a higher mountain. Ten years later, however, I am the one who has not recovered from the cleaving. I can't find the means to put it behind me. I can't seem to forgive myself for my subsequent lack of control, and I watch my ex-husband, married to a woman with pre-adolescent boys, and my sons, clinging to girls with intact families, and grieve and grieve and grieve.

Although I do not know it yet, in the morning I will decide that whatever part of my heart I came to collect from the anxious new generation of waters is no longer here. I will heat water and the shots of espresso I brought with me, on the small kerosene burner I bought thirteen years ago for my husband's thirty-fourth birthday, stand drinking it and staring at the ashes of tonight's campfire, wondering again where my brain was that I could assemble espresso shots but forget firewood, pack the burner but go to bed hungry for want of food to cook on it. I'll seal up the Rubbermaid "honey bucket" I brought on the off-chance there were signs of bear near the outhouse. And finally, abandon my campsite to drive the seventy-two miles farther west along Highway 82 and the Minam and Grande Ronde Rivers to La Grande, the town where we lived for most of our family's life and where I attended nursing school at the Oregon Health Sciences University School of Nursing outreach program on the Eastern Oregon University campus.

La Grande, where my husband once dropped a yardstick into the backyard drift of snow and we didn't see it again until April. The same yard in which our dog, Clipper, lay collecting flies on her pelt in the hours before her death. The town where my sons stood wearing graduation hats as they transitioned to kindergarten from preschool. Where they wrestled and played soccer and baseball and basketball and attended talented and gifted programs. Where the oldest marched in the band and worked on the school newspaper and the youngest once came sliding across a stage on his knees playing jazz with a bubble-making yellow plastic saxophone. Where I first discovered D.H. Lawrence and Joyce Carol Oates and gave up on Stephen King. Where I learned the difference between a hawk and a falcon, a sparrow and a meadowlark, a ponderosa and a juniper.

What I also do not know is that I will decide to sleep over in La Grande, renting a room in the same twenty-five-dollar-a-night mom-and-pop motel called the Quail Run, where I used to stay to save money when it was my turn to travel for child visitations. That I will set my bottles of Tanqueray and tonic water on the bedside table and drink until I vomit, while Mel Gibson in *The Patriot* fights his demons in the form of the British and laments silently over the Cherokee he massacred and buried as the result of an earlier segment of the same war, courtesy of in-room HBO. And at some point in the evening, after I've already had too much to drink, I will notice the two Wal-Mart paintings of White Buffalo Calf Woman and her medicine pipe hanging over my bed from either side of the narrow gauge room. I will wonder for months what those two paintings *meant*, and although I have long since left the Indian Health Service, whether the lesser ratio of my blood is once again speaking to me, whether the healer in me is calling me back into service. Or whether the time has finally come that it is myself I need to be healing. *Physician: heal thyself.*

Sitting here by the Lostine, however, this evening in 2001, I must look comical to the gods: the river and the stars have not changed order during this eon, much less ten or fifteen years ago, and my tent, silhouetted against the bank of firs, conjures that familiar duskiness of these woods, a thing I know has been here for a good portion of the earth's age, too. I found my stack of cordwood, after all, courtesy of the U.S. Forest Service and spring storms, so I wad balls of newspaper, arrange a tepee of kindling and two-fingers-thick branches in the fire ring, and wait for these to get going before I place the log and watch dead moss sizzle and pitch ooze in rusty dribbles, wondering who has the scrapbook holding the photo of my oldest son lying next to this very ring, the glow of campfire reflected off his face. He might have been about six then. The tinder ignites in a whoosh, and I recall my husband's quintessential camping joke: "White man build fire big—stand far away. Indian build fire small—stand close." My fire isn't all that big.

Remembering that my younger son stashed his new 35mm camera in the glove box, I grab it and snap shots of my blaze from several angles, turn and expend a similar number of shots on my pitched tent. Proof that, at the very least, somewhere along the way I learned about the mysteries of extracting fire from wood, an unforgiving but more or less reliable means of keeping even a lone, mostly white woman warm.

Holding the Line

Jenny Emery Davidson

When a range fire is crankin', you fight it by running alongside it.
You spray water as you run, pulling a hose from a four-wheel-drive
pumper truck that rolls along next to you. You push through
sagebrush and scramble over lava rock outcroppings, scratching a line
of unburned fuels into the black at the fire's heaving flanks, and then
you try to hold that line, while the fire licks your skin with ferocious
heat and wraps you in smoke. Sometimes ten-foot flames will subside
surprisingly fast, shrinking from the cold spray into smoldering
ash at your heels; other times a creeping fire can suddenly explode,
pushing you back hard and fast and irrevocably. Then you retreat.
You are always trying to read the fire, but you can never really know
what it will do. Firefighters get addicted to this dance.

I did not know this yet, during my first summer on the Bureau
of Land Management fire crew in Shoshone, Idaho. I grew up
with books and ballet lessons in the big Idaho town of Twin Falls,
and while I spent summers hiking and fishing in Idaho's
mountains, I was stepping into the unknown when I pulled on my
shiny new Vibram-soled leather work boots to join the fire crew
during my summer home from college. I missed the open desert
and high mountains while I was at school in Minnesota, so I
wanted to spend as much time outdoors as possible. Fighting fires
promised excitement and good money.

But the summer of 1993 was not a summer of fires. That summer, the high desert stayed green, following a spring and early summer of unusual rain. So instead of chasing smoke and flame, the fire crews worked on the trucks, played pinochle and gin, milled around, and built fence for days on end. The veteran firefighters got restless and cranky. For me, an eager and naive rookie, it was still an adventure. The fire world, with its military-like gear, trucks, and procedures, fascinated me. I was thrilled to be part of a crew, proving myself alongside ten strong men, guys like Tony, a fearless, freckled eighteen-year-old who had just finished high school with a heap of sports awards and no desire for college, and Russ, a lumbering, six-foot-five twenty-six-year-old who swung a pulaski with ease in the summer and drove truck in the off season. I had grown up with two sisters, so everything about the guys intrigued me, from the faded circles on their back pockets that marked their cans of Copenhagen to the way they leaned over an engine and talked about its horsepower.

And I was amazed by the landscape we worked in. I had no idea how big the desert around my home was until I started building fence across it. As my fellow crew members and I drove out to each new project area, I watched the roads and noted every turn, but after bumping down a couple of two-tracks that could barely pass for roads at all, I always felt lost. It was like being hypnotized: the radio droning country music, the wheels humming monotonously, and the landscape moving without seeming to change. We all stared out the windows, and several of the guys quietly spat sunflower seeds and tobacco juice into the empty cans from their morning Mountain Dews. For miles and miles, we drove through the same dusky sagebrush and pale dirt, then a narrow canyon fell from the side of the road without warning, and distant mountains seemed to sink below the horizon, while new mountains rose like a mirage in a different direction.

My crew spent weeks working on one particular fence project in the Kimama Desert, and I never really learned the way out there. On the first day of the project, after nearly two hours of driving, Larry, one of the bosses, somehow determined that we had reached our destination near an almost imperceptible bump in the middle of nowhere. "Yup, Wildhorse Butte," he muttered, and the trucks jerked to a stop. We all unfolded ourselves from the seats, stretching ourselves back into reality. The pungent smell of sage and a wave of heat washed over us as we tumbled out of the air-conditioned trucks. It was ten o'clock in the morning. White sun blazed across the desert with no shade in sight. Sweat surfaced on my forehead under my baseball cap and on my neck behind my ponytail. I rolled my T-shirt sleeves higher in defense against a farmer's tan.

Tony took a can of chew out of his back pocket and shook it deliberately between his second and third fingers, packing it. Squinting into the sun, he said, "Shiiit, if it stays this hot we've gotta get some fires soon."

The others were quick to disagree. It was common knowledge on the fire crew that a sure way to prevent fires from starting was to start predicting them.

"No way, man. We've had too much fuckin' rain. We're gonna be buildin' fence all fuckin' summer."

(On the fire crew, I quickly learned, one or two adjectives served all purposes.)

The can of chew was passed around while everyone stared at the desert and the sky and quietly reflected on the chances of dry lightning and careless cigarettes. Then we started unloading the fencing tools, steel and wood posts, and rolls of barbed wire.

I, too, was hoping for fires. I didn't want to return to college without some good stories to tell. But I didn't mind building fence. I mean, I didn't understand the purpose of this particular fence that seemed to be guarding one plot of brush from another—there were no houses for miles around, and I never saw any cattle, only jackrabbits and rattlesnakes, so the significance of the lines we were defining remained ambiguous—but the work itself was tangible and real, and I liked that. We brought in wood and metal, we stretched straight lines of wire across the desert, and we could see what we had done when we left. The fence work seemed somehow pure and honest to me: a true thin line to the horizon in wide open space.

And while the thought of wildfire excited me, it scared me, too. My shovel skills were marginal enough for digging post holes; I wasn't at all sure they would get me far in front of raging flames.

My fellow crew members, however, were not satisfied with the repetitive rhythms of fence work. Most of them had grown up building and repairing fences on farms and ranches; the testosterone coursing through their blood made them itch for the thrill—and money—of fires. What they wanted, as they often said, was to put some H-Z on their time cards, signifying the extra hazard pay for hours spent actively fighting fire. Building fence didn't qualify, and they grew impatient with the monotonous work. Still, they strode across the desert and through the relentless wind with such confidence, carrying a fence post on each shoulder, unwinding a massive spool of wire like it was thread, pounding a nail into the wood with two quick hits that punctuated the afternoon with certainty. They were beautiful to watch.

I admired them. I developed a number of silent crushes, and I tried in many ways to be more like them and less like the soft college girl I was. But I was long and lanky with arms my mother described as fettucine. I frankly could not carry one fence post or a roll of wire alone, and I had trouble hitting a nail on the head at all—not in two strokes or twenty. So, despite my determination as an oldest child and a budding feminist to be fiercely independent and strong, I found myself tripping along behind, carrying a pair of fencing pliers and stuffing extra nails in my back pockets, trying to look the part while I figured out how to do what they all did so readily.

They showed me how to pull the wire taut at each end with a fence-stretcher, how to clip the wire in place at each steel post, and how to slide the metal stays across the wires to hold them in line. Their instructions were always simple and matter-of-fact, more

a series of movements than words. They evaluated my work with a
nod or a shake, or they simply re-did it. Sometimes, at the end of
the day when we were all ready to go home, I would be pounding
the final nail for a line of fence—missing it, hitting it, and narrowly
sparing my own fingers—as they all stood around and watched.
Finally, when I thought I could not take the pressure and
humiliation any more, Jed or T.C. would start to cheer, "Come on,
Jen! You can do it! One more hit!" And I would wipe my hands
down the front of my jeans, grip the hammer harder, and pound
again, determined to hit the nail all the way in with each new swing.

Gradually, I fell into my own rhythm and walked along the line of
fence clipping the wire in place and sliding in stays like I knew
what I was doing, without side-glancing at someone else's work. My
leather work gloves broke down into familiar creases and soft spots,
and my forearms boasted thin red nicks from the barbed wire.

As we worked past each other down the line, each doing our own
task, jokes were passed along and stories would take shape in
the pauses between the thick thuds of posts being pounded into
the ground. Craig, a sinewy and plain twenty-year-old,
occasionally dropped details from last year's fire season, when the
crews didn't come home for weeks at a time as they hopped
from fire to fire across Idaho, Nevada, and Utah, "sucking smoke"
and racking up overtime.

This summer, firefighters had too much time at home. Tony, a
rookie firefighter, like me, but a natural on the crew, talked about
last weekend's party in the desert, when everyone was rip-roaring
drunk and he tried to light a clump of grass with a cigarette
lighter, just to test the chances of a fire starting.

"It'll burn," he drawled, with a crooked smile.

Blonde-haired, blue-eyed, rough-mouthed Dally talked about the
upcoming rodeo competition and how he thought he could win
the team-roping event if he had a better partner. He practiced
roping rabbitbrush and the rest of us on our breaks.

T.C. talked about his two-legged cow dog.

I rarely said much of anything, but I was usually impressed by
their tales, and a "Wow!" would sometimes escape me. I was
an easy audience. I offered a few stories of my own, making my
own awkward attempts to shock. I talked about college hundreds
of miles away, where the bathrooms were co-ed and students
played naked baseball and some people not only refused to eat
beef, they didn't drink milk. When I got a "You gotta be shittin'
me" in response, I chalked up a notch for the day.

This give-and-take was a kind of game, and it gave an electric
undercurrent to the long hours of repetitive work in sun and rain
and merciless wind. We tested how far we could push each
other, and it provided an outlet for the restless energy of waiting
for dry lightning in a green year. But sometimes someone
pushed too far.

We had been working on the Kimama fence project for what
seemed like weeks when one morning several of the guys found a
fledgling robin in the brush.

I wanted to see it. I felt a throb of sympathy for the young bird
in such a harsh and unlikely place, far from green lawns and trees. It
was alone, stranded. The guys held the bird up to me from a
distance but then fell into a tight circle around it. I turned back to
the fence work, not knowing what they were up to, but not liking
it. I tried to ignore them while they darted around to the trucks and
back, laughing smugly to each other. When we broke for lunch, I
walked back to the trucks a little slower than everyone else and
grabbed my lunch box last. When I opened it, a downy gray feather
floated out. A white blob of crap sat on my Saran-wrapped sandwich.

The guys howled. They had thought they would surprise me and
stick the bird in my box, but they had taken it out to preserve
my lunch.I threw my box in the back of the truck and spent the
rest of the break nursing my water bottle and brooding.

After the others had finished their roast beef sandwiches, potato chips, and Mountain Dews, we went back to work on the fence. I worked along, walking from one steel post to another, bending a clip around each wire at each post, trying to keep the wires straight and taut while ignoring what the others were doing. But I had to keep my eyes on them to mark my own pace, and eventually I noticed that Craig, Tony, Brandon, and Dally had stopped working and were standing away from the fence, guffawing and tossing something back and forth to each other. Craig held a thick stick. Brandon pitched the round object to him, and he swung wildly and missed. The object fell to the ground. I heard a soft, high-pitched squawk.

"Bird baseball!" they shouted to me. My mouth fell open and my stomach knotted. Craig picked up the bird and tossed it back to Brandon. Brandon pitched it again, and this time Craig hit it squarely with a *smack*. The little bird popped into the air, then dropped into the sagebrush thirty feet away. Dally chased it down. Tony took his turn at bat.

"Stop it!" I demanded. They laughed and kept playing. Over and over, they threw the bird, hit it, and chased it down. I stopped hearing squawks. Finally the crew boss called the game off to keep everyone moving on the fenceline.

I was trembling. My cheeks burned; my eyes welled with tears. Such a small thing, and vulnerable, and they just tortured it. I liked these guys. And I had tried all summer to be like them, feeling proud of the blisters and calluses I earned as I began to keep up with them. Now I thought I hated them.

On the ride home, a few guys muttered something about "It's just a stupid bird," but then the conversation stopped. Someone turned up the radio, and the same country songs we heard five times a day about lost lovers and dashed dreams rolled into a steady hum. Sagebrush and sunflowers blurred outside the window. I leaned into the seat and closed my eyes all the way back to the station.

Of course, the next day we had to load up again and go out to the same project together. We were on the same crew. We had to finish our fence. And if we ever got on a fire, we would have to depend on each other. No one played bird baseball again, and no one talked about it. There were no apologies, we just fell into telling the same stories between fenceposts—sometimes swearing, sometimes laughing, and always slowly moving down the line until we finished the square mile fence. Then we moved on to another project while we waited, still, for fires. My boots got bent and scuffed. The scabs on my forearms turned to fine white scars across my suntanned skin. The summer turned to fall and we all went our separate ways.

The next summer, most of us returned to the fire crew and got to see plenty of action and live flame. We chased fire into canyons and up hillsides. We watched fire whirls and blow-ups. We pushed each other along when we had gone forty-eight hours without sleep. At dawn in base camp, we wiped the soot and sweat from our faces with blackened handkerchiefs while we drank coffee and boasted about singed eyebrows. We would start thinking we were pretty good at working wildfire—until the wind changed direction and a fire whirl jumped a line and two days of work went up in smoke, and we were reminded again that you never really can read a fire. I, for one, learned this lesson more than once. In the morning, the sagebrush plain could lie quietly beneath a sky of endless blue. By the afternoon, it could be writhing in smoke. So I learned to keep my eyes on the horizon and my expectations to myself.

But the summer of 1993 we had no fires. We built fence, and—even I—talked tough. I took a picture of my crew when we finished the Kimama fence. In the photo, the guys stand in a staggered line, their arms folded in front of their broad chests, their mouths closed and serious. I sit on a crossbar, smiling widely despite myself. Our jeans and T-shirts are streaked with dirt, our faces tanned and flushed. We are proud. We had endured heat, wind, cold, dust, boredom, rattlesnakes, and each other. We had gone the whole summer without a fire. But we had drawn a line in the desert, and it looked straight.

Stick by Stick

Claire Davis

We tread water. Steam rises in cumulous stacks, and there's the smell of sulfur, and iron, and beneath that the peaty scent of wood smoke. Overhead a helicopter slices through the air, the concussion of blades pressing the steam back down onto the water. Beneath the craft, a bucket swings from the end of a sling. My sister, Mary, looks up, her brown hair pearled with mist. She calls this a vacation, although I know it is more than that—our father having recently passed away, and our mother as well, a short fourteen months ago. It has been a hard year, and now she has come west just in time to watch it burn. Ironically, this is also the first opportunity I've had to show the West that is my home to my sister. I take her to Coeur d'Alene, Bonner's Ferry, up the Selway River, and into the Bitterroot Mountains. Everywhere we go we are chased by fires. Today, we're near McCall, Idaho, soaking in the Burgdorf hot springs, a spacious log-lined hot pot the length and width of a goodly sized swimming pool. It's surrounded by a cluster of buildings: a rickety lodge, separate men's and women's dressing rooms, log cabins in renovation— several falling-down derelict remnants from the turn of the century. At our back, rising above this small pocket of buildings is a mountain, and over the saddle of the mountain the smoke from a 64,000-acre burn billows up and flattens in false thunderheads against blue sky.

Just a few hundred yards below us in the catch-basin meadow is fire base camp where khaki tents billow like oversized puffballs. Fire crews guide the bucket into the stream that cuts a yazoo course through a grassy field, through upstart stands of quaking aspen and tamarack. A handful of mule deer skitter out of the brush and flee up the road toward the highway.

It's a tent city down there with more than 1200 people manning the fire crews—mostly young men and women changing into or out of fire gear, or flopping down to sleep on open ground, or draping themselves over the hoods of vehicles to relax. Lines queue up outside the cook tent where the stove is stoked and the smell of bacon is slippery in the air. This is the front line of a fire that has been burning for close to a month, and one of a number of fires sweeping the West this summer.

We came to McCall because that fire was still some miles distant, and I wanted, more than anything, to have her experience sitting in hot springs on the side of a mountain. We'd driven along an empty highway, a clear summer day except for the narrow smudge of clouds to the north. It seems that even as we had been driving south out of Lewiston, the fire had been moving north. When we reached the Burgdorf cutoff, we found a barricade had been erected to stop traffic. A fire marshal walked up to my truck, leaned his arm on the open window, and smiled at us.

"You ladies going somewhere?" he said.

"Just into the hot springs here. Is it safe?" I asked.

He looked over his shoulder, up at the mountain, at the smoke. He turned back, shrugged, then flipped a palm down and up with a wavering, so-so kind of gesture. "Long as the wind don't turn," he said.

I glance over at Mary. She's wide-eyed.

"And if it does?" I ask.

"You'll be the first to know." He winked and laughed.

An hour later, we are paddling about in the shadow of a burning mountain, in a pool of water heated by fire in the earth.

The first time fire becomes personal I am eight years old. My sister is eleven. We're in the kitchen, and the last of the afternoon light slants through the window over the sink. If I stand on tiptoes, I can see out this window and into the backyard where our mother is kneeling in the garden. She's wearing, as she always does at home, a house dress with Mother Hubbard apron and nylons she will not forsake for any occasion or weather.

Mary is watching me, a job she begrudges. Who's to blame her? While her friends are playing baseball in the roughed-out side lot, she's tied to the house tending to me still recovering from measles. Mary decides to boil a couple of eggs, turns on the electric stove, and walks away.

Perhaps she leaves to play her violin. It's what I recall most clearly about Mary, the way she stood braced in a fighter's stance, her fingers around the violin's neck, her face screwed into a finely tuned ferocity.

She's playing "Turkey in the Straw." She's always playing "Turkey in the Straw." I'm looking out the window, watching my mother shake clods of dirt from some root vegetable. She's kneeling on the strip of overgrown grass—a hinterland between the tilled garden and nipped lawn. In the sky there's the scroll of clouds and a peppering of black birds.

Behind me, I hear the first sound, like ice cubes in water—the liquid squeeze that precedes the snap. Then silence, and then another sound, louder, a crackling like paper being crumpled. There's an odd cast of reflected light in the window—orange, and yellow, and strangely articulate. For a moment, I think it's a kind of backward sunset, reflecting from the wrong side. When I look over my shoulder, I see the fire.

Up until now, fire's always been managed, a small flame cupped to my father's cigarette. The merry glow of a birthday cake. The burn barrel my father keeps us clear of. But now, in the confines of the narrow kitchen, it's a pillar of flame that rises up and up over the stovetop, the black smoke rising like a hive of bees into the stinging air. Mary's turned on the wrong burner, under a kettle of grease. I'm past the first speechless moments and yelling when Mary comes running from the living room, grabs me by a sleeve, and shoves me backward.

"Get out of the way," she shouts, and I'm up against the wall as she heads for the stove. Her hands reach into the light, and there's a small sound, a kind of yelp, and then she grabs a pot holder to grasp the handle. She lifts the kettle, two-handed, and I see her arms wavering with its shifting liquid weight. She shuffles it onto a cold coil, but the flame burns with a life of its own, independent of stove or burner. Mary glances over her shoulder to where I stand. Her eyes have gone small and gray.

She takes a deep breath, picks up the pan again, then turns with it held in front of her at chest level, elbows locked. With each step the fire bends into her, and those small hairs around the side of her face, the ones that have escaped the bridle of ponytail, curl with heat and draft toward the flame, and still she keeps walking, marching.

I remember her long-sleeved, striped T-shirt. Her jeans rolled into cuffs over saddle shoes. I remember her lips pressed tight, and how close she is to crying, though I know she will not. I remember the flame and how it washes over her with each step, as if for those few moments she becomes part of the luminous package she bears. I remember the feel of the wall against my back and shoulder blades, too frightened to do more than watch her cross the entire ten steps to the sink. Then she is lowering the pot into the porcelain basin, and breathing as if she's come up for air after

a long immersion. Her hands shake as she reaches around the
flame to turn on the faucet.

A grease fire.

The water hits, and the flame—all hiss and fury—glazes the glass,
and clings to the sheers over the sink. Mary's driven back by
heat and steam and spitting grease. And then she's slapping at her
arms where the stinging bits of grease darken her shirt. I know
this look; she's angry now. She's up on the balls of her feet and
ready to go at it again when our mother comes running in through
the back door. Her apron's spilling a trail of vegetables as she
marshals Mary out of the way, grabs a lid, and drops it over
the pot. She's a practical woman, and in this her movements are
utterly economical. Even to the way she bats out the curtain
flames with a dish towel in one hand and pulls the last smoking
wisps into the sink with the other.

Smoke hangs in a false ceiling throughout the house, and Mother's
throwing open windows and doors, and still my sister stands on the
balls of her feet, with hands at her side, in the place between stove
and sink. Mary's trying to explain. About the fire. The water.

Mother stops long enough to plant her hands on hips, looks over
the stove top. "You never turn a burner on and leave." She flips on
the appropriate burner under the eggs.

"You never pour water over a grease fire." She's not really yelling;
it just feels that way. Mother looks out the dining room
window where the lawn hunkers in the twilight. She sinks into a
chair, and I see she is not as composed as I'd believed; her hands
are shaking. "My God, you never walk with fire in front of
you. If you got to carry it somewhere, walk backwards so the
flame moves away. *You* could have caught fire. A grease fire." And
wonder of all wonders, it's our mother who's crying, and my
sister standing at her side now, patting her back, her shoulder
and arms.

It's then my mother sees the blush on my sister's hands. Mother's up on her feet again, tears forgotten, and holding the smaller hands under cold water. After that she applies the only remedy she knows. A stick of butter. Bandages.

She keeps my sister close the entire night.

I pull at the swimming suit strap that slips down my arms. The air above my shoulders and sternum wavers with heat, my skin radiant. My sister and I sit on the log-lined edge of the hot pool, letting the breeze cool our pinked skin. The same breeze is brisking through the tops of the firs, coursing up the mountainside like fingers raking through hair, and in the moments between gusts, in the lull when the firs sway slowly back toward the hollow, the smell of wood smoke is bright. There's no other indication of the fire that burns steadily just the other side of the ridge.

Below us, activity in the fire base camp peaks and lulls as well, between departing and arriving convoys of trucks. Between the flight of helicopters up and back. The Oregon Hotshots are somewhere down there—the elite team of Native American smokejumpers. We passed their rig when we pulled in. I think about the men and women standing alongside the road, how impossibly young they looked. Their eyes ringed with dirt and hollow with exhaustion, staring after us, following our progress up the dusty drive, wondering who these two middle-aged women were, driving through the middle of camp. What did they think when we drove right past the cook tent, past the supply trucks, and the medical tent, past the units' headquarters, choosing instead the right fork, up and into the hot springs grounds with its shabby resort. *Tourists.*

This must be what the front line of war looks like, and to those down below we must appear like something out of a book, *War and Peace*, say, when the townsfolk bearing picnic baskets drive in their Sunday carriages to the front to see the war played out for their entertainment.

For Mary, the West has turned wild again, and she's having an honest-to-God adventure.

Me? I'm feeling sheepish. This is my home, after all, not a ten-day vacation I'll recall in three-by-five photos. I feel I should be doing something. Something other than floating on the Styrofoam tubes that litter the pool, or shepherding my sister through the unfired portions of the state. Something other than sitting mute on the edge of a pool while my toes pucker in the water. I should be helping. I feel guilty. I feel helpless. I should pray. Or something.

For it appears that the sky has fallen, the clouds—just over the tops of trees and houses—are gray-green and tumble in a wad like laundry dimly seen in a dryer window. There's a flicker and glow on the foreshortened horizon and then a muted rumble long moments later. The roadside oaks begin to stir, leaves twitching on thin stems, and the wind returns, and about the base of the trees and down into the ditch a cluster of mayapples invert their parasols. The wind snatches our hair, twists it up and over our heads and faces. We're shrieking, Mary and I, laughing and stumbling into the wind. "Come on," she yells. We run for the house, dirt flinging up into our faces, while in the weedy no-man's land between our trim lawn and the farmer's fields, the winds bob and weave and wave through the long uncut grasses.

High summer, 1955. A workday, midday. Friday. That narrow belt through the nation affectionately known as Tornado Alley. When the storm comes upon us, it is slowly over the long hours of an afternoon that follows on the heels of a sweltering morning, humidity so high mosquitoes tread the sweat on our arms. I am six years old, playing in the dirt lot next to our home, and when the wind starts, it's with a single fierce gust that layers us in a patina of dust—up under our nails, in the crack of eyelids, our nostrils. (Later on, when stripping for baths, we will discover it has sifted down into our clothes as well, a fine red line of dirt delineating where our underdrawers begin and end.) The wind falters, stops.

My sister and I look at each other. She wipes a sleeve over her face, her eyes, and looks up at the sky. She stands staring.

On the front porch our mother's turned mime, clutching her apron in a hand, and with the other, a big, gestured wave. Her mouth is opening and closing. She's clearly shouting, though we can't hear anything. We tip into the wind like drunks, enjoying the sheer physicality of what we can't see.

When we hit the porch, her words are broken up like static, so that all I hear is *storm*, and *inside*, and *something, something radio*. Clearly it's not as funny as we'd thought. She bustles us in, but I look over my shoulder to see her, one hand blindly feeling for the screen door that has slammed back on its hinges while she scopes out the oncoming storm, leaning over the flower planter crammed with pink and white petunias, their delicate trumpets flailing. The bitter smell of their shredding fills the hallway.

She struggles with the screen door, then locks the inner door as well. She stands with her hands braced on the frame, head bent as if she's listening, or as if she's feeling the pulse of the storm through the wood. When she steps away, the smile she wears is the one that's supposed to convince us everything's okay. I'm running back and forth from the living room's big Thermopane window to the smaller one in the dinette. Here and there the clouds glow and dim with an incandescent green like the belly of a firefly. Mary's standing across the room from the window, the back of her knees backed against the sofa. Her hair is a windy snarl that she pats down.

We watch the trees outside; the sturdy oaks twist and resist, branches fall, mostly dead wood. The dark intensifies and the firefly light becomes violent flashes; the rumbles are replaced by hard cracks. Mother tells me to stop running, and then the room lights flicker and go out.

When we stop yelling *the lights are out, the lights are out*, it's because Mom's returned from the bedroom with the blessed candle in hand. It's in a candle holder that's a cruciform Christ

molded in glass. I know this candle holder. It's the one that held
the nub of beeswax burning at the bedside of my dying
grandmother—the small flame sole illumination in the shade-
drawn room for an assembly of aunts and uncles and cousins, for
the hollowed husk lying prone on the bed whom I am made to
walk past and kiss a last time.

The storm deepens. The windows are being pelted with twigs and
leaves, rain and even small hard bits of grit that turn out to be ice.
I suspect the presence of this deathwatch candle, feel it does not
bode well. Mother sets it on the highest point in the living
room—the TV cabinet.

My mother was a native of Wisconsin, who had lived through any
number of storms. She knew what we *should* do. As did my sister
and I. Every home in the midwest, any house worth its weight,
had, at the very least, a root cellar or storm cellar. Our home
had a full, ten-course, concrete brick basement—my father's pride
and joy—where there were no windows to blow out. Where the
walls wouldn't fold in. Where there was no roof to collapse down
upon its concrete slab floor. It was a clean, new basement, spacious
and free of the clutter—the coal bins and chutes of the older
houses. My mother's wringer washer was down there, the
dual wash sink, and the sump pump that kicked on with the big
rains. There were clotheslines strung the length and width
of the basement from the metal pillars that supported the home
we lived in. There was no reason we shouldn't go down there in a
storm of this intensity.

She struck a match. There was the sting of sulfur and the sweet
smell of beeswax, like sin and salvation hand in hand. The small
flame wavered as the wind outside walloped the side of the house,
and sucked back, drafting air from the slim cracks beneath the
door, and up the chimney, and through the slits of rattling
windows. And then in all the dark and our growing fear, the flame
became a clean, small pillar of light that cast a bright oval against
the wall, and over the mahogany cabinet and the pebbled carpet
we knelt on as our mother handed us each our rosary.

We knelt before the blessed flame with the fire of crystal beads in our hands, praying, "Hail Mary, full of grace——." The three of us pitting our faith against the air about us, against the engine that ramped down upon our house with a head of steam built in its headlong run across the great plains. We could hear the storm, and above it my mother's voice. Perhaps this is what she meant to teach us. That leap of faith. To put ourselves in the hands of something greater than the works of man.

Perhaps she was putting us to the fire so that we might know the concrete experience of faith. I remember concentrating on the small flame, willing it to stay lit, for that meant the walls must remain intact, the windows whole, and the roof attached as the train bore down the long tracks overhead.

It occurs to me all these years later that this is what fire has mostly been for me, a referent in a place of greater mysteries. My first and most lasting perceptions of fire have to do with faith cultured in the landscape of churches. St. Matthews where I was baptized, with its full-sized statue of the crucified Christ whose nailed feet we kissed after dropping our pennies in the offering box and lighting the vigil flame. St. Lawrence where I was married. Sacred Hearts of Jesus and Mary—a church built with the stones hauled by my grandfather's team of horses, set in place with his block and tackle. Holy Apostles, Jesu, Holy Hill, St. Josephat— the Basilica.

St. Francis Friary in Burlington, Wisconsin, where I am a toddler on a pilgrimage with my sister and parents. We wander the arboretum and flower gardens the monks tend, then follow the paths that wind down into an underground grotto where banks of vigil lights flare against the backdrop of wrought iron bars encasing a life-size diorama of Romans—centurions whipping Christ, whose plaster flesh was peeled back in full color like ripening fruit. The smell of incense from the main church and the monks' chanting reaches even here in this twilight tomb. And

when staring at the rendered flesh becomes too much, my refuge
is the small ruby votives, the trembling cups of flame.

When we leave the hot pot, our limbs feel deliciously *al dente*. We
clamber into my truck, having stowed damp towels and suits in
the pickup bed. We tool back down the drive, past yet another
flurry of activity as a helicopter approaches and crews rise to their
feet again. You can almost hear the groans. At the highway, the
barricades are still up, but there's been a turnover of personnel,
except for the smart-aleck marshal who smiles at us and tips a
finger to his forehead. We have a forty-minute drive back to
McCall, to the state park where our tent is set up for the evening.
Mary dozes, head against the window, mouth dropping open. It's a
thing she's done since she was a child—an almost automatic
response to riding in a vehicle. Just days before, she drove with me
the 1700 miles from her home and stayed awake to keep me
company the entire way. A marathon of will. But now she sleeps,
her head rocking back and forth on the glass. I drive the winding
road, comforted by her confidence.

Though I want to wake her and point out the unfired beauty of
Lake Payette in the early evening hours, the waterways that
parallel the road, the island stands of Douglas fir and ponderosa
pine, I do not. Instead, I watch her from the corner of my eye and
think, *She is smaller,* thinner, folding in on herself in a way I don't
recall from our youth, and I see how the death of our parents, and
her long vigil over their declining years, has taken its toll.

In the resort town of McCall she wakes, blushes when I tease her
about drooling. We stop for dinner at an Italian restaurant,
both of us weary, and ravenous, and only too happy to pack in
pasta with its hearty tomato sauce and Italian sausage, warm
garlic bread.

Later, at the campsite, I build a small fire in the iron grill the park
provides for cooking. We are allowed this frugal blaze, but the

larger campfire pits rimmed by stone rings are dark and cold and will remain this way throughout the long summer of fires. I feed the flame stick by stick. It's hardly enough to warm our hands, but I persist. It's curious—the heavy smell of wood smoke paired with the unnatural dark of the campground. No glimmering campfires, no bonfires, no families grouped in lawn chairs about roaring blazes. I am amazed at how restrained the campers are, children sticking close to parents, parents speaking in quiet tones. There's no electric in this park, so even the strings of owls and colored tiki lights are missing.

All about us, the woods are dark and deeper than I recall, and in the upper canopy, among wind-tossed limbs, is a spangling of stars. We sit deep in our chairs, letting the lassitude of limbs dictate the evening. It is companionable, and we talk about home and our children. After a long while, we talk of our parents so recently deceased: our mother's slow decline, and our father's sudden passing from cancer. We fall silent. This is unfamiliar territory. We sit across from one another in the night, feeling alone, as children will without parents.

Because we camp on the lee side of the mountain, in the shadow of fire, when we speak again it is of kitchen fires, and storms, of tiny flames, and faith. We sit the long hours, feeding each other these stories, staving off sleep and doubts, for at a level deeper than reason, we are just beginning to comprehend the ways in which our lives— even the ways in which we have always seen ourselves—are being as cleanly redefined as the hills after a burn.

When at last we grow silent, we remain seated, my sister and I, already half dreaming in our chairs. In a short while we will put to rest the struggle to stay awake. Housed among the pillars of trees, tips wicking the light of a full moon, we will find our way to the tent where we will say our *good nights*, and *sweet dreams*, and each *I love you, Sis*. We will burrow into sleep, content to take on faith that the night will pass, and that the winds will remain as constant as the woods about us.

An owl hoots from the perimeter, and somewhere outside our circle of knowing, the misplaced deer bed down in thickets, and coyotes whose fur smells of wood smoke and singe range the hills nosing through grasses, startling up small droves of rodents even as the fire roots about the sides of the mountain, sending its own waves rippling outward.

But say instead, that is not what we do. Say we stir ourselves, step out of this rim of woods, beyond the parked cars and darkened tents, say we walk the pitching paths through the trees, over root and rock, cutting clear of the wild rose and salmon berry to cross over into the small meadows that lie just beyond so that we might lift our faces to where the wind blows. Say we raise our eyes to the narrow belt of sky with its pinkish gloaming, like the atmosphere over some distant city, that is fire on the mountain. Fire on the mountain contained by the vigilance of young men and women suited in soot. Contained by the grace of whatever hand directs the wind. Say we raise our eyes to fire on the mountain, a flicker in the distance. Flame trembling in a cup of green.

Strawberry Blonde

Phil Druker

The State of Idaho had not hired us to have water fights
with its fire trucks. So on that surprisingly hot June day we didn't
pay much attention to the guys from the other crew when
they parked their truck on the dirt road in front of our lunch
spot while we relaxed in the shade. Nor did we give their
efforts to start the pump engine any heed. However, when cold
water sprayed us, that did get our attention. I leaped up and
ran for cover while the five others in my crew jumped
onto our truck and started the pump. The two crews soaked each
other, hurled insults, and laughed until long after lunch break
was over.

When we returned to work, our crew leader mentioned we would
have to head into town early to fill the water tanks. Since piling
brush wasn't what anyone called a good time, the prospect of
heading to town early didn't exactly trouble us.

During the previous winter, a crew had thinned the twenty-year-
old stand of Douglas fir, grand fir, tamarack, and white pine
by cutting down the small trees, the misshapen trees, and
the trees crowding out those growing fast and straight. Now, our
job on this firefighting crew was to remove the slash left behind.

It was tedious, hot work: bend, pick up, throw; bend, pick up, throw; bend, pick up, throw.

Those who had worked on the fire crew in previous summers got to cut the slash with chain saws. While they had the honor and privilege of running a saw, their job was no less boring and difficult. They spent their days humped over a noisy, vibrating machine, and their breaks came when they needed to refill the saw with gas and chain oil or when brush caught in the chain, which could throw it from the bar. In the mid-1970s, sawyers didn't wear safety chaps. They were too hot, and besides a woodsworker wasn't supposed to look like a cowboy. Neither did the saws have the automatic breaks and guards that saws have today. So, the sawyers had to watch what they were doing and keep their hands, thighs, and boots away from the chain. It was hungry even when dull.

The rest of us threw the cut slash into piles that would dry until fall. Then, we who had spent the summer protecting the forest from fire would walk through the forest with propane burners or cans of diesel and set the piles on fire. This, unlike our present work, was immensely entertaining. Sometimes the brush piles didn't want to ignite, but when they took off, their blue and orange and yellow flames leaped and danced through the pile of dry branches and sent embers high into the gray autumn sky. The incense of burning fir and pine filled the air and permeated our clothes. The end of the work season was drawing near. Hunting season, Thanksgiving, and fall layoff approached. Even if it was raining, it was a good time to be in the woods. You could always dry off with the warmth of a just-set fire.

On this hot June day, we were not thinking much about fire—it was too early in the season for that. Somehow, however, a fire flared up in some of the dry slash we had piled. Maybe a chainsaw overheated and no one noticed. Maybe a sawyer spilled gasoline and a spark from his saw ignited the gas that flared up in the dry, dead, cut limbs. Maybe it was a cigarette. Given the way things went back then, maybe some kid was trying to light a joint on that hot, windy afternoon. Maybe someone set the fire on purpose thinking to make some overtime or hazardous duty pay. Maybe he wasn't thinking. Anyhow, a fire began to burn in the stand of timber we were supposed to be improving.

We ran to the fire truck, rolled out the hose, and started the pump engine. The spray of water arced onto the flames and quickly knocked them down. Then, the water stopped—the tank had gone empty. The other crew couldn't get their pump started—they had run out of gas. By the time they got their pump running, the fire had a good start and was already blowing up into the crowns of the firs and pines and making a run despite our efforts to stop the blaze. It raced up the ridge, leaping from tree to tree, whipped by the stiff afternoon breeze.

For a moment, a stream of water from the other crew's hose slowed the fire's spread. Then their tank went empty. The fire crackled back to life. We stood in disbelief. Fires weren't supposed to take off like this in early summer. At first the crew chief was too embarrassed to radio for help, but now he had no choice.

Someone mentioned the water fight and the crew chief said to forget that. We had to get the fire out.

Guys with chain saws headed up the ridge and started felling trees in an attempt to make a firebreak. The rest of us worked on the edge of the fire with our shovels trying to smother the flames with dirt. The wind freshened and the flames created their own draft. Desperately, we worked against the flames. Cinders burnt through our shirts. Smoke stung our eyes and choked our lungs. The heat singed the hair from our arms. My heart beat as if it were ready to burst.

The fire spread quickly and we were in danger of being surrounded by fire. In our zeal to stop it, we were working too close. It was too hot. We had to get out of there. So we regrouped, headed farther up the ridge to cut a fire line, and hoped the Orofino office would send us the help we needed soon.

With our hand tools and chain saws, we couldn't work fast enough. No matter how quickly we cut and dug, the fire gained on us. The sweltering heat, the choking smoke, the crackling flames pressed ever closer. The fire began to overrun our hand-dug line. We were losing the battle, and it looked like we were going to lose the whole stand of trees—a stand that the state had spent huge amounts of money on thinning and preening for timber harvest.

Just as we were about ready to give up and get out of the fire's way, a D6 (a good-sized Caterpillar bulldozer) came roaring up the hill. Its silvery blade knocked over small and medium-sized trees. Then the Cat backed up and scraped the duff to expose damp, brown soil. Working this way, the Cat skinner gouged out a fire line far wider than we ever could cut with our hand tools.

We moved out of his way, waved, and went back to reinforce the fire line the bulldozer built. The Cat skinner smiled, waved briefly, and kept rumbling up the ridge building the firebreak. We cut roots that might burn, felled trees near the line (downhill into the fire), and put out smokes that windblown embers and fire brands started across the line.

Tanker trucks arrived with other crews. We rolled out hose, dragged it up the hill, and started the pumps. The water doused the flames. Then we aimed at the hot spots. The cold water wet our hot gloves, shirts, and pants. The cool spray gave relief from the heat of the flames, the heat of hard work, and the heat of the day. The water hissed in the smoldering fire and steam mixed with smoke.

By dinnertime, we had the fire out. Some men stayed to tend the fire by dousing hot spots and flare-ups through the night. The rest of us, as we rode back to town, calculated the couple hours of overtime pay plus hazard pay.

I said, "fiyer." Barb, my then wife, who was from the Orofino area, teased me about my Minnesota accent. She said the word had one syllable: "fir." Even though I had worked in the woods as sawyer, even though I could buck six or seven truckloads of timber to send to the mill in a day, even though I drank a six-pack of beer on the way home from the woods each night and smoked a pack of Camels each day, I was still an outsider.

With Barb's Uncle Lester, the man operating that bulldozer that saved the day years earlier after the water fight in the woods, I dipped into my mother-in-law's whiskey while Lester told stories about playing baseball, raising barns, fighting fire, and labor strife in the area's mills. Still I was an outsider.

I said the property we owned on a bench above the Clearwater River not far from Orofino was dangerously built up with an accumulation of dead grass. We needed to burn some of it off. Lester didn't say much. Barb said I was nuts. I was a city boy who didn't know brass from gold about fire.

I, like most foresters and extension agents, considered controlled fire to be a great cleanser. To eliminate slash left behind by logging operations, which harbors insects and disease that attack trees, foresters employed fire. Plus, fire offers a good way to return nutrients and minerals to forest soil after it has been logged. Extension agents and state foresters urged landowners to keep dead grass and other burnable material from building up in ungrazed pastures and woodlots or along roadsides. The best way to do that, they said, was to set controlled burns.

I had some experience with this: I had helped touch off controlled burns with the Forest Service. Plus, I had burned many a field with another of Barb's uncles who had a 1500-acre wheat ranch near Nezperce on the Camas Prairie. He hired me to help run the place. He lived in town; Barb and I lived in the family ranch house seven miles southwest of town. A magnificent home built near the turn of the last century, the six-bedroom house stood on a hill that offered a view that extended from White Bird Pass in the south to the Selway Crags in the east and to Moscow Mountain in the north. During the summers, I worked raising wheat, barley, canola, and Kentucky bluegrass seed. Each August, after we harvested grass seed, we regularly burned the mile-square fields. Or sometimes, when a harvested field of wheat was filled with so much stubble we couldn't easily plow, we burned the stubble off.

This field burning was a time-honored practice and nearly as common as plowing. In the 1970s it was part of farming landscape even though we knew it left fields bare and, thus, in danger of eroding more than when stubble is left in the field. We also knew burning eliminates the organic matter healthy, productive soils need. Still, some farmers reasoned—whether rightly or wrongly, but mostly wrongly—that field burning killed insects and diseases along with offering an expedient way to clear a field. More importantly for farmers, bluegrass needs fire to produce large quantities of seed. Nowadays, much to the dismay of bluegrass farmers, the practice is forbidden in many states and somewhat controlled in Idaho. Air pollution from field burning has killed people and makes whole areas suffer under a pall of smoke. In the 1970s, however, we didn't worry much about those sorts of things.

Burning a dry field of stubble is one exciting process. After circling the edge of the field with a disk to expose bare soil and create a firebreak, we would wait for a still day or a day with a little wind. When conditions were just right, I attached a section of harrow to the tractor and drove through the field to fill the harrow's teeth with dry stubble. Then Barb's uncle lit the stubble in the harrow, and I drove the tractor along the windward side of the field pulling the flaming harrow.

Flames spread with amazing fury. The holocaust of flames rushed across the mile-wide section in a flash—in ten minutes the mile-square field was burnt. The smoke rose to form a mushroom-shaped cloud as if from a nuclear bomb. The roar filled our ears, and we could only hope that our firebreak would hold. The thought of someone being caught in this conflagration was beyond imagination.

The fire left the field smoldering, blackened, and bare. After the fire cooled, rough-legged and red-tailed hawks appreciated our work. They gorged themselves on so many mice and voles they could barely fly.

Based on my experience with field burning, which I considered extensive, I assured Barb that burning a little dead grass alongside a road would be easy. So on a glorious spring day, the first clear day after weeks of storms and rain, we decided to head up to our land for a visit and to do a little clean-up work. Barb got some food and beer together. I threw the fencing tools and a couple shovels, a rake, and a pitchfork in the pickup. Why, she asked, was I bringing a jug of diesel? To burn off some of the old, accumulated grass, I told her. She rolled her eyes and shook her head.

Our twenty acres faced south and afforded a view down the Clearwater River canyon. Half the acreage was flat and cleared years previously for farm ground. The other half rose steeply up a hillside covered with good-sized ponderosa pine mixed with Douglas fir. We mended fence and cleaned up some old junk. As we ate lunch in the warm sun, birds sang in the pines and firs, and off in the brush, grouse were mating and booming. A couple of red-tailed hawks soared in a thermal above the river canyon and disappeared into the clear blue sky.

Barb was 23; I was 30 when we met. She was from Peck, Idaho; I was from St. Paul, which seemed like a big city. She wanted kids; I didn't. She liked the bar scene in Orofino; I liked hanging out at home. We were, despite our differences, in love. Barb was wild about me. I don't know how many times I tried to douse the embers of love. I ignored her, went out with other women, and tried to forget about her to make her forget about me, but she wouldn't give up. When I rented an old homestead on the breaks above Big Creek, she moved in. We had a yo-yo relationship: when she drifted off, I pulled her back in; when I drifted off, she reeled me back in.

She was a wild one. Long before tattoos became popular, she had a long-single-stem rose tattooed down her back. She stayed in town partying late, got drunk, argued with the cops. She collected black animals: a black lab, black cats, and black chickens. For a while she even had an injured raven with a broken wing that we found on a logging road not far from home. That raven, which smelled like burnt wood, ruled the menagerie with its black eyes and beak. My nickname was "Animal" because with my long hair and beard the loggers I worked with thought I looked like the crazy Muppet. Friday nights Barb and I would close the bar, go to a friend's house, and party until dawn. Then we'd drive home, never once questioning the wisdom of driving when we were so drunk we barely could walk. Still, compared to Barb, I was a wet blanket and some friends called me "the old fuddy duddy."

One Friday evening, I came home after a week of work in the woods. Barb came running out to greet me. She wore a pink dress with little pink elephants on it—her party dress. After a big hug and a kiss, she said she couldn't stay in that house anymore. Why not, I asked, crestfallen. Because pack rats had invaded the house. She screamed as she told me about a rat running over her as she lay in bed trying to fall asleep.

She had her party dress on, so we went to town, got drunk, partied till 3 A.M., drove home (our guardian angel kept us on the steep, narrow, winding road up the canyon to our house that night), and in the morning, despite a roaring hangover, I ripped up floor boards until I found the rat nest, then set traps and poison bait. We got rid of the pack rats and Barb stayed. Her folks were not exactly happy with this. Still, she persisted. I persisted. We persisted. The spark flared. We went to Coeur d'Alene to get married and stood nervously in a judge's chambers as he intoned the marriage vows. When he paused, I blurted out "I do." The judge said, "Okay, but not yet son." He finished my part of the vows, nodded to me, and I repeated "I do." Barb said her vows, I gave her a ring, and we went to the bar to party.

In the shade on our twenty acres near Orofino, we lay together and talked over plans for our future house. We finished our beer

and dozed in the spring sun, a few flies buzzing, a neighbor's
rooster crowing, and warblers singing in the trees. With
lunch over, I decided it was time to burn off the dead grass, so
I raked up a pile of brown grass, soaked it with diesel, lit a
match, and set it to the pile. Nothing happened.

I raked up more grass, doused it with plenty of diesel, and lit it.
The pile smoldered and finally flames licked through the pile.
With the pitchfork, I spread the flames to grass lying dead
alongside the dirt road that cut across our land. The fire went out.

Barb kept saying I was nuts. The dead grass was fine. This place
had looked like this for years, she said, and it hadn't burned. I,
however, was insistent and kept trying. Come summer, I said, it
would be a fire hazard. Better to get rid of the dead grass near the
road now.

After about an hour of fooling around with piles of grass and
diesel, plus a little gasoline, I still hadn't burned more than a few
yards along the road. But we had run out of fuel. So I convinced
Barb to drive back to town with the empty plastic jug to get
more diesel and beer while I tried one more time to get things
burning. She left, repeating I was nuts, and I continued my
mission. The day was warming. The wind was rising. I set another
pile on fire. It took off. I spread the flames to the next clump
of grass. Slowly it began to burn, and I spread the flames farther.

Soon the grass was smoldering and burning on its own. Then,
instead of trying to encourage the fire, I started trying to keep the
flames contained to the grass near the road. I put out one spot,
but the warm afternoon wind blew the flames to another, then
another. I tried to stand in front of the burning edge of fire and
beat the flames out with my shovel. The flames, however, put out
so much heat I couldn't get near them.

The wind picked up. The flames raced across our field and headed
up the hill toward the adjoining property. I dropped my shovel
and ran like hell to the nearest neighbor's house, praying to

heaven that my fire wouldn't hurt anyone. Cows looked at me curiously as I sprinted up the road. Magpies cackled from the brush. Dogs barked. At the neighbor's door, I knocked furiously and waited. No one came to the door. I shouted hello. No one answered. Hesitating a moment, as I had never been in the house and had talked to these people only once, I tried the door. It was unlocked. I ran in, found the phone, and dialed 911.

The operator was amused. April was too early for fire season, she said, and no one had any fire rigs ready. I begged for help. She said she'd see what she could do.

Defeated, I hiked back to our property to see what destruction my fire had wrought. The fire had galloped across our field and up the hill, burning through the grass in the lower part of our ponderosa pine stand. Then it continued across the grassy hill on to another neighbor's property, met a gravel road, and burned itself out.

The area smelled of burnt grass, soot, and burning pine. A few stumps smoldered. A clump of brush crackled as it burned.

I walked around beating out hot spots with my shovel. Men from the fire protection district arrived in red pickups. They commented on what a good job I had done burning off the field, talked about the weather, and mused this was one field they wouldn't have to worry about when things turned dry in the coming August. As the red pickups departed down our road, Barb returned with the jug full of diesel. She said, "I guess you won't need this now." I shook my head and answered, "I'd be glad to take one of the beers you brought." She looked at me like I might not get one.

That summer, we had a beautiful stand of grass. Although my plan had worked, and happily I had not destroyed any property or burned up any timber, I forswore setting open fires. The theory made sense, but the practice was too scary.

A friend once told me that I was playing with fire marrying a redhead like Barb. Actually, I said, she was a strawberry blonde, but he insisted that was close enough. Years later, before we divorced, I told Barb that it seemed the fire had gone out. She said I still didn't know how to say "fire."

Textbooks tell us that fire requires air, fuel, and heat. Based on my experience, even with all three you still won't have a fire unless conditions are just right. Experience also tells me that once a fire blazes enough to create its own heat, if it has enough fuel and enough air—in the form of wind—there's darn little you can do to stop it.

Like fire, love sometimes is difficult to get started and requires fuel to keep it going. When love is burning bright, it's like a raging blaze that is nearly impossible to put out. But when love's fire turns to cold ashes, it's darn hard to rekindle the flame.

Trash Burner

Susan Glave

The house was by any standards tiny. Two bedrooms and a
bathroom scrunched together to form the house's north side. A
giant's step, if you were a child, across a strip of worn linoleum
separated the bedrooms from a living room. A left turn through a
small doorway led into the kitchen; the kitchen tumbled down a
step and into the utility room—an afterthought room housing a
hodgepodge of outdated appliances: a hot water heater, a
refrigerator with only an ice box, and a wringer washing machine.
No room in the house, save the bathroom, had a door partitioning
it from any other room.

The primary heat source for the house was an oil burner. The oil
burner was a copper colored behemoth hunched up in one
corner of the living room. The stove's guts consisted of a metal
cylinder. A valve switched to the "on" position slowly
drizzled fuel oil into the stove's belly. A stick match sparked the
pooling fuel into a tiny oil-fed flame. The oil burner was
inefficient; when temperatures hovered in the thirties it might
heat one room. When temperatures dipped into the teens,
to stay warm you had to huddle against the stove.

Oil heat was dirty—even with weekly house cleanings, by spring a
pernicious film of black filth oozed its way into cabinets and

closets. My mother hated the oil burner. It needed meticulous tending. Should the fire go out, fuel oil continued to drip into the belly of the stove, filling the house with a nauseating petroleum stench—to say nothing of the fire hazard it created. When fuel floods occurred, which they did with regularity no matter how closely the stove was watched, it did not matter what my mother's mood might have been before. Frustration chiseled lines in her face; every muscle of her small body tensed. A stack of newspapers and a tandem of dented, dull, galvanized buckets appeared stove side. My mother, on hands and knees, a mountain of wadded up newspapers in her fists, sopped oil from the belly of the stove until, once again, the fire could be rekindled safely.

On the west wall of my mother's kitchen was a second stove. About three feet high, it perched on cast iron legs; the exterior was white enamel. The top was cast iron, as was the boiler portion of the stove. An I-shaped lid separated two round lids. The whole top could be removed to expose the fire that smoldered in the stove's core. It was too small to be a real wood-burning stove. My mother called it the trash burner. The stove was designed to take care of excess debris. Beneath the stove's boiler, a grill sifted ashes into a catch pan. Every few days, my mother would empty the ashes into one of the galvanized buckets, then spread them across her small garden space where, come spring, they would be tilled into the soil.

The cobwebs of sleep cleared ever so slightly. It was pitch black in the tiny bedroom. I recognized the whistling breath of my older brother sleeping soundly on the bunk overhead. My mother rustled around the kitchen, familiar sensations flooded my half dreams—the sound of paper being crumpled and stuffed into the trash burner, the acrid smell of sulfur as a match ignited, the flicker of light across the ceiling as the fire caught, then grew to a flame. I listened as she stacked kindling wood into the yawning mouth of the stove. Then the sound of water drowned the sound of fire as she filled the coffeepot and set it to percolate at the back of the trash burner. Next she refilled the teakettle that was a permanent fixture of the stove's posterior. I felt the warmth as it seeped around the corner of the kitchen and eased its way into the bedroom. The fire was going in the kitchen and things were okay. I pulled the blanket tight around my chin and drifted back to sleep.

When I was young—old enough to have moved out of my parents' bedroom and into the room my brothers shared—my parents went to bed at the same time. They would lie together, side by side in the dark, talking. Exact words remain a mystery; it was the cadence of their voices, the rhythm of conversation that lulled me to sleep. In the middle of the night I might awaken to whispers, rustles, the sighs of threadbare sheets. I rolled over, an ear pressed against the paper-thin wall—murmurs, soft as flannel blankets, hummed along the walls. In the summertime the windows would be open. Night flowers blossomed. Time slipped through lily-of-the-valley scented nights. But as nights crept into crevasses of the past, my parents' conversations stalled, their whispers less and less frequent, until silence alone flooded the night air. Unease, like mice on padded feet, crept through the darkened house. Sometimes I woke when the back door creaked open. Streaks of pink swirled across the worn utility room floor— the door unable to hold out the dawn before it clicked shut. My father's night conversations now belonged to other women.

Most nights I did not hear my father come home. If I woke at all it was to the static of television after the national anthem had concluded. Or perhaps I stirred when my brother slipped over the side of his bunk, tiptoed into the living room, shut the television off, then gently shook my mother awake, "Mom, it's time to go to bed."

My mother's voice beckoned me to get out of bed, to get ready for school. I rolled over, my face pressed against the window, and lifted a corner of the plastic shade to see if it snowed during the night. Fingers of frost etched the edges of the sill like silent frozen flames. I dragged myself from beneath the blankets and pulled on a dress. There was a decided iciness to the house—an iciness not from winter's temperature alone. In the kitchen, my father had not yet left for work; he perused the daily *Statesman*—a morning ritual—and finished his breakfast of bacon, eggs, toast, and coffee. He nodded good morning. My mother sat a bowl of cold cereal in front of me. No words passed between them. My mother took the cast iron handle from the hook at the side of the stove and lifted one of the trash burner's lids. She prodded the fire with the handle; sparks shot toward the ceiling like a miniature fireworks display. The fire gulped air and flared, tangerine flames licking the stovepipe. The chill of the room melted away. My father stood to leave for work. My mother knew he had run out of money. It was days yet before payday. He would be home for supper tonight.

Hard years were nothing new in my mother's life; most of her years were hard. There were the years Huntington's disease gnawed away at her father's life, the year cancer took her mother's life. There were dirty black years of the Dust Bowl, years of the Great Depression, war years. There was the year her firstborn daughter died, and other years her brother spent in a mental institution. There was the year her best friend stole away under the cover of night, leaving two young daughters on my mother's doorstep. In her forty-first year, with two sons half grown, she learned it was me kicking against the insides of her womb.

Perhaps the hardest thing in my mother's life was being my father's wife. It's not that my father was a bad man. He was a diligent worker; he tried hard to provide for his family. My father was a competent mechanic, and a mechanic's wage might put hamburger on the table, might put jeans on his sons and dresses on his daughter, might pay for water and electricity. It was a wage that enabled him, with his own hands, to build the house that sheltered his family. But my father had dreams, big dreams. Dreams that would never come true for a man with a wife, and three children, and a mechanic's wage. Then too, my mother and father were such different personalities. She tended toward martyrdom as her main coping strategy. My father found solace in an opaque bottle or between the legs of women who were not his wife.

It must not have seemed unusual to my mother when 1960 began a downhill barrel roll and picked up speed only to stop hard against a brick wall. My father was supposed to come home drunk on Christmas Eve—that was a fact of life. He was not supposed to collapse in the bedroom, too dizzy to stand up, too light-headed to get himself in bed. It was the first time I saw fear on my father's face. He had been sick for a long time. Every day he ate breakfast, read the morning paper, plucked his lunch from the kitchen counter, got in his car, and drove to work. His illness was something he never revealed to his children. Then two days after Christmas, a doctor came to our house. He looked at my father, immobile on the bed. The doctor said he didn't know what was wrong. He wrote a prescription for a sedative and told my father to stop drinking coffee and stop smoking cigarettes. He said he hoped he got better soon. He left, on the kitchen table, a bill for my mother to pay. It must not have seemed unusual to my mother when 1961 dawned hard, and as the pages of the calendar rolled one over the other, the year stayed hard, bashing itself against the brick wall.

Each fall, before Halloween, a tanker truck from Purcell's Oil Service pulled down our driveway. Louie, the driver, jumped out of the truck, wrestled a hose around the side of the garage, and pumped fuel oil into the big red tank. In a good year a tank of fuel lasted until spring. Fuel oil came in two grades—number one heating fuel and diesel grade fuel. Diesel grade was the cheapest form of heating fuel. My mother said it would be a cold day in hell before she used diesel fuel. The fall of 1961, Louie filled our tank half full with diesel fuel. Diesel fuel reeked; when it burned, black noxious smoke curled from the chimney; black sludge coated the hairs on our heads, the hairs in our noses, the little hairs that lined the inside of our lungs.

By Thanksgiving, icicles hung long toothed from eaves. Snow covered the ground, and it did not melt the next morning or the next, or the next, or for most of the winter. Hulking gray clouds, like frigates, became permanent fixtures anchored against Boise's foothills; at night they cracked open and big, wet, white flakes drifted, like partridge feathers, through moonless nights. In a few days the snow would be a sooty, dirty gray until the low, fecund clouds would again spill and wrap the world in a white quilt of snow. Steamy clouds of breath stalled, masking the faces of the people behind them. Whenever I came into the house my mother searched my cheeks for whitish patches of frostbite. Her delicate touch seemed enough to shatter the frozen skin of my face.

Each afternoon my mother sent my brother out to the fuel oil barrel. He climbed a ladder with a long stick in his hand, inserted the stick into the opening at the top of the barrel, pulled it out, read the markers along its side, then relayed to my mother how many gallons of fuel remained. Each afternoon my mother set the thermostat on the oil burner one degree lower. At night, in attempts to squeeze another degree of heat from the oil burner, she would open the furnace door, revealing the metal cylinder and exposing the orange flame dancing behind the boiler's glass porthole. It reminded me of a poem I read in school about Sam McGee, a man who lived in a furnace but could never get warm. Soon I began doing homework at the kitchen table instead of on my bed. It was the trash burner now, for most of the day, that radiated heat into the rooms of the house.

My mother had a woodpile: odds and ends of lumber gleaned from neighborhood handymen, plywood scraps from construction sites, tree trimmings. She hoarded any combustible that might warm a cold winter morning. This winter, my mother's woodpile began evaporating at an alarming rate. The M&W on Overland Road was the neighborhood market. They had, in front of their store, a stack of Presto-Logs—logs of compressed sawdust. The logs were manufactured at lumber mills in northern Idaho, then shipped by the truckload to the Boise Valley for resale. My mother liked them because they burned longer than wood scraps. But at five for a dollar they were too expensive to burn on a daily basis. Sawdust logs were fragile commodities, sometimes breaking in transit, casualties of a shifting stack. My mother finagled a deal with the store manager to buy broken logs at a discounted price.

In elementary school, the week before Christmas vacation was an exciting time—parties, caroling, special lunches, Christmas plays, and holiday art projects. That year, freezing cold put a damper on even those activities. The coal furnace lodged in the school building's basement could not compete with the fury of a north wind hurling ice and snow at the city. Girls were allowed to wear jeans beneath dresses. The denim barrier separating skin from the wooden desk seat felt peculiar.

The school day finished, I barged through the back door. The house seemed chillier than usual. On the trash burner, one round stove lid perched atop the other; the flame in the trash burner flickered feebly. My mother must have just rebuilt the fire. She sat at the kitchen table, shivering, wrapped in a bulky sweater I recognized from a Junior League rummage sale. One hand held a cigarette, ash dangling from its end, blue smoke curling toward the ceiling; her other hand was wrapped around a green coffee cup half filled with a coffee, milk, sugar mixture—my mother's constant companions. No steam rose from the cup. A stack of bills spilled across the table—the same stack that shrouded the table's surface when I left for school earlier that morning. I wondered for a minute if my mother had been crying. But this was my mother, and my mother never cried.

"Mom, I'm home. You need me to go to the store for anything?"

Maybe I just wanted to snuggle down behind the comic book rack for an hour or two and read the latest *Dennis the Menace* and *Superman*. Maybe I hoped the girl who worked in the bakery, the one who liked to chat about hamsters, would slide a white paper bag containing legless, armless, mangled gingerbread men across the counter—"no charge" printed across the bag front. Maybe I just wanted to get away from the chill of this house.

My mother said she needed to go herself, if I would get her coat we could go together. The M&W store was a short, easy walk even in the foulest weather. Before we stepped through the store entrance my mother stopped at the stack of Presto-Logs, hoping, I knew, to discover a few broken logs. One or two broken Presto-Logs and some small two-by-four ends were all that remained of our meager woodpile. I was not too naive to realize that in a few days, or even a few hours, there would be nothing left to burn.

The pile revealed no damaged logs. The creases at the corners of my mother's eyes deepened, widened. She stared at the stack, hands dropping to her sides; a frozen sigh, question mark shaped, hovered around her lips. I had never before seen her brown eyes pool such emptiness. As she drifted slowly toward the prescription counter, I sprinted toward the comic-book rack, then instead, veered out the automatic door. I knew from watching older boys committing minor acts of vandalism that if you pulled a log from the bottom corner of the Presto-Log pile chances were good you'd create a small avalanche, and chances were even better some of the cascading logs would break. The trick was to dislodge the proper log and create an avalanche yet not roll the whole pile to the ground. I jerked at a corner log halfway up the stack; the pile wavered a little. I jiggled a lower log. Eureka! A dozen or so logs tumbled from the stack, and a half dozen broke with a crack as they rumbled to the concrete. I sauntered back into the store to rendezvous with my mother.

As we left, she glanced toward the pile, hoping a miracle might have occurred during her fifteen minutes inside the store. She stared at the broken logs scattered around the base of the pile as if they were a mirage and fairly floated back inside the store to make her purchase. Out she came, a smile on her face, a small box in her hands to collect the broken treasures—logs to warm two or three mornings, logs to stretch the precious fuel oil a few nights longer.

Christmas Eve morning dawned cold but cloudless. The M&W market had cleared the snow from its parking lot. A sign taped on the entrance announced the store would close at noon to allow employees to enjoy Christmas Eve with their families. Only three cars were parked along the west edge of the parking lot, cars belonging to store personnel. A snow-free parking lot was too much temptation. I dusted accumulated snow from my hibernating bicycle and headed across the street. This was the first opportunity to bicycle since snow began falling in early November. A racetrack, the product of my imagination, took shape in the parking lot. I circled around and around the oval. With each lap I went faster and faster, pushing my racetrack wider and wider.

I must have known how close my widening ellipse was taking me to the Presto-Log stack. Still, the crash, the dull thud of my shoulder meeting wood, the rumble of the logs—these sounds came as a surprise.

"Are you okay?"

The store manager towered over me. I scrambled to untangle arms, legs, pedals, and spoked wheels.

"I'm sorry, I didn't mean to do this. I'll pick it up—restack it. I'll pay for the broken logs . . . ."

Words spilled out with the identical cadence of my heartbeats.

"Don't worry about it. You just gave us a scare."

I picked myself up, picked my bike up, and trudged toward home.

"Make sure and tell your mother to come get the broken logs."

Christmas was a low-key celebration that year. If my mother had her way we would have canceled the entire holiday. Except that my father was not about to break with one tradition.

He came home drunk Christmas Eve—drunk and late.
Maybe he wanted to escape into a fantasy world, escape the
polycythemia he finally had been diagnosed with. Maybe
his disease failed to thrive in the surreal worlds of taverns. Maybe
he hoped bartenders and drinking cronies would keep free
booze flowing all night. Maybe he just wanted to escape the chill
of our house.

Emptying ashes from the belly of the trash burner became an
everyday chore. Although I found the chore distasteful, my
mother never seemed to resent buckets filled with wood ashes.
Nor did she resent trips to the snow-covered garden where she
disposed of the ashes.

A popular psychic authored one of my favorite books. The psychic
claimed she could tell the future by reading patterns of tea
leaves or patterns of ashes. My family were coffee drinkers and
there weren't many tea leaves available so I interpreted the
future as told by the wood ashes—those sprinkled across my
mother's garden.

Raven-black ashes etched furrows deep into alabaster-white snow.
Steam rose, and, in an intoxicating winter tango, melded with
silver filigreed snowflakes swirling through the air. It was the most
beautiful sight I ever saw. Ashes traced loops and curlicues,
flourishes and embellishments through the snow. I thought how
much it resembled the flowery script of my mother's handwriting.
When I came to the outline of an ashen crucifix carved into snow,
I wondered, was my mother not writing her own future?

In late August of 1996 an errant tracer bullet set the foothills
above Boise ablaze. Long orange fingers of fire snaked up gullies
and draws, caressing, then consuming sagebrush and cheatgrass
but never satisfying its insatiable appetite. Angry clouds of chalky

gray smoke billowed, ash rained down on the city. The night sky glowed an eerie, electric, burnt orange.

I watched the foothills burn, my foothills, foothills that nearly every single day for the past forty-four years had defined the boundaries of my life, had formed the backdrop of my seasons, had been the first thing I saw each morning and the last thing I saw each night. I watched fire blacken familiar landmarks of my hometown, watched fire in images flickering across a TV screen in a motel room in Corvallis, Oregon. I had come with my husband to Oregon looking for a new job, looking for a new city to call home—looking for Camelot in the lush landscape of Oregon's Willamette Valley.

Days later we flew back to Boise, outrunning a setting sun, just enough daylight left for shadowy silhouettes of Boise's foothills to unfold in front of the eastern horizon. The fires had abated. They had consumed everything in their path before sulking behind surrounding mountain ridges.

A pomegranate sun climbed the backside of Table Rock, peering tentatively at the charred landscape below. I gazed out the bedroom window, my eye tracing familiar outlines that define the eastern skyline. Foothills rise and fall, rise and fall, rise and fall, their symmetry matching exactly the cadence of my respiration. Raven-black sweeps of burned hillsides, soft velvet gray of ash, flaxen expanses of spared grasses, wisps of thin smoke rising, melding into a tango with dry barren air—these are images that fire my memory. Charred lines—loops and curlicues, flourishes and embellishments—scrawled their way across the hillsides.

I remembered the ashes in my mother's garden. It would be melodramatic to say my mother's memory rose like Phoenix from the ashes of the Eighth Street fire. I often think about my mother. But that morning I felt closer to her. I realized my future was not in the faraway landscape of cedar and rhododendron. This is my future—this place of sagebrush and cheatgrass. What I wished in that moment was to say, "Mom, I'm home."

I was not there when they pulled her from the fiery oven. I was not there when my father and two brothers claimed the ash-filled urn. I was not even present the day they interred my mother's ashes in a small cemetery on the outskirts of Meridian, Idaho. I was somewhere—the Oregon Coast, Puget Sound—trying to ignore the pain.

Reading the Glow

DiAnne Iverglynne

I hold a quartzite rock between the thumb and index finger of each hand. One rock I found while hiking the Hot Dry Hike in the Bennett Hills. The other I toe-lifted from the bottom of the hottest water of Burgdorf Hot Springs. They are similar but dissimilar enough to create sparks when struck one against the other.

I dangle a small rectangle of charred cloth from earlier fires over the back of the fingers of my left hand. It drapes in the windless air just below the Burgdorf rock. Lifting my right arm two feet above the left I pause for a moment of concentrated inner aim. I disallow the soft mew of a nearby wood duck, the layered voices of the river currents forty feet away, and the scorch of sun-heated sand as it sifts past the leather on my sandals and burns my right arch. My arm, hand, and the Hot Dry rock come down fast and hard in a large sweep past the Burgdorf rock, close enough to graze its edge. A strike. A spark. The charred cloth sends a sharp pain to the back of my middle fingers, and I know the spark is caught.

The seed of heat grows outward on the cloth with dull rings of gray, then with a dark red and a thread of smoke. I nudge the new ember gently to the center of a twisted bundle of dried bark that fell loose from dead sage, then pinch the bundle slightly, cradling this most ancient of treasures. Now I see a growing life, edged with a bright yellow ring, hungry for fuel. A gentle smoke curls upward into my eyes and nostrils. One long soft breath, steady as any operatic aria invoking a lover off stage, passes through my lips and into the cloud of smoke in my palms . . . we have a flame, as we always have known flame to enter . . . almost as if from another dimension. A burst of excitement and a quick lowering to the waiting crib of twigs that welcomes flame.

We have fuel and a purpose. A large pile of cow pies waits to be added to this small warming fire. A small hodgepodge of unfired clay pots surrounds the fire. They are warming before being brought to nineteen-hundred degrees under the burning cow pies. I turn the small orbs slowly around the flame and am inspired to count the seasons I have fired pots in this way. I shake that thought to wonder how many seasons I will fire pots in this way. The dung has been allowed to dry for days on the hot sand. The pots have been drying for months. A canteen or two, a few small bowls, a bird-shaped ocarina, and one long cylindrical flute. I imagine the flute as the comet in this miniature galaxy. Wandering thoughts are natural at this stage of any fire, when the sun is hot and the river is suggesting a cool swim. We can swim soon, but right now we are working as our ancestors have worked: outdoors and with fire.

We need this fire to make clay hard enough to hold water, so that it will not dissolve back into the water as unfired clay would. I imagine the river stretching greedy fingers toward my pots to slurry them down the current to the next bank. I laugh aloud and mentally slap its muddy mitts. "Stay out of this story, you will always have a turn," I say. These pots, once fired, will live thousands of years, though perhaps in shards, even in the depths of the river or at the bottom of oceans. Firing pots is what I do to have a place in the imagination and hands of those still to come.

We want the flute and ocarina to be smooth and not to crumble and slime in our mouths when we trumpet the arrival of dignitaries. We want the porridge to stay in the bowl for all Goldilocks of all times. After that, we will want differently shaped pots to clean our dishes in, excrete in, build houses and floors with, and protect us from electricity; and furthermore we will want keystone-shaped pots to keep us from disintegrating when we fly ourselves home from space. This inoculation of fire will change the clay. We also will change with years of firing clay.

The pots are getting too hot to touch. The smoke names me the fool. I have no time to argue as I fumble the hot pots to the center of the fire. I pile them like a house of cards. Flames now are leaving sooty trails where they lick the clay. For the first time I notice my hands. They have been licked and licked and licked. Soon I will scrub them in the river. The cow pies are looking like stunned eyes, and I imagine them asserting that surely we are making some pyrotechnic mistake. "Nope. Sorry, pies," I respond, and put the first one at the base of the fire. I say a little prayer to the kiln gods as I work quickly to surround the pots and the fire with a large dome. The fire begins to munch like a dreaming cow along the edges of the pies.

Now it is time to sit and watch. When a cow pie slips on its flame, I prop it back in place. The familiar smell of wood fire shifts to a grassy, heavy, and somewhat foul odor. But the cleansing of the flame makes it acceptable. All our ancestors in times past smelled of smoke every day of their lives. My mind wants to linger in the past but is momentarily distracted by gleeful yelps of teenagers pushing one another out of a raft and into the eddy. I had expected them. Five minutes earlier, while building the dung kiln, I had lifted my eyes to mergansers flying downriver at a rapid pace and knew that boaters would soon arrive.

One of the young men runs from the river to the fire and stops about ten feet away when he sees the burning cow pies. "What are you doing?" he asks with one lip slightly curled.

"Making clay pots the way our ancestors did."

A raised eyebrow indicates only a little curiosity. "Oh, huh." And he runs back to the river. "They're doing weird things over there," I hear him say to his comrades. I chuckle.

The kiln is now engulfed in flames four feet high. A sound somewhat sharper than a thump comes from the fire. Sad. A pot has popped. My thoughts are with the bird-shaped ocarina. Please do not be that one. Nor do I wish it to be the turtle canteen. But the clay is committed to the fire, now. What is ready and dry will come through this passage. I should not, but I retrace my steps: I dried the dung for days on the hot sand, so dampness in the dung should not transfer itself to a pot during the building of the kiln. Check. I thoroughly dried and warmed these pots. Double check. Made sure that in the building of the pots the walls were kept an even thickness. Well . . . the head on the bird could be a problem . . . . oh dear; I think it is the bird.

I wish and demand and want this fire to draft a little bit through the flute—just enough to play a brief note. I always want that when there is a flute in the fire but have never experienced such a magical moment. Another fire, perhaps. With the slightest breeze, a primitive firing should be called off because the breeze side of the kiln gets hotter too fast and lots of pots pop. Maybe every pot in the firing will be lost. In Southern Idaho along the Snake River, I have learned to fire in the early morning when the air is still on warm summer days. The breeze picks up on the river around ten o'clock, and the kiln needs to be smothered by then.

This fire is ready to smother with sand. It is at its hottest point. I can tell by reading the glow. At first, when the cow pies are whole and the kiln is tall, we can see into the center only in a few places. As the fire grows and the cow pies are reduced, we can see a glow clearly in several places. The heat softens contact lenses as I get close enough to inspect the center, which at first is a dull red, around seven to eight hundred degrees Fahrenheit. As the temperature climbs, the glow takes on an orange edge or crustiness to the solid embers. Hotter, and it turns a bright orange, like an orange popsicle in the bright sunshine. Hotter yet, and it takes on a crust that is bright yellow, like a neon sign. We have that neon yellow edge in this fire. This is good. This is a hot fire and will soon start to die down. Had the flames been dying when the glow had only reached orange, I would have been forced to smother it early, and my pots might not last as long. But this is perfect. A pyrometer placed in the center of this pile will show nineteen-hundred-and-eighty degrees. But I prefer to use my eyes and experience.

I quickly shovel sand all around the base, on top of the pile, and all over the flaming kiln. Not one thread of smoke do we want to escape this mound. If smoke comes out, air is going in. Air will allow red spots on the pots. We want the pots to be robbed of oxygen so they will turn black, like black wrought iron. This is not soot from the fire and will not wash off. If the fire was hot enough and smothered at the right time, the color will go entirely through the clay wall of the finished pot. So watch carefully. If we see a thread of smoke, we shovel more sand.

An hour passes at an hour's rate on the river. I watch the shadows of the ripples as they move across the pebbles. The little waves in the eddy magnify the stones on the front wall of the wave and sometimes mesmerize me for hours on a warm summer day. Today I am anxious to dig into the kiln. I go for a quick rinse of the smoke and a few laps of the eddy and return to the hot-to-the-touch mound of sand. Deep inside, it is still dangerously hot.

Gingerly, I move the first shovels of sand from the top. Like digging for buried treasure, I continue down through layers of smoking coal and sand. The shovel clinks against something. I use the tip carefully around the area of the sound. Up comes the bird! Intact and lovely it is! I set the ocarina in the sand with great elation of creation, and welcome its arrival to the world beyond fire.

Turning back to the kiln, I focus on the turtle. Slowly, a shovel-tip-ful. Another shovel-tip-ful. Clink. Again I ease the pot up through the coals and sand, and it is the turtle! Now I stop and consider what magic and synchronicity is at work. What could this parade of thoughts and creatures from the fire mean? Or does it mean nothing? And what broke? The Tao says the road takes a thousand directions, but the truth knows only one. Something broke. I will continue to shovel.

Several more clinks and everything is out of the coals, intact. I take the flute to the river and scrub it with sand. The surface of the clay holds without dissolving. It is crisp with a metallic ring when hit with a stone. This fire is a "red letter" primitive firing: partly because we have shared it, partly because of the mew of the wood duck, and partly because it will leave me forever musing over that knock I heard in the flame. A sound I was sure of from times past.

I am in no hurry to clean up or fuss about. I sit down. I play my new flute and think grateful thoughts about Hot and Dry Creeks and Burgdorf Hot Springs. I remember fondly my hikes and how my new spark rock undulated beneath the surface of Hot Creek when it was swollen with spring waters. The smell of the fire turns acrid as I pour water into the high hiss of the coals. A few spitting sputtering sounds and it goes back to wherever it came from until next time. I lie down for a nap in the shade and look across the beach at my little circle of pots in the sun and doze off on a trail of marvels: of water to stone to spark to fire to flute to music to us.

What I Know of Fire

Robert Coker Johnson

I remember the smell of cigarettes, my mother's hands cool against my face, and I would come back to the room, the rough sheets, the other children bleating in the ward. I lived on shots. They fed me through the nose. Sometimes a nurse brought a bottle of distilled water with an aluminum shaker top like my mother used when she ironed clothes. The water was room temperature, but when the nurse peeled the gauze from my legs—I was always on my stomach—and sprinkled water on my wounds, it burned like ice, as though I were still on fire.

My memory is full of holes regarding those early days and weeks I spent in the hospital, but I remember the day and year it began: February 14, 1962. The day before, I had watched the gardener down the street burn a pile of brush and clippings in the vacant lot behind our house. This was in Lewiston, Idaho, a small town then, surrounded by wheat and pea fields, and just south of town the single, cutover ridge of Craig Mountain rose out of the Camas Prairie. When the gardener lit the brush pile and left, no one paid any attention. Except me. I went back the next day and found a pile of ash glowing orange deep beneath and an occasional small lick of flame.

No one in my family has ever been able to explain why a boy barely three was out of sight of his house. I imagine I just wandered off; perhaps I followed our white collie on her rounds. More likely I was simply drawn to the fire, the small flames easy to step on, something I could control. What I remember is not what I remember. I see myself running up the hill to our house, my blue corduroy overalls ablaze and my dog crying. I don't remember my father coming down for breakfast, perhaps kissing my mother, and seeing through the window behind her their son trailing fire; I don't remember him smothering the flames with a blanket. What I remember is sitting beside him in our '58 Chevy Biscayne telling him, *It hurts*, and him saying, *I know*. The mind, the blessed mind, took away the worst memory of the fire and pain; what it could not take away is the memory of the smell.

All the children were in a single room, a ward, and one child had what I recognize now was polio. I don't remember her; how do I know it was in fact a *her*? I remember going in for surgery and waking with the ether, like burned rubber, on my lungs. I drank 7-UP from a Captain Kangaroo cup and ate saltines. The lights were never off. I closed my eyes for a second and it was day again. I forgot my toilet training. I cried myself to sleep and awoke to my parents' faces and the aroma of stale cigarette smoke that now, even on strangers, still comforts me; or I awoke to a nurse with a tray of syringes. I had my stuffed gray kitty that played Brahms's Lullaby, a song that still makes me a child, like the smell of baby lotion or the laundry detergent some hospitals and motels use. One day when my parents came, three children followed them as far as the waiting room at the end of the ward. They kept looking at me and smiling. They looked familiar, but . . . Finally I asked who they were and was told they were my brother and sisters.

Time did not matter. We simply existed in our cribs and things happened to us. We had our temperatures taken. Our bandages were changed. Winter became spring, and sometime before summer I went home. I was back a year later for skin grafts. My right leg from ankle to midthigh had third-degree burns. My left leg suffered only a small patch burnt on the inside of my thigh, and from this leg the surgeon took skin for the grafting. If the graft looked perhaps like a map of continental drift, then the burn

looked red and bubbly as a lava flow. The grafting scars have
faded a bit; they stretched as I grew and a fair amount of hair
covers them, but the burn is still barren and lifeless. I was better
prepared the second time I went to the hospital. I had a green
metal steam shovel I kept in my bed; a workman promised to
bring me some dirt. I had my stuffed animals, a plastic and cloth
doll in overalls and a cane pole I called Johnny, my father's name.
I had books—one, *Stop That Ball*, in rhymed verse. It must have
been a favorite, because I soon memorized it. I still seem to have a
knack for remembering poetry. Finally I went home again, but I
had to endure months of saltwater baths, which crusted the gears
of my windup boat, followed by exercises in which my parents
turned me over on my stomach, grasped my ankles, and
manipulated my legs like slot-machine levers. They finished by
rubbing lanolin into my new skin to keep it supple and healthy. I
still can't stand the smell of lamb. I don't recall nightmares, but I
hid on the floor of the car whenever we passed the hospital. And
later at the swimming pool, I served as a point of instruction for
many a parent. Photos of me then show a boy with—how do I
describe my legs: Angry? Fire red? They *are* fire. They *are* embers.
They are what's left of the fuel when the fire's passed.

"What happened to that leg?" my friends' daughter asks when she
wakes me on the couch. "Don't you know about *stop, drop, and
roll?*" "No," I tell her, "we didn't have that then." And I remember
awakening in Weippe, alone, where I lived for a time when I
worked in the woods, as the fire engine sped past on the highway.
Something about the town siren fanned some terror within me,
and I huddled in my blankets until morning.

I seldom wear shorts. The scar tissue will not tan, and after
adolescence I never felt comfortable with my legs exposed,
although I know other people have much worse burns. Once, a
tall, slender young woman came into the library where I work. She
had long, dark hair. She wore shorts, and she had burned legs. I
could not believe it. I would have fallen to my knees in worship. I
wanted to tell her, *I know your body*. But of course I said nothing,
and she got her books and left.

When I was a teenager, a large wart grew on my ankle, and my parents thought it serious enough to warrant a trip to the doctor, who burned it off as I watched. He said it would smell like burning chicken feathers, and it crackled and blackened under the electricity's pulse.

This is not the smell that still comes to me sometimes. I might be at a stop sign at night with the windows rolled up, and my right leg will heat up—not burn exactly—and I smell what I know is a three-year-old's flesh and pants becoming one part of the fire equation. My first recollection came when I was ten or twelve and watching a sci-fi movie about alien children called *Village of the Damned*. A villager with a torch means to burn the children's school, but the children confront him and with telepathy make him drop the torch at his feet and hold him there in the flames. I am more amazed than frightened when my own leg begins to burn, because it is only a physical sensation, but where does the smell come from? The terrifying part is that I don't know what sets it off or when it will occur. It smells like a wet wool coat permeated with propane.

What I know of science is this: fire is rapid oxidation—rust speeded up. And I know this: fire needs three things to exist—heat, fuel, and oxygen. Remove any one of the three and the fire dies.

I was a bitter, unmotivated student who wanted only one thing from high school—out. In 1979, with the help of a friend's father, I landed a summer job with the U.S. Forest Service as a forestry aide. My job mostly consisted of cutting and piling logging slash to make a fuel break around timber sales, and later I worked the trail crew. But it also involved fighting fire.

Not that I was ever afraid of fire, exactly. As a boy, I was as much a pyromaniac as any of my friends, perhaps more so. I was fascinated with the burn barrel. After all, fire and I knew each other intimately. My eldest sister was a blue baby. When she was old enough to tolerate the procedure, she had open-heart surgery in San Francisco, the only place on the West coast where it was performed. She was always behind in school, and New Math gave her fits. One day, for whatever reasons, I stuffed her math homework down the hot ducts of our wood-burning furnace and watched the flames consume it.

Still, I had to wonder when, after a couple of days' instruction, I found myself holding a hand tool called a pulaski as our fire dispatcher strapped a propane torch to his back and lit a small logging unit for a practice burn.

This was in north central Idaho on the Clearwater National Forest, 1.7 million acres that stretch most of the way across the Idaho panhandle. I was now responsible for the Pierce Ranger District—270,000 acres of multiple-use land that accounted for most of the forest's total allowable cut, and so varied I have trouble calling it to mind. Basalt gives way to granite, meadows are blue with camas and white with the tall plume of beargrass in spring. The dominant trees are fir—Douglas and grand—a mix of larch and lodgepole pine, a few disease-scarred white pine and, along the creek bottoms and cool slopes, western red cedar. Also along the creeks grow willow, alder, narrow-leaf cottonwood, and low bushes of red osier dogwood. And almost everywhere else on the steep slopes of the district, a tangle of huckleberry, snowberry, and thimbleberry, and patches of doghair cedar and pacific yew. But there are open areas, too. Cedar groves blanketed with fern and the dark green, heart-shaped wild ginger leaves that smell of lemon when you walk through. Farther up, around five thousand feet, the vegetation thins to lodgepole and false huckleberry, thins enough that you can walk without zigzagging continually. The ridges and peaks aren't knife-edged as they are above the Salmon River; they're more rounded and eroded, but when I carried a chain saw or a pack filled with three hundred feet of inch-and-a-half hose and clambered through the brush and over downed logs, they always seemed plenty steep to me.

During the summer of 1910, most of north Idaho burned in a series of fires called a complex that stretched from a few miles south of the Canadian border to the North Fork of the Clearwater River, well within our forest's boundary, and involved more than three million acres, much of it covered with the highly prized western white pine for which Idaho was once known. The 1910 fire pumped so much smoke into the atmosphere that a ship off the California coast had to wait three days before it could get a safe bearing to land. Eighty-five people died, and the land still shows its scars. Idaho then had few roads, which slowed access to the fire and made supplying the fire camps a logistical nightmare. Firefighting equipment of the time consisted of two-man crosscut saws called misery whips, axes, shovels, and a combination pick and grub hoe called a mattock. Finally, though, the fall rains put out the fires.

North Idaho burned again during the Sundance Fire of 1967. I have a dim childhood memory of this fire, and later I learned it burned fifty thousand acres and killed two firefighters. It was the first firefighting effort supplied completely by air. Embers falling from the fire's convection column started spot fires ten miles ahead of the main fire front. In one area during a blowup—an explosive run—the fire released the energy equivalent to a Hiroshima-size atom bomb every twenty minutes. The heat warped quarter-inch steel deck plating on a bridge.

One of the heroes of the 1910 fire is Ranger E.C. Pulaski, supposedly a descendant of Count Pulaski of Revolutionary War fame. Ranger Pulaski led his crew of more than forty into a mine shaft when he realized they would be overrun. Acrid smoke poured around them, but he stood in the entrance with his back to the fire and a pistol cocked in his hands and kept his panicked men from running back into the flames. Only five of his men died, from smoke inhalation. Later Pulaski invented a new fire tool that is the best piece of equipment to have in the woods. And it is so simple, so basic, it is a wonder no one thought of it before. It has the curved blade of a grub hoe where a normal axe has merely a butt end. In some parts of the country, it is known as a forester's axe, the best combination of two good tools. With the axe, you can fell small trees or cut logs and brush; with the grub hoe you can scratch in a fireline. But I've used one to dig trenches and to remove rocks from a trail bed; the hoe end is perfect for scraping out open-top culverts, and with a shovel it does a fine job of peeling bark from a log. Two people armed with a chainsaw, shovel, and pulaski can perform almost anything that needs doing on a fire or trail.

I carried a shovel and pulaski whenever I cut firewood on my weekends and always felt prepared. Like a pair of good boots or a pair of leather gloves, the pulaski is a necessity. And it is something more. I had not hefted one in years until recently when I found myself drawn to them among the other hand tools in a ranch supply store. I picked one up, checked its head for tightness, sighted along the handle to be sure it was true, and felt the weight of it in my hands. And there beside the birdseed I meant to buy, and the mundane posthole diggers and pitchforks, I got a good grip on the handle, bent over, and tried a few strokes as though scratching in a fireline. It was all still there. The wood remembered my hands.

We were so many, and the fire so small, we could have surrounded it in a human chain, but our supervisors started a line of us with one on each side of the fire's base, each person spaced about ten feet apart, and alternately gave us shovels or pulaskis. Three or four people with pulaskis started off, following a sawyer and using the hoe end to break up grass, duff, and litter and to scrape down to mineral soil. Then a couple of people with shovels jumped in behind them, scraping the debris *away* from the fire (so the fire won't creep under and ignite any fuel covered by dirt) with an easy, pivoting motion using only their hips and locked arms. Then the rest of us, a few pulaskis and then a few more shovels, cleaned up so that we left a line free of fuel about eighteen inches wide in our wake. Even roots must be cut out of the line, or the fire might smolder across the root and take off on the other side of the line. It is not uncommon for stumps and deep roots to smolder underground all winter, popping up again in the summer heat. What a sight that must be in midwinter. Thick snow on the land, small trees bent at odd angles to the earth, the wrens threading their way through the brambles, and the chickadees with their *tee-dee-dee*. Everything as it should be, except just there, where the bare ground smokes and steams.

This is basic line construction for any fire. If the fuel is heavier, make the line wider (lines on California brush fires are routinely two hundred yards wide; they are called cat lines because they are put in with Caterpillar bulldozers). On a steep slope, the fireline has a cup trench with a high berm of dirt on the downhill side to catch rolling embers or rocks that burn loose and tumble away.

While we dug line, others set up pumps in a nearby creek and ran hoses to the fire; they learned the language of the lateral line and the gated wye. They learned to spray water from the perimeter in, because water can blast coals across the line. Still others used the most traditional method of putting out a fire: they threw shovelfuls of dirt on it, practicing an overhand throw accurate to about twenty feet.

Once a line is constructed around the perimeter, a fire is said to be *contained*, but by no means should it be called *controlled* or *dead*. Containment should come by 10:00 A.M. of the day following the initial attack, that being when the morning winds usually begin. Control comes when the flames are knocked down and any hazards such as burning snags have been dealt with. Slowly we combed every inch of burn, running our bare hands over every stick, log, and ash pile. Any place that was still hot was treated with dirt until cool to the touch. Ordinarily, a fire is not called out until two hours after the last hot spot is found. But it was early in the season, it was late afternoon, and no one was getting overtime for a practice burn. Besides, camp was only a mile away, and someone would be back to check the fire the next morning.

So we learned our trade. About forty of us stayed at Musselshell Work Center, about fifteen miles east of Weippe, Idaho, population eight hundred, on the edge of a three-thousand-acre clear-cut that was still being replanted after almost twenty years. A large meadow sits across the road from camp, and for untold years the Nez Perce Indians have been coming here in late summer to gather the bulbs of camas, whose blue flowers make a pale sea in spring. Just south of Musselshell—Mothershell, we called it—the Lewis and Clark Trail descends the ridge and proceeds out onto the larger meadow of the Weippe Prairie. Within sight of camp, the Nee Mee Poo Trail climbs into the mountains toward Montana, the trail the Nez Perce followed during the 1877 war.

We lived in bunkhouses—a few locals keeping alive the tradition of woods work in their families; college students, of course, from Kansas and Vermont, Michigan and New York; a few old hippies who came as part of the Green Revolution of the seventies. One of the bunkhouses was of the modern dormitory style with two beds per room, and two others had two pairs of bunk beds per room, with wooden lockers and a bathroom between. But two bunkhouses were the barracks type—one long room lined with beds and lockers. These had been built during the 1940s to house Italian prisoners of war who were working on U.S. Highway 12 between Missoula and Lewiston. Only one bunkhouse survives today. It was sold for a few dollars and moved to Weippe to house the library. The other we tore down to make room for a combination office and recreation building. Between the walls we discovered the hatch-marked attempt at a calendar, beer cans (obviously not from the Italians), and in pencil on lined notebook paper, a portrait of a woman with a wide mouth and the full, perfect lips of memory.

John from Montana was rumored to have spent the Vietnam War in Canada. Don, a permanent employee, had been a member of the SDS (Students for a Democratic Society) and had been at the Chicago Democratic Convention and at the Moratorium on Washington. His record kept him out of the war. My friend Dave, also from Montana, is the only man I know who actually *lost* his draft card.

Most evenings Dave and Steve and I walked down to the pond below camp to watch the moose or practice our ornithology. Steve was a scientist's son, and he bought cassette tapes of bird songs and memorized them. Or sometimes we sat on the bunkhouse porch watching stars and listening to coyotes. Virgil was always there with a thermos of coffee, and he kept up a running commentary on how many satellites and falling stars he'd seen. He'd been there forever. Actually he'd been there since 1963, but to us he seemed as ageless as the woods. A Nez Perce, he spent several years as a young man on an Indian Hotshot crew, a group of highly trained firefighters that was airlifted around the country. Later he worked on a district fire crew. Before he was old enough to fight fire, he carried two five-gallon containers of water on a pole across his shoulders to the men on the line, from one ridge to another. When I met him, he was on the brush crew and just leaving his prime. But when we dug fireline he had to be in the lead or he would run over whomever was ahead of him. Once I tried to race him digging line, without letting him know, and almost killed myself before I gave it up.

He could tell you how many games of pool he'd won or lost, or give you the lifetime batting average of almost any player in the major leagues. He loved math and spent hours in his room inventing problems and solving them. But he was naive, and the stars and planets mystified him. It never occurred to him that the satellites he watched night after night were the same ones.

He knew some of the plants his people had depended on, camas and biscuit root, and every summer he picked huckleberries and in the fall dug wild celery, good in soup or stew, he said, and he chewed a small chunk when he had a cold. He told great stories, but whether this was something he learned as a child or came by naturally I never knew. When he repeated a conversation with a friend, he shifted between speakers, taking on the voice of his friend as well as himself. Malapropisms gave him trouble—a *conviction oven*, for example—and once when his crew had finished a project, he said they had reached their destiny. His own destiny is approaching all too soon: both his parents are dead, and out of eight children he is the only one living. His heart is failing.

But things change. One season is never like the last or next. People work a season and move on. After a while, I could look at the new people and figure out who wouldn't last the season. Those who were fired or mysteriously not hired back were seldom mentioned, as though we considered it bad luck to say their names. And after a while it seemed the people themselves were repeated; someone new one year reminded me of someone who worked a few years before. Now I know only a few people who still work on the district.

Things change: the cookhouse closed in 1981 to be remade as kitchenettes. In some ways this was good because it allowed us the freedom of eating when and what we liked. The cookhouse was heavily subsidized, and as the budget cutbacks increased, it finally became too expensive to maintain. But it was one of the last two on the Clearwater Forest, perhaps on any forest, and its closure meant the end of a tradition that had existed as long as the Forest Service itself. We lined up out front, and the cook or her helper, known as a flunky, came out and rang the triangle made from the bit of a rock drill. We filed in, got our food, and sat down. The cook was never friendly as we went through the line, but once we were all eating she came out of the kitchen and stood there quietly, arms folded, a thin, satisfied smile on her face. We didn't talk much at meals, also in accordance with tradition, and when we finished eating we quickly left.

The Forest Service cookhouse had the same roots as its counterpart in the logging camps, and they were generally run by the same type of cook, but ours had a tradition behind it,

something from the boom days of the agency when the world was
a known, comfortable place, before environmental impact
statements, before RARE 1 and 2, before Fire Control
Officers became Fire Management Officers, when the budget
allowed money for Forest Service china. I have managed to
collect a few pieces, bought at antique stores: coffee mugs, heavy
and white, with a green ring around the lip and the F.S. seal
on the side; a cereal bowl, with the ring but without the seal; and
my prize, a covered sugar bowl, also white and with both ring
and seal. As utensils they are functional, nothing more. Yet
like the pulaski I found, they are a link to a time that will never
come again.

I learned to cook once the cookhouse closed. I went the usual
route, some kind of meat covered with some kind of soup and
baked until it was dead. I soon gave it up, though. Pork chops
baked under cream of mushroom soup almost made me sick, but
not because I poisoned myself. It was the sight of it. The meat
looked too much like my own legs. It was the flesh of my flesh.

We lived for storms, black towering cumuli from the west and
south, following the river canyons upcountry to where we
waited, adrenaline and overtime in our eyes. We'd catch the first
smell of rain and see the first flashes of lightning—some
cloud to cloud, harmless and hollow sounding, and then ground
strikes, thick-forked and cracking, the flashes white and
blinding in absence. Once, in a fire camp on a ridge above the
North Fork of the Clearwater River, I watched a storm roll
in, the sky incandescent. Most of the strikes were the usual—a
single strike or a main strike with smaller forks branching off,
but occasionally there were thick-bodied strikes that glowed and
pulsed for what seemed like seconds. The Forest Service
measures a thunderstorm by its Lightning Activity Level (LAL),
a scale from one to six. LAL three is routine for our region, and
six is almost unheard of. This storm had to be a five.

We stood looking across the river at the strike and flare-up of fire that erupted and then died down. We stood on that treeless ridge in the rain and hail until someone had the good sense to order everyone to abandon camp.

I met a man that night who had been a lookout during such a storm. He happened to be watching a tree as it was hit by one of these super strikes, and when the flash dissipated and the smoke cleared, the tree was gone. And we all knew the stories: lookouts perched on glass-footed stools as the tower around them glows blue; the old-timer who started to reach for the hand crank telephone to call in a fire, became distracted, and watched the phone blow apart when a strike hit the line; the pack mules tied to a tree that was struck, fusing their shoes to their hooves. Once I was sitting in the office during a storm, listening to the chatter on the forest radio, when lightning struck the radio repeater miles away. The familiar voices became the otherworldly squeal of transistors and circuits frying, the radio crying in pain. One of my friends in the bunkhouse said he'd been in camp when lightning hit close enough to make the phones ring.

Sometimes the strikes are cold, that is, they don't start a fire but are beautifully destructive anyway. Another friend told me he had come upon the remains of a tree struck but unburned. Outward from the tree, spears of wood from the fractured trunk formed a perfect circle around the tree like a warning: I'd go back if I were you. I saw for myself the crazy corkscrew scars lightning made up a tree, leaving it so damaged it would be a hazard to fell. A leader of ionized particles travels down from a cloud, but what we see as a down strike is actually the return stroke to the cloud. I have seen trees blown into pieces no larger than fence posts.

After lightning came fire, radioed in by a lookout or by a spotting plane. Then it was a matter of finding the fire, which could take several hours depending on how much smoke it put up and the accuracy of the directions we were given. Sometimes our noses guided us in. Then we dug a fireline to contain the blaze, threw shovelfuls of dirt to knock it down, and dug up and turned over every inch of black. When we were lucky, we had water close by and could use pumps. Depending on the size of the fire or its fuel, it could take hours or days to put it out, and our enthusiasm, mine at least, quickly waned, for the whole process became a matter of working as hard and as long as possible, baking during the day and freezing at night; no matter how much drinking water I carried, it was never enough, and what I had grew hot from the fire and the sun; and I swore I would find another job.

The morning after a fire, after a storm, was often cold. After getting wet from the hose or from sweating all day and then sleeping in the dirt, we'd wake cramped and stiff. We'd have a breakfast of cold Army-surplus C rations from the Vietnam era (complete with insect repellent that warned against getting it on watch crystals or plastic) or, later, MREs (Meal Ready to Eat). Dave Johnson often poured a packet of instant coffee on the chocolate bar from a C ration just for the jolt it gave. Then we'd have a warming cigarette and go out in our wool Mackinaws to hunt for hot spots to put out.

Usually a hot spot consists of a few smoldering embers. Occasionally, though, it may be a large area, where a stump or large log has rotted, and this punky wood is a chore to put out, even with water. In fact, water alone will often make a protective coating of mud over the coal, thus keeping it alive. Eventually, the mud turns to dust and wind breathes life into the ember again. We resorted to crushing each ember between the fingers of our leather gloves.

If an area is truly hot, especially if the fire has burned intensely, the dirt will contain air bubbles, as though the ground itself were boiling; water hitting such a spot will explode in steam and ash, filling your eyes and lungs. But some places must be tricked into revealing themselves. I learned if I got down close to the ground and looked across an area toward the sun, I could see clouds of gnats hovering over the hot spot for warmth. Sometimes all you get is a whiff of smoke, and then you must cast about like a dog on a scent, running the smoke to earth. But the most reliable way is to run your bare hands through the ash. If you find a spot, it must be dug up and mixed with cool, moist dirt until it's cold to the touch. So there we'd be, two people or two hundred, tired and cold, on hands and knees in the damp earth, listening for the morning weather forecast on the radio, daydreaming about going home, as the ravens scoffed at our work and the olive-sided flycatcher taunted us with its call of *whoop-three-beers*.

I found beauty in the fire, not just in the flames, but in the living thing and its aftermath. I loved the various shades of gray and black of the ash and trunks, the black standing trees against the gray and white ash; the contrast of blue sky against the brown then green edge of the fire; the small islands of vegetation that did not burn; and the animals alive in them, chipmunks and garter snakes, or the gray jays that followed us, and the huge, dangerous-looking blue-black insects we called stumpjumpers that lay their eggs in newly burnt wood.

Fire a living thing? Yes. It reproduces. To survive, it must have food and oxygen. The best part of Ron Howard's film *Backdraft* is its depiction of the fire as a thing the firemen hear moving inside a building. A large fire creates its own weather, but it is still dependent upon its environment. It is less active at night, generally, when the temperature drops and the humidity increases. At night the wind that has blown upslope all day turns and blows downslope into what has already burned. A fire won't burn without adequate fuel. Just like us, it must consume to live. I've watched fires burn upslope through thick fuel until a cloud or the smoke column blocked the sun. Suddenly the fire lies down, the flames shorten, and instead of making a roaring, it makes a low muttering, as though cursing its luck. Then the sky clears, and the fire becomes its old self again, taking what it needs and moving on.

We kept our fire shelters, which we never used, and the leather gloves we seldom used with us because one would not protect us without the other. During the bad fire year of 1979, we heard a rumor that a group of firefighters in south Idaho somewhere,

Mortar Creek Fire or Ship Island maybe, were overrun and had to deploy their fire shelters—small pup tents of reflective metal we called brown-n-serve bags. We heard temperatures inside went above 120 degrees—not unusual—and everyone survived except the one who had no gloves. He couldn't hold the shelter around him, and later his buddies found his body beside his melted radio and the exploded cans of his C ration lunch. But we loved our yellow and green fire clothes of Nomex, with its wonderfully reassuring chemical smell, and most of the time worked small two- or three-person smokechaser fires. Before 1985, we had few fires of any size, except for one *hot* ninety-acre blaze at the south end of the district at Yakus Creek, and a ten-acre fire in cedar slash that melted my boot heels.

Our chance at the big time came in 1985 when twenty of us were dispatched to the Sand Point Fire in Montana's Lewis and Clark National Forest. The fire was as hot as we could want, overrunning our lines, growing from one thousand acres when we arrived to thirteen thousand acres when we finally contained it eight days later. At the peak, twelve hundred people fought it. At one point we dug a line and pulled "back to the black," the already burned land, and waited for the fire to make its run. Then the retardant planes shot through the canyon, four-engine tankers just above our heads, spraying everything with borate. After four days on this minor section, we went to the head of the fire, about a six-mile walk, during which red-haired Jane Tonkin and I occupied ourselves by singing bits and pieces of every show tune we could name. We were not appreciated.

We spent the next four days at a spike camp beside the North Fork of the Judith River, where the land rolled between meadows of short grass and steeply rising hillsides of Douglas fir and clumps of juniper. The fire made minor runs the next couple of days and then blew up, burning five hundred acres in less than two hours. It began with a wind shift, the fire coming to life minutes before a planned burnout of fuel near the line. People streamed past me out of the trees, someone yelling, *Get out! Get out!* The tops of trees bowed toward the new center, their branches pulling free, my hard hat nearly lifted from my head, and from within that center a noise like locomotives in a house, roaring through each room, bearing down from behind the last wall. From a safe meadow, we watched the forest vanish beneath flame. This was the fire's last run, and two days later we contained it (although it wouldn't be declared out until nearly Christmas), and some of the crews were sent home. The fire had been phenomenal—the convection column looked like a mushroom cloud and towered so high the smoke fell finally as rain.

We flew out on National Guard helicopters, the old HU-Is used in Vietnam, and I was lucky enough to get a seat on the side facing the burn, the doors locked back, the ground dizzily gone. Only then did I understand the size of the fire. On the ten-minute flight back to base camp, I saw acre after acre of burned meadows, ridges, and draws, a bare and seared patchwork that resembled my legs. That night, as we sat up late, drinking coffee heavily sugared and knowing tomorrow would be an easy day of travel, I saw the aurora borealis for only the second time in my life.

What brought me to fire? Was it because I was burned? I don't hate fire, certainly: fire is one of the best things that can happen to a forest. It clears out undergrowth, gives seeds a place to start, and creates browse for deer, moose, and elk. Even when fire burns through a stand of trees, some will survive. Douglas fir, western larch, and ponderosa pine have bark thick enough to withstand the high temperatures of a fire. Ponderosa pine bark is layered like scales, which flick off as it burns, keeping the fire away from the delicate cambium layer between bark and trunk.

Nor do I fear fire. I've felt apprehension and concern, but I have also walked through a fire at night and felt a kind of wonder, as though I were deep inside the earth and nothing could harm me. I've watched snags burn and fall around me in a silent shower of spark; a little *whoosh*, and another tree comes down. I've felt awe at

the beauty and known this would be as close as I could get to
death without crossing over—without crossing the line. A lifeline?
A fireline perhaps?

My dictionary says *bonfire* comes from the Middle English word
bonefire, a fire to consume bones. It does not, according to
the Oxford English Dictionary, refer to the time of the plagues
but rather to the practice of saving bones to burn on
Midsummer's Eve. But Johnson claims it comes from *bon*, meaning
good, and *fire*—literally a good fire. Isn't that a Midsummer's
Eve fire? Is there a difference? The deeper meaning is
there somewhere, hidden in the word. *Let's go to the beach and
have a bonfire!* And how we love fire, how comforted we are
watching the flames, whether campfire or woodstove. Along with
the small knife sharpener and first-aid kit I keep in my pack, I
carry a film canister filled with shredded birch bark and sealed
with waterproof tape and a magnesium striker. Just in case. Others
say we love fire because it "eases our aching forebrain," and I have
to agree. Only while staring into a fire can I let my thoughts run
and not worry about what they'll uncover. Fire is the great leveler,
reducing everything to its origin, a transformer working the
diamond back to its first element, carbon, the base of all life.

One fall, late in my time with the Forest Service, Kevin Held and I
worked the Sylvan Saddle Trail. Late September, the elk beginning
to bugle mornings, the weather changed. Gone was the easy weather,
the red-tingeing frost; we awoke to mixed snow and rain that
continued as we worked, miserable now, our feet wet, leather gloves
sopping. At lunch we built a small fire of white pine and tried to
wear it, not caring that the wood was wet, grateful for the warm
smoke. Its coals glowed red, it gave heat, and that was all we cared.
Finally, though, I suggested we should do some work. My
partner agreed, and we put out the fire almost as carefully as if it
were August, and we kept the memory of heat as long as
we could.

Some nights I go walking in the early dark of a Lewiston winter,
dinner over, a switch engine shunting cars down by the river.
Cassiopeia hangs like an M in the north, and Orion begins
his climb from the east. And I swear, I know what type of wood
people are burning just from the smell of the smoke. There's
birch, perfume sweet and foreign; lodgepole and white pine,
slightly pitchy and delicate; larch, heavy and strong, like a
chimney fire in the making; Douglas fir, strong but not as sharp as
larch, mild as its green needles against the darker green of the
forest. I know when the wind blows wrong. I can pass my hand
over ash and feel the fire hidden within like a memory.

Warmed Twice

William Johnson

When my wife said we ought to get rid of the stove, I balked. She has her reasons—we heat with gas instead of wood now; our children have left home so we don't gather around a fire; and the stove takes up space we could use for a stereo or chair. My wife knows I'm attached to the stove, and that moving it will be a chore, but she didn't mention her real reason: she thinks the stove's ugly. From an aesthetic point of view, she's right. It's the size of a recliner, blunt and boxy, made of quarter-inch steel, with head plate, skirt, four stubby legs, and an L-shaped sheet-metal pipe that once carried smoke to a cinderblock chimney. In a den filled with potted plants, a sofa, chairs, and a hardwood coffee table, the stove's an eyesore, and useless to boot.

The trouble is, I don't see it that way. To me the stove isn't junk that takes up space, but a source of fire. And it triggers visions: a man and his son splitting wood on a crisp fall day; flames crackling from a log on the grate; a family together on the sofa eating popcorn and reading stories, with no TV in sight. And I'm hearing things: the snap and roar of flames; our voices in shaky unison launching into "The Little White Duck" with Burl Ives' scratchy tenor caught on an old 33 while it's snowing outside. To my wife the stove is in the way. To me it recalls the life of a family. And we're both right.

As I get ready to remove it, the stove calls me to winters past. Before the drone of television—we had no set in those years—fire accompanied our voices. When the door of the stove was ajar, firelight rippled off the wall of the den. Sap boiled to a hiss, and pockets of gas exploded like gunshots. Wood heat is dry heat. When a fire burned in the stove, the den felt like a desert. For a remedy, we bought a cast-iron pan, filled it with water, and placed it on the head plate. Now steam moistened the air, mimicking smoke that rose from the chimney. The stove got hot enough to fry eggs on. When our youngest two were toddlers, we erected a barricade of chairs to protect them. Like the old Roman oven, or *focus*, the stove was the heart of our house, and fire its pulse. In combustion, carbon and oxygen marry to give off heat and light. But the effect, or spirit, of fire eludes scientific explanation. It speaks of a mystery I barely fathom.

In our early years in the house, my wife wanted to see the fire in the stove. The kids agreed—hearing the flames whetted their appetites. I removed the panel from the door and took it to a glass shop. A man there cut a piece of tempered glass, fashioned a copper frame for it, and welded on a handle. Now the door of the stove was also a window. I'd catch one of our children sitting on the floor, mesmerized by the flames. Heat could lull you into a stupor, or spark visions. Our oldest boy would lie on the carpet gazing into fire, charmed by the ever-shifting light. If imagination transforms what we see, fire is its living image.
Like Blake's tiger, it burns in the forest of the night.

A fire in the stove was like an unruly child—it had to be fed and cleaned up after. But in return, it kept us warm and tricked us into seeing things. I'd place crumpled wads of paper on the grate, frame them with kindling, strike a match, and when the fire grew, roof it with a length of larch. Soon the flames fumed and spat. Thoreau wrote, "you can always see a face in the fire," but to do that I had to keep the panel clean. After a few fires, the glass was coated with creosote. Each week I'd take the panel outside, spray it with oven cleaner, and with newspaper rub off the grime. The fire sparked images that startled me. I saw Rome burning, a volcano

erupting, the leap of a forest fire. I saw what at first I hadn't words
for—the alchemy of carbon born and dying, in the flash of a
moment. In Hindu legend, Shiva, the destroyer god, dances in a
halo of flames. *Nirvana* is derived from the image of flame. It
means "blown out" or "ceasing to draw breath." The flame of
desire is quenched, the soul released from suffering. The fires in
our stove evoked memories and longings. Sometimes we tasted
soot in the air, as if the dead hovered around us.

I first met fire in the house where I grew up. A coal furnace near
my basement room would lull me to sleep with the hum of its
forced-air fan. If I couldn't sleep, I'd get up, shuffle into the hall
and stare through a glass peephole at the flames. Clinkers glowed
at a white heat, and ashes swirled like comet tails. Coal is solid
energy, fire in a stone. In the coal bin I once picked up a chunk of
anthracite. It smelled like burnt motor oil, and the smudge it left
on my fingers took many scrubbings to wash off.

In those days there were fires all around us. We lived in Spokane,
Washington, during the 1950s, and many nearby towns had
sawmills. Each mill had a burner for sawdust and slash, which at
that time were considered waste wood. The burners were tall,
inverted cones made of scrap metal that could stand seventy-feet
high, like great blackened wigwams. Flames licking the rivet holes
made a burner seem to quake, as if it might explode. Nights after
fishing when my father drove us home, the ovens were lit. Sparks
rose in flurries to the night sky, and the air stung with smoke.

Once as I lay in the backseat half asleep, the moon rose. I lifted
my hand to find it dappled with glitter. I thought I was dreaming,
then realized that fish scales stuck to my fingers caught the moon's
reflection. My skin looked milky, riddled with light, like mica-
stippled granite. When I sat up, we passed a burner roaring, the
sparks like those flecks on my hands. The sky was thick with stars.
For the first time I felt the mystery of fire. It came out of the
night, but also out of me. Flesh, wood, and sky were laced with

sparks, beautiful and terrifying. I thought of clinkers in the furnace near my room and remembered seeing clips on the Movietone News of the night fire bombings of London or Germany, and Nazi ovens belching an impossible smoke to the sky.

Fire was a character in the drama of my childhood. It yawned and spat from the roof of a burning house. It snickered in the fireplace, and its smoke stung me to tears. Fire fluttered from the Christ candle in church on Christmas eve. It sprang from a match like a flower blooming in a speeded-up film. Fire was the anger in my father's eyes. It was taboo, risk, a wild attraction. When I singed my fingers with a match, the pain was a reckoning. When paper wilted into wispy flakes of ash, I took note. Was this the fate of all things in the world?

Fire not only kept us warm; it linked us to the natural world. Our woodpile held fir and larch I'd cut in the mountains. Over the years, woodcutting became a ritual. Sometimes my oldest son went with me. We'd cruise logging roads looking for a dead tree to fell. I'd cut wood in June, after snow had melted, before the fire season prevented using a chain saw. We'd meet mushroom pickers, or see whitetail deer browsing early grasses. The cry of a Steller's jay set the woods on the alert. When one flew, a patch of sky darted through the trees.

Cutting wood was hard work. I'd choose a midsized fir or larch—a tree no more than three feet in diameter and up to a hundred in height. With the chain saw I'd make a kerf in the trunk, about three feet off the ground, saw halfway through, and drive in a felling wedge. A good sawyer would have done it all with a chain saw, but I was green and wanted to be sure which way the tree would fall. After the tree came down, I trimmed off branches and bucked the trunk into stove-sized lengths to split. If I worked on an open slope, I'd roll each length to a wood-hauling trailer. If not, I had to carry them, one at a time. By the end of the day, I was spent, but in the lingo of old-timers, I was "making wood."

I never got comfortable with the chain saw. I learned the right mix
of gasoline and engine oil, how to lubricate and sharpen the chain,
and I had the strength to lug the thirty-pound saw around in the
woods. But the machine unnerved me. At high speed it whined
like a banshee, and it bit through wood at a furious pace. If I ran
into a knot, the saw kicked violently, and if the bar got pinched,
the chain wound bind and trap the saw, its engine idly gargling.
Once as I worked a steep slope, a standing snag pinched the chain.
As I struggled to free the bar, the snag suddenly snapped. I leapt
from its path just in time. Afterward, blood pummeled my throat.
But it was fear I tasted. I chose not to work on steep ground again
and realized the lunacy of cutting wood alone. I could have bled
to death before I made it back to the truck.

Still I wanted to know fire. Cutting wood made me feel I'd earned
the right. And there were little bonuses. Once I forgot to
retrieve the axe. When I came back a week later, it leaned against
a stump where I'd left it. In the duff a few feet away, a
mushroom had sprouted—a stinkhorn, blunt and phallic, sprang
toward the sun. Brown ooze trickled from its cap, and a faint
malodor hung in the air. The fecundity of the woods startled me.
In the topsoil, new life smoldered. Dew steamed like smoke,
lilies unfolded, and shoots of grass appeared. Wood from the
forest had warmed our home, but now the earth itself heated up.
Other lives were waking—paintbrush and lupine, gnat and
butterfly, and the brash, unsavory stinkhorn—all warmed to the
planet's inner fire.

My work followed a seasonal rhythm. I cut wood into stove-sized
lengths in the spring and split it in the fall. It was good work, and
full of purpose. Splitting wood, I rediscovered what I'd known as a
boy working in the potato fields or as a carpenter's assistant—the
pleasure of hard labor. I used my back and hands, sweating for the
fires to come. Swinging an axe, I understood why chain gangs set
their work to song. If I forced a stroke, wood got stubborn and
thwarted the blade. I'd pause, take a breath, relax, and start over.
Soon the axe was an extension of my arm, its stroke a rough
music. Chuang Tzu's butcher came to mind. He became so good

at cutting meat, his knife never touched bone. Finally, the blade became invisible, and the meat fell away untouched.

To cut wood is to follow nature's way. The grain and growth rings in a log are paths, like the Tao, the "way" of things. Writing demands similar patience and precision. You follow the paths of words, tracking invisible meaning. But in life, as in writing, sometimes it's best to say nothing. When I tried talking my oldest son through his axe stroke, we both got impatient. By suggesting a "right way" of doing it, I made him feel inadequate. Rules were not the Tao. When I stopped talking and got back to work, he began to get the hang of it and soon was splitting wood on his own. On good days our strokes found their rhythms and the work seemed effortless. The *tunk* of an axe was its measure, like a drum sounding an overture to winter.

A forest holds subterranean fire. The dead feed the living and the living each other, in the dance of biomass at work. Windfall rots to become rich turf, and the term "dead wood" finds new meaning. The forest is a laboratory in which work is always in progress. Once we found cedar saplings had sprouted from a parent log rotting back into duff. They grew in a row, straight as the moss-cloaked trunk, faithful to the body and spirit of their elder. It was the way of the natural cycle, the fire of new life rising from decay. Where a cut bank exposed them, we found nodes of fungus clamped to fir roots, in mutual symbiosis. Fungus and wood feed each other in a vegetable barter. A tree feeds the air with carbon dioxide, feeds us with fire, and fungus feeds mice, shrews, or voles, which in turn are eaten by owls, foxes, or coyotes. I wanted to burn wood so I could come back and cut more. Seeing the journey of seed, sprout, needle, and cone, and the turning of wood into flame, I felt whole. I was an agent of real estate that would burn, an instrument of fire, who brought the forest into our home as light.

Our woodpile held other worlds. Each fall I covered it with a tarp to keep it dry, and over the winter neighbors moved in. Crickets, ants, beetles, and spiders nested in crevices of bark. Night crawlers squeezed under damp wood, and moths hatched from cocoons wedged into woodpecker holes. There were doors and windows in wood. A split log held cricket caves, ant roads, and the stubborn whorls of knots. Our cat used the woodpile as a scratching post and left her scrawls in the bark. Termites and carpenter ants gnawed wood to a spongy dust, and on the inner bark, beetles carved labyrinthine paths that looked like logging roads I'd seen from the air, or designs in Celtic art. Larch bark is a crazy quilt of flaky orange layers, thick and scablike. It looks like the pattern of a jigsaw puzzle, or a topo map of rugged terrain, and smells like turpentine. Pitch is the forest's tart perfume. Writing, too, recalls the pathways of wood. Originally "write" meant "to carve." Scribble in a field book and you score the flesh of trees.

Each fall, before lighting the first fire, I'd clean the chimney. I'd screw together fiberglass rods with the ends threaded to form a long, pliant pole; tie on a square wire brush; and attach an iron weight from my son's gym set. I'd lug the wobbly contraption up a ladder, place it on the roof, then haul myself up. Holding the pole over the chimney, I'd lower the brush down into the blackness as far as I could, then, as if I were pumping water, jerk the pole up and down so the brush scraped creosote off the chimney's inner walls. A flash fire might spit cinders onto our shake roof, and my wife knew it. She made sure I cleaned the chimney. To her, a house fire would be Armageddon, and I honored her fear. As I yanked the pole up and down, wisps of soot floated into the air. Each fire season left its residue of creosote, like a trace of the past or a hint of what we'd become.

Though the stories are culturally determined, each of us has a personal history of fire. Hawaiians honor and fear volcanic eruptions spewing magma and ash. In Ohio or Pennsylvania, steelworkers trudge past blast furnaces that roar like the devil, while giant vats pour molten ore into trays, in a version of hell's factories. In the Northwest, smokejumpers risk their lives parachuting into the backcountry to put out spot fires. Near large cities, the domes of nuclear reactors etch the skyline, and people pass them uneasily, sensing the fire inside. In South American rain forests, as land is burned for farming or grazing, smoke clouds out the sun. The flames are bad omens. Corporate greed threatens clean air, water, plants, and animals that could provide cures for cancer, AIDS, or plagues as yet unknown. If I could choose my own role, I'd be a Native American firekeeper, who selects rocks to be heated in the sweat lodge. He or she must choose carefully. Fire releases not only sweat and impurities but also the wisdom of earth as stone.

I try to think back to the original fire—before the woodstove and the furnace of my childhood. Back so far I can no longer think, only envision. I'm a boy being led with others into a cave. It's pitch dark except for the light from a torch ahead of us. The dark soaks into my skin and wants to swallow me up. Now we are in a vast room. Torch light flickers off the walls. I'm inside the belly of a great stone animal that has swallowed light. And now pieces of light begin taking shape. In the stone a sabertooth tiger flashes awake. A herd of bison stampedes across the wall. There are antelope and deer, hunters with spears and bows, and figures part-human, part-beast. In the dark, I witness the hunt that happens above me, in the country of light. Thanks to fire, I discover who I am. Cave paintings tell a story fire lets me read. I'm attracted not only to the beasts themselves, and the stone that holds them, but the flames that bring them to life.

Fire kindles a child's curiosity like nothing else. When our youngest turned seven, it charmed him. I'd find burnt matchsticks under his bed or in the washroom downstairs. I warned him about the danger and, luckily, he never had an accident. But for six months he couldn't help himself. He wanted to see the blue kiss of a spark, when phosphorous leapt to flame. Seeing fire he was mesmerized. He honored its candor and savored its risk. Playing with matches he flirted with the creative–destructive force and like a would-be Prometheus, conjured its power.

2

Recently, my father told me he'd like to be cremated when he dies. In life he was a shrewd businessman, and in death he wants to follow suit—be tidy and efficient, and not buy a casket or plot. He said my sister and I could dispose of his ashes however we liked. We could scatter them near our mother's grave or into the Idaho lake he loves. How we treat the dead reveals our take on life. Mummification turns on a belief that body and soul are inseparable. Christian burial looks not to this life but to the resurrection of the body in the next, when the flesh shall be made incorruptible. In India, a corpse burned near the Ganges becomes ash on sacred water, and the soul returns to Brahma. Some Native American tribes raised the dead on scaffolds where, through the work of birds and insects, they returned to the air as spirit.

My father's decision fits him, and I'll probably choose it for myself. Fire will lick me clean, bonemeal perchance make fertilizer, so I'll be put to use. A sealed coffin only holds an idea of life, and a strange one at that—as if we could preserve the body in some permanent way; as if we'd want to. I'll rot as worm fuel or be cast on the water as fish food. After death, I'll get back to work, let my calcium add its ounce of energy to creation. I won't burn in hell, but smolder in the only heaven I know.

My mother died young, and none of us thought beyond a conventional burial. Now I think she'd have preferred fire. It would have been a fitting response to the cancer that consumed her. Recently, visiting her grave, I remembered our church pastor. He was a stocky, balding Scotsman named Redfield, who delivered impassioned sermons, a man my mother called "fiery." At first I thought she referred to his complexion, which had a bright reddish tint (I later learned he suffered from acne rosacea). But she was probably thinking of his voice. The lyrical force he gave to the Psalms (read in the King James version) reminded her of fire.

Language is a fire that can warm and illuminate, or chill and confuse. At Pentecost, when the spirit descended, the disciples spoke with tongues of flame. In his New Testament letter, the apostle James writes, "And the tongue is a fire. With it we bless the Lord and Father, and with it we curse men who are made in the likeness of God." James knew that the power of language required responsibility, that words can either heal or destroy. When I tried to tell my son how to split wood, he grew impatient, but when I was quiet and taught by example, he found his way. My mother loved language and wrote colorful letters. With time and practice, she might have written poetry, been fiery with words. The poet Dickinson compared the restless soul to a flame in the blacksmith's forge, whose "impatient ore" burns with "unanointed blaze."

So, the stove has to go. We no longer rely on wood heat; smoke has become a major source of pollution in this valley; and the forests where I cut firewood have been badly over-logged. Recently I sold my wood-hauling trailer to a neighbor, and now it's time to part with the stove. I regret it, but I know what I have to do.

Home from college, my youngest son volunteers to help. I place newspapers on the concrete slab where the stove rests. When I loosen the stovepipe, soot falls like inky snow. I'm closing a chapter in the life of a family. After removing the pipe and gathering the soot, we edge the stove off the slab and jockey it through the back door. In its temporary home on the patio, the stove looks desolate, but a part of our life has gone up in its smoke. What before had seemed alive, is now inert, mere steel, bolts, and paint. As we hauled it through the door, I felt the stirrings of this essay. Whatever their residual statement, these words reach for volatile truth. Like Thoreau, who dug stumps from his bean field and later split them to burn in his fireplace, I'm warmed twice.

On a bright June morning, we hoist the stove into the pickup. The steel is cold—the stove has been out all night. As we wrestle it into the truck, my skin tingles. We work up a sweat getting it on board. On the drive to the recycling yard, I glance into the rearview mirror. The hole for the stovepipe gapes like a throat severed from its head. No rational part of me can explain this. A psychologist would say I'm projecting. A literary type would accuse me of the pathetic fallacy. But I can't help it—the stove not only looks out of place, but betrayed. It holds an emptiness as black as it is terminal. What defies logic, lives in my imagination. Though I can distinguish fire from steel, I can't, or won't, separate them.

When I stop on the platform of the weigh scale, the woman at the window waves me back. I pull off and drive on a second time. Somehow, I've triggered the alarm. Electronic sensors in the scale registered the presence of radioactivity, but this time no bell sounds its warning. I think of the stove again. The alarm signaled dislocation, a rent in time. My cargo isn't scrap metal but rather an artifact that kept a family warm.

I drive into the scrap yard, past mounds of junked iron and steel—oil drums, the driving wheels and rails of trains, cracked girders, housings of table saws and lathes, stacks of rebar, steel poles, hubcaps, and buckets—all the molded metal imaginable lies in a mountainous graveyard by the tracks. A young man wearing overalls and heavy boots sits in his car eating a sandwich. When he sees me, he gets out and points to a dumping spot. "Nice stove," he says, and helps me slide it out of the truck. I nod in silence. Just now the recycling yard is still. The driver of a front-end loader is also on his lunch break. The stove topples from the tailgate, lands hard on the dirt, and tips on to its side. The door flings open and coughs a mouthful of soot on the ground. As I turn to go, bits of it hang like smoke in the heavy summer air.

Fireworks

Jeff P. Jones

I.

*[T]ake a brasse pestle and mortar, and dipping the pestle in oyle of
Almonds, put it to your Camphire, and so stirring it by degrees, it will
powder; which when you have done, keepe it very close from ayre, till
such time as you use it, otherwise the Camphire will lose his spirit, and
become of no use.*

—John Babington, London, 1635

That night, in the summer of 1982, on the sidewalk outside my
grandfather's house, I huddled against the wind over a small match
flame and a tiny black pellet. There I was, a small creature, a ten-
year-old child on his knees, coveting a tiny spark, wishing for the
flame to ignite the pellet, to teach me something about the
mysterious powers of fire and gunpowder.

The flame burned down to my fingertips and winked out, so I
struck two matches together and held their flame to the black
pellet until it awoke. A tiny black creature grew before my eyes,
robed in smoke, twisting and coiling. The smoke was sweet and
dark and I inhaled deeply. When it stopped growing I took its
black husk in my hands, cradling it like a broken-winged bird. I
started to carry it inside, but the wind tugged it apart. It was a

momentary thing, too delicate for this world. I crushed what was left and its body blacked my palms with ash.

This is how I will remake it. By taking a fountain in hand, peeling back the layers of blue touchpaper from around its tip, and touching a spark to its fuse. This is how I will remake it. By giving coolness to grass, clarity to the sky, hushed exchanges between my parents who must have been nearby. This is how I will remake it. By gazing into the night sky as a silver star rises like a beacon on a trail of sparks and bursts into a sphere of gold that expands even as it hangs in the air, turning from gold to green, green to purple, purple to red—a new universe of possibility and light.

This, then, is where my fascination with fireworks began: on a summer night in our neighborhood park, when I was four years old, I leaned back against the hill and felt each cool blade of grass under my palms. The clear Colorado sky stretched overhead with its pale specks, beckoning toward something of great promise. I listened past my parents' low murmurs for that liquid hiss, that chest-thumping boom. I watched for stars. Not just any stars, though. That bouquet of exploding stars that would become my first memory.

Charcoal. Sulfur. Saltpeter. A mealed powder rolled tight inside a tube of pressed paper. Clay nozzle. Quickmatch fuse. Flame. The brightness of sparks.

The human fascination with gunpowder is traced to the eighth century when Chinese alchemists mixed honey with sulfur and saltpeter to create a concoction that, when heated, would ignite into a wall of flame. Various historians and scientists since then have claimed the discovery of gunpowder as the most significant of all time. In 1313, it was the fascination a monk named Berthold Schwarz had for gunpowder that led to the invention of the firearm, the impact of which is difficult to underestimate. Schwarz's obsession with the grainy gray and black substance is well-established—he was called the Powder Monk.

2

The screen door slapped shut behind me and the first thing I felt
was the cool air of the shop against my sweat-moistened skin. Ten
years old, I had just walked the half mile from my grandfather's
house to the country store along State Highway 64 in East Texas. I
grew up in Colorado, but every summer we returned to my
father's childhood home in the Lone Star state where, for two
weeks, my life narrowed to a singular focus—fireworks.

Along my walk I basked in the strangeness that was East Texas.
Pine trees grew everywhere, and the robust scent of pine needles
dissolving into the earth spiced the air. The soil was a mineral-rich
red earth that clung stubbornly to everything it touched. Iron
horses, some rhythmically pumping, others motionless, were
constant reminders that deep belowground awaited vast reservoirs
of oil. During the day, birdsong filled the air, most notably the
tune of a forest dweller calling its name with a lilting rise—*Bob
Whi-ite*—again and again from a hidden perch.

Inside the country store, though, the humidity and sweltering heat
and birdsong washed away. The air tasted of cool beads trickling
down the sides of Coca-Cola bottles and peanut-studded Big
Hunk candy bars.

"Well, there's my Colorado friend. I was wondering if y'all was
going to make it down again this year." The shop owner was a
small lady with a friendly smile. "I'll bet you want some fireworks."

The wall behind the counter was chock-full of ordinance: Saturn
Missile Batteries, Air Travel bottle rockets, Black Cat firecrackers,
Catherine Wheels, Camellia Flowers, Ground Blossoms, Red Rats,
Satellites, Birds.

It was hard to swallow and my stomach felt airy, as if punched full
of tiny holes.

"Would you like a soda water while you're looking? It sure is hot today."

"Yes, ma'am." I fingered the dollar bills and coins in my pocket, the cash I had saved for weeks in anticipation of that moment.

The next day, armed with a brick of firecrackers, a handful of M-60s, and a bag of multicolored smokeballs, I scouted an enemy structure near the base of a pine tree and initiated an attack with a single firecracker poked into the center of their bunker. Immediately, tiny red pismires climbed the explosive. Their singed bodies fell like passengers from the sides of a doomed ship as the fuse burned down. I ducked for cover just as the explosion tore out a hole the size of a Matchbox car. The pismires teemed madly over their hill. When I stuck in the next firecracker, they swarmed so thick that their bodies snuffed the fuse. But I persisted. Once I had excavated a sufficient chasm, I dropped in an M-60 that ripped a gaping hole and exposed their inner chambers—caverns and rooms filled with mealy white eggs. I pinched a lit smokeball and aimed its steady stream of green smoke into the exposed tunnels and chambers until their entire network became a smoking heap. I hated the little monsters. My father called me in for dinner and the war was put on hold. The fire ants busied themselves with reconstruction.

Inside, we tucked into my grandmother's chicken and dumplings, green beans flavored with bacon, fried okra, homemade cornbread, fresh tomatoes, and sweet iced tea. Every so often I glanced out the window, willing the sunlight to fade and dark to settle.

That night I lit the punk in the blue flame of the oven's burner. My hands trembled. I raced outside. My grandmother and grandfather were already faces at the side window. My cousin Gary rifled through the bag of works while I grabbed a fountain and placed it on the sidewalk.

There I was again, a child with one palm pressed to the pavement, the other holding a red-hot tip to a thick green fuse. I bent closer and blew on the cherry tip. Though I didn't think about it, I was aware on a level deeper than thought of the damp earth rising about me, boggy and rich, laced with sweetgum and pine and carrying on it the sharp timbre of cicadas and low rumble of tree frogs. In my mind no one was watching. It was only me, a boy leaning intimately close, almost embracing, that shell of cardboard and packed gunpowder. The fuse ignited. Sparks and cinders blossomed, golden and brilliant, a dance of lights that streaked and glittered and pushed back the darkness from the porch, burning a ghost image into my vision that lasted long after the fountain extinguished.

After we launched all the big fountains and rockets, the others retreated inside. Our grandparents went to bed and Gary and I stayed to finish off the small stuff.

There the child was yet again, hurling a Super Bee into the night. This particular firework, a tourbillion, was meant to be launched from the ground. Instead, hurtling through the air, it zoomed horizontally across the highway, a tiny ball of whirring flame, and landed among the pine trees. I made a mental note to check it again shortly.

Ten minutes later I noticed the glow in the forest.

Sparks flew against my face and singed my jeans. Flames leapt up a tree trunk as high as my throat. Hot smoke scorched my lungs. Soot stung my eyes. My father and I, along with several neighbors, thrashed the burning tree trunk and ground with wet towels while Gary shoveled dirt onto it. My lungs and arms burned and I stepped away. Outside the circle of flame I found fresh air. With hands on knees I coughed until it felt like part of my stomach lining had come loose.

The others beat the fire into submission. Their sweat-soaked faces and clothes were smudged and filthy. My father inspected for cinders. The fire had burned outward in a perfect circle, ten feet in diameter. I stood nearby, stunned, and wondered what my father would say.

Our relationship was not what I imagined existed between most fathers and sons. He was thirty-eight when my mother had me. I was his third child, a smart but sensitive second son. He reasoned with me from a young age, and I soon learned how to act mature with him. Our favorite activities were mental games—trying to guess the opposite of a word, figuring long division in our heads, solving wind-speed problems. Because my father had always played with fireworks as a boy they were an acceptable indulgence, especially when in East Texas, and he even encouraged my fascination.

He looked at me as I wiped my ash-blackened hands onto my jeans.

"If it had gotten up that tree this whole forest would've caught." He didn't need to say more.

Roger Bacon, a thirteenth-century monk who studied divinity and cosmology at Oxford, gives us insight into the fascination fireworks held for children in the Middle Ages. Though he didn't invent it, he refined the gunpowder recipe, purifying saltpeter, which provides the all-important oxidant in gunpowder, and adding sulfur and willow charcoal. When wrapped tightly, the result was a "toy of children" about which he wrote: "So horrible a sound is produced at the bursting of so small a thing, namely a small piece of parchment that we perceive it exceeds the roar of sharp thunder, and the flash exceeds the greatest brilliancy of the lightning accompanying the thunder."

Mrs. Galbraith presided over our seventh-grade homeroom. This was the teacher who wore bulbous eyeglasses as thick as binocular lenses and who couldn't hear well enough to recognize when students called her "Mrs. Cow Breath" to her face. Yet, one morning, I discovered this tottering old lady deserved more respect.

Just about anything went in her class—gambling, cussing, pencil fights—so I had no qualms about dissecting a firecracker at my desk. I poured the fine gray powder speckled with pinpoints of black into a cone of notebook paper on my desk. I had plans to unravel others and make a single mega-cracker. I'm sure it was the fuse that gave me away.

"What's this, young man?" she asked on a routine stroll through the classroom.

"Oh, nothing. Just something I found," I lied.

"Looks like the makings of a firecracker." She scooped it up and scuttled to the front of the room. "Come with me, Jeffrey," she said.

In the vice principal's office, I stuck to my story—that it was a single firecracker I had found on the floor of the music room. Mr. Morgan leaned across his desk and fixed his heavy gaze on me. Silver sprouted through the gold of his eyebrows, and I was certain he saw through my lie, heard my fluttering heart, and somehow knew that, in my locker, I had a whole brick of Black Cats—that right then, in fact, I had several more firecrackers in my jeans pockets. I could feel their hard edges poking my thigh, prodding me with their possibility, and all along I knew that, if he didn't suspend me, I would find all sorts of objects to blow up in the alleys I traversed after school on the way home.

On the electromagnetic spectrum, which ranges from gamma rays to radio waves, only a tiny segment is visible to the human eye. When a Roman candle burst sears across our vision, we see only a fragment of its emitted radiation. The bursting shell releases light that ranges from the ultraviolet, includes the visible, and covers all frequencies of the infrared. When we see a shell burst, it is only natural to assume that what we see is all that's there. To an omniscient eye, however, the bursting shell would be a thousand times more spectacular.

In high school, some kids dealt pot. Others dealt speed. I dealt fireworks.

Like the best suppliers, I kept a good stash in my locker. Mostly, it was just the basics—firecrackers and bottle rockets. Colorado state law prohibited any fireworks that left the ground or exploded, and Aurora's city code prohibited any fireworks at all. So, besides most of my supply having been highly illegal, it was also popular.

One day in tenth grade, two friends dared me to light something inside the school. It seemed too easy. I strolled to the end of the hallway, paused briefly to light the fuse, tossed the tiny jumping jack by a set of lockers, and bolted. As I hit the door at the end of the hallway I heard the electric whir followed by what I knew would be a five-second display of a bouncing ball of red and green fire with plenty of smoke.

I burst into Honors English, took up a seat behind a bookcase, and pulled my sweatshirt hood over my head. Ten minutes later the hall monitors came for me. Because I was a good student and that was my first offense, I received only a three-day suspension.

After my suspension I discovered Time-Life's eight-volume series titled *The Unexplained* in the school library. These were black, oversized hardbacks with red question marks blanketing the covers. They were the best books in the library.

On a night in 1952, Mary Reeser sat in her favorite armchair in her St. Petersburg, Florida, home. She wore her most comfortable black satin slippers. Nearby were delicate lace curtains and a pile of newspapers. Somehow that night, Mary Reeser caught fire and burned to death without bothering to get up from her chair. When they found her body the next day, she had been reduced to a blackened liver fused to a vertebra, a heat-shrunken skull, and a single foot inside a satin slipper. The rest of her was ash. The temperature required to consume an adult human body, according to the International Cemetery and Funeral Association, is between 1400 and 1800°F. Mary Reeser's drapes and newspapers, within arm's reach, weren't even singed.

I pored over every volume in *The Unexplained* series, studying, instead of English and algebra, ley lines in Ireland, ectoplasm spewing from people's navels and ears, frogs and fish falling from the sky, and people bursting into balls of flame. Spontaneous Human Combustion (SHC) intrigued me, and I spent many afternoons in the library studying the grotesque photos that contained hands and feet, perhaps a skull, but always, where the torso had been, only ash—a blackened hole of soot. In the case studies, a brown oily substance, the residue of burnt body fat, often covered the walls and floor. I could imagine no more incredible event than the sudden fusion of the body with fire, the suggestion that some of us may contain the chemical makings to combust into living flame.

I had never heard an adult talk about SHC. It was a subject I couldn't imagine my high-school teachers or parents discussing. I wondered why it was kept such a secret. Having discovered it entirely on my own, the knowledge felt somehow elicit. (Years later, I discovered the scenes of SHC in Dickens' *Bleak House* and Melville's *Redburn*, as well as Job's proclamation: *My skin is black upon me, and my bones are burned with heat.*)

As *The Unexplained* were cataloged as reference books, they could not be checked out. One day, as I was reading volume eight in the school library, the fire alarm sounded. The librarian began ushering students out the side door and, with barely a moment's hesitation, I slipped the book into my backpack and committed my first act of library theft.

At home, I studied the entry on ball lightning. In 1958, the Reverend John Henry Lehne recorded an event that happened in his York, Pennsylvania, home when he was twenty-four: while he was seated in the bathroom, a ball of yellow fire the size of a grapefruit entered through a screened window, rolled around his feet, and bounced up into the washbasin, where it melted the steel chain attached to the rubber stopper and disappeared down the drain. A few weeks later, he experienced the same event and the ball of fire again melted the new metal chain.

I longed for the chance to witness these supernatural phenomena, partly to prove to myself, finally, the existence of such things. But it was more than that. At fifteen, I believed myself to be on the cusp of adulthood, and one of the things that dismayed me most about the adult world was its skepticism of the peripheral. There seemed to be no room in the mainstream for ghosts, which I had seen, dream control, which I had undertaken, and ball lightning, which I believed was real. Yet I already sensed in myself a hesitancy to acknowledge such beliefs. I knew without trying that the topic was off limits to discuss with my father—my fascination wouldn't have been acceptable but merely seen as a distraction from my studies. I longed for proof of a world that adults, with all their high sensibilities, had overlooked. In retrospect I understand my fascination with fireworks to have grown out of their extraordinary power to inspire belief in the potential for mystery and wonder. My ensuing interest in things "unexplained" grew out of this desire for a world still open to childlike awe.

The smell emitted by fireworks, the smell of sulfur forming hydrogen sulfide upon combustion, the smell that still touches off realms of possibility within me, the smell that is intimately linked with the rich scent of earth around my grandfather's house and all that place was—family (now passed), dinners (now memories), moments (now gone)—has remained the same throughout history. A millennium ago, when Arab children detonated their "fire crackers," they smelled the same scent of possibility; they extolled in their own ways the gifts of gunpowder and fire. The child huddling over the tiny flame, willing it into a greater reaction with the powder, is an image at least a thousand years old.

II.

And all is seared with trade; bleared, smeared with toil;
And wears man's smudge and shares man's smell.
                                        —Gerard Manley Hopkins

In the summer of 1991, after my first year of college, I landed a position as a retail fireworks manager. As far as I was concerned, there could be no better summer job: pulling the cardboard boxes with red-inked Chinese characters off the semis that had hauled them from the California coast, cutting open the shrink-wrapped packages, stamping each individual product with a price gun, taping labels to their boxes, imagining which fountain would burn longest or throw its sparks highest, testing each product after hours, and, of course, keeping, for personal use, the illegal bangers and rockets that couldn't be sold.

That first day, I pulled up to a barren field on the southeast edge of Aurora, Denver's largest suburb. A few workers, mostly twentyish, milled around. The field was near the highest point in the city and commanded an expansive view—downtown Denver and the Rocky Mountains to the west, and the desiccated plains to the east. Yellow scrubgrass sprouted between anthills and discarded Big Gulp cups. The dry soil was packed hard from the eastern plains' copious high-altitude sunshine and lack of water. We erected what would become my tent. The red-and-white striped canvas we stretched out flat over the field and then lifted into place with ten-foot perimeter poles and a thirty-foot center beam. We lashed it to the ground with stakes and ropes and pulled the shell taut.

The tent carved something out of nothing. A barren field suddenly became a new space with a roof and removable walls, a

place of protection from sun, wind, and rain. Ostensibly, it was a
place of business filled with product and cash registers, but for
those of us who worked there on that patch of dirt and anthills, it
became a place where you drank your first cup of coffee in the
morning; a place to listen to the radio while setting out boxes and
checking labels; a place to play catch; a place to help moms and
dads find just the right assortment pack; a place to eat fast food
and meet friends; a place to do a drop, carrying $500 or more out
to the glove box of your car in case you got robbed later; a place
to fire up the gas generator and watch the string of yellow safety-
caged light bulbs come to life; a place to have pizza delivered to,
which you paid for in trade; a place over whose shell you crawled
at night, all the way up the seam until your hands wrapped around
the center pole's stake thirty feet aboveground, the canvas bending
and stretching underfoot, to see Denver spread out pell-mell in
the distance and, on the Fourth, the colored splashes of light
gushing in several spots across the nightscape; a place that quiets
during the dinner lull and affords you the chance to pull a cold
beer from a cooler; a place to tell stories; a place to lower the
sides of; a place to count the day's earnings; a place from which to
haul products into the nightly lock-box storage bin; a place to
drive away from, knowing all the while you'd be back in less than
ten hours. This place is your life for three weeks.

Even in the thirteenth century, Roger Bacon was himself obviously
enamored with the possibilities inherent in gunpowder. He wrote,
"By the flash and combustion of fires, and by the horror of sounds,
wonders can be wrought, and at any distance that we wish, so that
a man can hardly protect himself from it." For his efforts in
alchemy, the Church imprisoned him for ten years. Nevertheless,
in 1252, he preserved his illegal recipe for gunpowder in an
anagram which, when deciphered, reads, "of saltpetre take six
parts, five of young willow charcoal and five of sulfur and so you
will make thunder and lightning." No doubt this was the recipe
later used by the Powder Monk.

My fascination with the surreal and peripheral continued throughout college. While outwardly studying anthropology and English, I pursued a shadow education in biblical archaeology, UFOS, and cryptozoology. I sought out reputable sources that proved the world still held mystery.

Meanwhile, the retail fireworks job lasted five summers. Starting in June, each year my life became one of breathing the field dust inside the tent, managing cashiers, and, of course, handling money. With each new season, the job became more and more about the cash—the ones, fives, tens, and twenties that coated my fingers with inky residue each night during the till count.

By my fifth summer, I no longer sought out customers to whom I could extol the virtues of a particular fountain. I didn't even bother trying the year's new products but relied instead on others' reports. Coworkers stopped hassling me to come out to dead-end streets in new developments to shoot off illegals. I was no longer interested in the bursting of sparks, the crackling of powder, the bothersome explosions. What interested me were fully stocked bins, the ringing of cash registers, and apprehending shoplifters.

For the most part, these boys were under sixteen so they stole what they were too young to buy, usually pocketing small stuff—smoke crackers, Snap-N-Pops, booby traps. At nightfall, I would send two of my best workers up onto the shell of the tent. Peering through tiny holes in the canvas, they were my security system. As soon as they saw someone steal something, they slid down and reported. The first time I busted a shoplifter I was nearly as scared as he.

He was a scrawny kid about fifteen, with well-combed dark hair. He had stolen two magnum poppers and a pack of crackling balls. I was angry and wanted to get word out that I was no pushover.

"Why'd you steal this?" I asked stupidly.

"I don't know. I'm sorry, mister. I'll pay you double for it."

"You know, I can call the sheriff on you. He can decide whether or not to arrest you. Either way it'll go on your record."

"Oh, man. Please, mister. Don't. Please."

Sometimes the boys cried. Sometimes they pleaded. Sometimes they became angry. Whatever their response, it never melted my resolve, and I always called their parents or the sheriff.

The authority I held over those boys frightened and exhilarated me. When I told them to sit in a chair and wait for the sheriff, they did. At times, when a boy either glared or looked pleadingly at me from that corner chair, hoping for a reprieve, I remembered the times I had shoplifted—candy, library books, and yes, fireworks, on a trip through Missouri when I was thirteen.

My best friend had come along on a family trip and, when we stayed the night at a motel next to a small fireworks tent, the temptation was too strong. We snuck out in the middle of the night, and I slipped under the tent flap while the only worker slept in his car twenty feet away. It was pitch black inside. My fingers brushed over the sides of the bins, then dipped into their contents, fingering the cool sides of mini-fountains, the chalky round shapes of smokeballs with their springy fuses, and the lipstick-shaped ground blossom flowers. I felt each item separately and made sure I knew what it was before either putting it back or pocketing it as I moved from bin to bin.

"What took you so long?" my friend asked when I finally slid into the ditch behind the tent.

"I wanted to make sure I got the good stuff."

With the boys I caught shoplifting at my own tent, I didn't allow the past to interfere. My duty was to protect my tent and show no mercy.

One time I wrongly accused two boys of having shoplifted. It was the middle of a hot, dusty afternoon when there were no customers and their lollygagging over my products aroused my suspicion. They emptied their pockets, eager to prove their innocence and seemingly glad, even, for a diversion in their day. After I let them go, they hung around the tent and I eventually hired them. They became two of my best workers and, since it was illegal to employ underage workers, I paid them in fireworks.

Legend holds that Catherine was a fourth-century virgin in Alexandria condemned to be tortured to death by a spiked wheel for refusing to marry the emperor Maxentius. When they tied her to the wheel, it flew apart, killing her torturers. After being fed by a dove through her prison window, she saw a vision of Christ before finally being beheaded. From her experience, the Catherine wheel arose. This firework is the same as a pinwheel, with a gunpowder-filled tube spiraled around a central pivot, which is nailed to a post and, when lit, spins rapidly, throwing from its edges showers of sparks.

At my grandfather's one summer day after the Fourth, I collected the residue from several spent fireworks into a heap. The pile of black ash extinguished every match I dropped onto it.

The remnant of fireworks is a sooty powder that mars sidewalks, stains clothes, and darkens skin. I now understand that this soot is the residue of several chemical reactions within gunpowder, including a spray of molten potassium salts that leaps from grain to grain during ignition, activating potential energy. During the combustion of a single pyrotechnical device, numerous physical changes occur within gunpowder, including the rapid expulsion of gases that causes the fuel's ingredients to decompose, as well as the reconfiguration of the crystal structure of its molecules. In the end, though, what remains always after fireworks is ash—an incomplete reminder of the showers of silver and gold, the colored balls of light, the bright flashes that went before it.

There's a certain slant of light,
Winter Afternoons—
That oppresses, like the Heft
Of Cathedral Tunes—

The longer I contemplate these words of Emily Dickinson, the better I understand how things familiar and comfortable can become despicable. Her words expand and blanket my thoughts with a hot air that stultifies, but at the same time births, out of sheer frustration, a new sensibility that pushes upward to break through an older one.

The explosions and showers of lights have remained the same, but they carry different meaning now. I didn't choose to become disillusioned with the mystery of fire and gunpowder, and I don't fully understand why it happened. I know it had something to do with the faces of those boys I caught shoplifting, whose zeal for packages of gunpowder I knew intimately; it had something to do with learning to desire the familiarity of dollar bills in my hands more than the surprising weight of a Sunburst fountain; and, it had something to do with an elementary pleasure simply fading with age. Nevertheless, the sensation of lost joy persists.

In my last summer as manager, my tent shattered all previous sales records. On July 4th alone, we hauled in more than $30,000. The owners were ecstatic. They gave me a $250 bonus . . . which wouldn't have been quite so insulting if I hadn't counted every dollar of my tent's $60,000 after hours each night when I was bone tired and desperately needed sleep.

At around midnight on the Fourth of that last summer, Brad, one of the owners, appeared at my tent. By then, the dust kicked up by the herds of customers had settled, leaving a few empty bins and an exhausted silence. The day before, from the top of the tent, we had suspended forty feet of red, white, and blue ribbon from a massive helium balloon eight feet in diameter. That night, we reeled it in. Brad cut the ribbon so that a length of about ten feet hung from the balloon's nipple. He tied the ribbon around a Sunburst, lit the fuse, and released it.

"What do you know? It worked," he said. The fountain burned furiously as we watched it pull away from us.

"Just hold it," I used to say to customers as I placed the Sunburst in their hands. They could feel its heft, loaded with gunpowder.

"It's the most bang for your buck. Five-ninety-five and it'll burn for at least four minutes straight, guaranteed." Though I'll likely never return to retail fireworks, still, I often recall that last night of that record-breaking summer.

As the balloon pulled the fountain into the night sky, I realized that my desire to cradle packages of gunpowder, to hold them and touch flame to their potential, had extinguished. Still, the Sunburst's stubborn refusal to relinquish its light was impressive. Brad ducked into the tent, to boxes and dust and Budweisers. I remained outside with my gaze transfixed by that soft, radiant star and its slow burn, imperceptibly diminishing, so that it was impossible to tell the moment when its light matched that of the stars decorating the blackness into which it rose.

With part of the $1200 earned from that first summer working retail fireworks, my girlfriend and I took a trip to Yellowstone National Park. It was three years after the fires of 1988 and we stood in the middle of a forest of blackened trunks, surrounded by stark branchless spires. The desolation stretched as far as we could see, miles of skeleton trunks blackened into a seeming mockery of living things. Even the ground was black with soot.

We found a single black beetle flipped onto its back, pawing the air, and when we stooped to help it we noticed the shoots. Almost imperceptible because they were so small, tiny bright green cotyledons had pushed upward, their tips just breaking the soil's surface. When we looked closely, we saw that they were everywhere, a subtle but verdant reawakening.

Rendering Gold by Fire with a Master

Steve Koehler

Fire is the test of gold; adversity, of strong men.
—Seneca, Moral Essays

Assaying rocks for gold by fire is rooted in the antique world of alchemy. Vestiges of that world still survived in 1972 at the University of Idaho College of Mines. Back then I was a graduate student in the geology department and had come to study the art of fire assaying under an old master, Joseph Newton.

Newton was the college's assistant dean and venerable author of *Extractive Metallurgy,* an authoritative 1959 book on recovering metals from their ores. He enjoyed correcting students who called him Dr. Newton. He was Mr. Newton—had a master's but never a doctorate degree—and was proud of it. I asked him if he would teach fire assaying, a class he hadn't taught in years. Though near retirement, he said he would, if I'd clean up the furnace room.

The place looked like a dump—a storage room into which stuff had been haphazardly piled and left to collect dust on a floor littered with pieces of slag. Even so, I was delighted to perform the task; it was like being turned loose to explore a foreign museum.

I found chemicals in cans, bottles, brown paper sacks, and a wooden barrel; boxes and boxes with orange ceramic crucibles—the size and shape of medium paper cups, but much thicker—and long, black-iron tongs for holding them. In the middle of the room, on a waist-high iron table, stood three oil-fired furnaces—domed, black-iron boxes with reddish and bone-white stains—to which were connected large and small black-iron pipes. The monsters gave the room the appearance of a crematorium for small animals.

And there were brass balances, like the Scales of Justice, each enclosed in a glass-windowed wooden case. A control knob on the outside unlocked the beam with its two hanging pans, leaving it to balance on a knife-edge.

Only one other student signed up for the class. Instruction began in the sample preparation room, with its cast-iron marvels of the Industrial Revolution: electric motor-powered jaw crushers and pulverizers. Under Newton's watchful eye, the other student and I crushed and ground hard rocks into fine powder, then weighed out samples into the crucibles for assay.

Then we went to the furnace room. Despite his diminished health, Newton became animated as he explained how to light a furnace.

I put on heavy, elbow-length fireproof mittens, and the other student tied a rag on the end of a six-foot iron pole, soaked it with fuel oil, and handed it to me. The moment he lit it, I became a Lucifer ordered to set fire to Hell.

We flipped the switch on an electric black-iron blower on the floor, as ugly as the furnaces to which it was connected. A black, elephant trunk of a pipe joined all the monsters. The roar of that blower terminated casual conversation. Newton moved well back toward the corner, from where he watched me with an encouraging smile.

I opened a fuel-oil valve, and aerated mist sprayed into the furnace's firebox. Then I stepped back and touched the flame to it. The spray burst into a coughing orange flame that rumbled like thunder over the roaring blower. I thought my job was done, but the flame suddenly went out. I glanced over at Newton, who repeatedly thrust out his arm to tell me to relight the furnace.

Raw fuel was soaking the firebox. The moment I touched the torch to the spray, orange flames and black smoke exploded from the furnace. I jumped back and looked over at Newton. He was doubled over with laughter.

The flame coughed and sputtered and resumed its rumble. Then poof: it went out again. We had no time for swearing. An ominous white cloud was crawling out of the hot firebox. The torch I held had become a flickering candle, but it would have to do. I crouched and grimaced fiercely as I charged the stove, holding that pole as far from me as possible, the pitiful rag-candle bobbing like a drunken bird. I thrust the pole at the white cloud. An explosion rocked the room and the furnace roared to life. The flame popped, banged, and sputtered, but mercifully it stayed lit. The fireworks exhilarated Newton to tears.

Meanwhile upstairs inside the college, fine soot was streaming into the reception area, professors' offices, and classrooms. An unfavorable breeze was guiding the plume of black smoke spewing out the furnace-room chimney to its neighbor—the air intake on the college's ventilation system. Newton had forgotten to tell us about this potential problem, but later on, others didn't. They grumbled about our using antiquated technology, the smell, and fouling sensitive analytical instruments.

After some minutes, however, the rumbling flame became a steady, roaring blue fire with a yellow crown. When the furnace chamber became orange-hot, I picked up a long pair of tongs and placed each of twelve crucibles inside it. Then I closed the door.

Mixed with the quartz samples were various chemicals. These included soda ash (similar to baking soda), litharge (orange lead oxide), a teaspoon of wheat flour, and a grain of silver. The chemicals melted like butter in a hot skillet and dissolved the powdered rock like sugar in the butter, but with much more drama. The molten pool inside each crucible was the scene of a hellish dance of atomic love and hate: molecules broke apart and new ones formed. Sodium in the soda ash united with quartz. Carbon in the flour stole oxygen from the litharge, and the two joined and fled up the chimney as a gas. Left behind was metallic lead, as countless tiny droplets. This liquid lead then picked up the gold and silver, and finally the alloy settled to the crucible bottom.

We poured the contents of each crucible into a mold, an object that looked like an Iron Age muffin pan with six egg-size cavities the shape of inverted cones. The lead alloy settled to the bottom beneath the slag. As the last of the red heat faded from the slag, it became opaque glass colored in shades of green and brown. As the slag continued to cool, it unpredictably cracked and shot hot, sharp projectiles through the air. Wearing a clear plastic face mask and heavy gloves, we emptied each mold onto a heavy iron plate and, with a hammer, pounded off the remaining slag. Then we beat each lead cone into the shape of a cube, to make them easy to pick up with tongs.

Into the glowing furnace I placed cupels—squat, inch-and-a-quarter cylinders with dished tops—made of compressed bone ash. I don't know whose bones they were, but they had the essential attribute that bones have and that we needed for our purposes: they would absorb lead. When they reached the correct heat color, I placed a lead button on each cupel and left the furnace door ajar to let in air. Each button melted into a puddle. Then its silvery surface transformed into fluid iridescence as the lead oxidized back to litharge, in liquid form, which the cupels absorbed. The moment the last of the lead vanished, the remaining gold and silver bead would "blink"—a tiny bright light that went out after the bead solidified. We then removed the cupels from the furnace to cool.

Using tweezers we picked up the silvery beads from atop each cupel, flattened them with a small hammer, rubbed them clean, then weighed them on an elegant antique balance. Levers on its outside operated fine weights so that we could balance the beam behind the glass door, which we kept closed so air currents would not affect the weighing.

Each bead was then dropped into a "parting cup"—a plain, doll-house-size China cup—and we poured nitric acid in to dissolve the silver. Any gold remained as a sponge-like disk. After rinsing it clean, the gold was fused inside the cup by heating it to incandescence over a gas flame. Then we weighed the gold to determine its value in the sample, in troy ounces per ton of rock.

Though we learned to shut off the college's ventilation system before relighting the furnaces, that class turned out to be their swan song. A year later I asked Newton if I could borrow tongs, crucibles, iron molds, and other things, so I could do fire assaying with the electric furnace I bought for the laboratory I had built in Grangeville.

He looked me in the eye and said, "You mean to tell me that you're a graduate student and haven't learned to steal?"

"Yes," I stammered. "I was raised not to do that."

"Okay," he said. "Write down what it is you want, and I'll sign a note that says those things are on indefinite loan to you." And that's what we did.

Shortly after that, most of the contents of the furnace room were put up for auction—a first step in the flowering Age of Environmentalism. I bid on many of those things, except the furnaces, and got them cheap. I must have been the only bidder. The last time I saw the furnaces, they were sitting dismantled in a fenced university lot, rusting in the rain.

The College of Mines is now but a memory. What remains of fire assaying at the university resides inside the College of Engineering, where a microwave oven with a specially enclosed crucible is used to teach the principles of the method; but should a sample require a fire assay, it would be sent to a commercial laboratory.

Newton went to meet his Maker in August of 1974, and though he was a good and helpful master, I believe he'd be happy only if he landed in a place where they let him play with fire.

Black Butte Jump

Robert McCarl

Instead of wearing peace signs or shoulder-length hair and
making a pilgrimage to Haight Ashbury, I spent the summer of
1968 wearing White logging boots and running five miles every
morning, getting ready for my last summer of smokejumping.

We began each day hungover. As we lined up on the airport apron
and began our jumping jacks and push-ups, you could hear
the previous night's beer sloshing in our guts. The smell of hops
mixed with the aroma of stale booze wafted over us as we
stretched, yawned, bent, pushed, farted, and began our
daily stumble around the airport. The only one who never had a
hangover was Davis. No matter how much abuse he had taken
the night before, no matter how many exhausted go-go dancers he
had mauled or pulled out onto the dance floor of the 86 Corral,
no matter how many pitchers of beer he had consumed, Davis was
ready to run our sorry asses into the ground. And he did.

It was often a contest to see who was going to get sick first. Usually
it was Edmonson or me. We would just get started into our run, our
boots clunking on the broken pavement of the apron, when one of
us maimed veterans of the bar wars would dash into the sagebrush

and juniper to pay for our debauch. The others—eyes squinting into the laser of the morning sun—would trudge by, trying to breathe without smelling their own foul breath.

About a mile into it, the stale beer pouring from our bodies would turn into something approaching actual human sweat, and if you made it that far without dying or passing out, you began to feel a bit better. If we could have stopped, we would have. But no, Davis kept us running. Adding insult to injury, he would jog backward puffing on a Marlboro and laughing like hell at all of us "candy asses" dragging our sorry behinds across the morning desert. Somehow having the Three Sisters looming over the horizon made it easier to accept a death from overexertion.

On this typical day, we had just finished policing our rooms and checking the barracks for garbage, old underwear, and stray contraband when Tony Parsons, our squad leader, called us to the loading dock. He smiled the knowing smile of the confirmed sadist as he explained the drill: "Okay you dipshits, Pat is already on his way to Black Butte, and he is gonna find the smallest, nastiest jump spot in those big ponderosas over by Camp Sherman that you guys have ever seen. You pussies have been sitting on your butts for so long you don't know a guideline from a shroudline, but this little jump is gonna separate the men from the boys."

When he finished, we walked to the ready room to get suited up and check our equipment. We traded the usual frantic ritual of getting our gear for the more relaxed joking and ribbing associated with a practice jump. I started pulling on my jumpsuit: first the pants with the large leg pocket for the let-down rope, followed by the jacket with the oversized collar. Because I knew we were not in a big hurry—unlike a real fire jump—I did not button everything up but slipped on my harness, wandered over to the wall where the parachutes were lined up, and picked up the one labeled with my name. Although I had the usual butterflies in my stomach, it was a great day for a jump. I was looking forward to a lazy morning of jumping followed by a leisurely drive back to the base for lunch. This promised to be easy duty.

The Beechcraft was squatting in the crisp morning air like an ugly pelican ready to take on a load of fry. Our pilot, Howard, sat casually in his seat doodling with the instruments and cooling his heels while we got ready to go. We had an impressive group of pilots—all of them experienced backcountry fliers. Many of these guys had flown bombers or fighters during WWII or Korea, and they had never lost the itch for taking the stick of a DC-3, an old Ford Tri-Motor, or the Beech. Legends circulated, and heated, beer-laced arguments ensued over how many times Howard had actually ditched a plane in the French or German countryside and walked home through enemy territory to get another plane and try it again.

In the 1960s, more than half the guys I was jumping with would go to Vietnam. Some would go to kick cargo and some would pilot their own planes, but a good many of them made the trip home in a black body bag. Others of us—myself included—planned to oppose the war and resist the draft. We rarely talked about it among ourselves. Periodically, former jumpers or recruiters visited the base or sent letters to one of the crew. We were constantly reminded of the inevitability of the *choice* we would all have to make about Vietnam. No matter how we felt or what we decided to do, we all knew that the war would engulf us.

Parsons wandered out of the loft, turned toward the windows of the dispatcher's area, and aimed a majestic middle finger toward the guys not jumping that morning. He then proceeded to check us out as we tightened our harness straps, checked the static lines, and assumed the ape-like crouch of the fully loaded jumper as we crawled into the belly of the Beech. I preceded Anderton, Waldren, and Franks as we loaded in reverse jumping order. Parsons put the thin canvas strap on the open door of the plane and yelled to the pilot to get this goddamn thing off the ground.

Belching smoke, our plane bumped across the apron as we rode out to the main runway. There was not much of the usual banter and bullshit because most of us were still nursing hangovers. Franks and I talked a bit about the cool morning air and how it would give us more time during the jump. Jumpers know the slow descent of a cool morning jump contrasts sharply with the thin-air jolt of a late-afternoon landing when the air is drier and the chute falls more rapidly. The Three Sisters and Broken Top disappeared under our wing, and we banked around Black Butte while Parsons made his way over our outstretched legs to stare out the door looking for the location of the jump spot.

During a flight like this, whether we were jumping a fire or just practicing, I often felt conflicting emotions. At this point in my life, I had worked wildland fire crews for six years—since my sixteenth birthday. I had fought a number of fires, from smoldering county dumps to full-blown house fires and once, a spectacular barn fire that to this day remains a vivid memory of sweltering heat and stench of burning horseflesh. I had begun my fighting career with the old Arboretum crew outside of Corvallis, an early Hotshot crew that trained sixteen and seventeen year olds in progressive fire line construction. Our twenty-man crew could build fire line almost as fast as we could walk around the fire. I quickly became enamored of the camaraderie and adventure of the trade so, on a whim, I applied to become a smokejumper. Apparently one of the rookies did not show up for training, so I got the call. My training progressed well with regard to the physical conditioning and parachute handling, but the tree climbing nearly washed me out. I just could not imagine myself hanging in one of those towering ponderosa pines a hundred feet above the ground while trying to get my climbing rope over a limb before my climber's gaffs slipped through the tree's bark. Finally, Parsons took me to Sisters on a couple of Saturday mornings so that I could practice. He would climb up the tree beside me and have me kick out my gaffs at forty or fifty feet so I could understand how the climbing rope actually would stop me from falling by pulling me into the tree. Without his help, I would never have made it.

This morning, we circled a tall stand of ponderosa pines just southwest of Black Butte. Parsons had spotted the small orange X in the trees with just barely enough room to allow one parachute canopy to slip between the crowns of the two-hundred-foot trees. Chuckling to himself how this jump was not going to be the typical "candy-ass" flop in a plowed field, he stripped the rubber bands from the crepe paper drift streamers and on the first smooth pass over the jump spot he tossed them into the slipstream of the Beech. Immediately the pilot put the plane into a tight left-hand circle, and we all kept our eyes on the red and yellow streamers as they made their way to the ground. Weighted with a short section of wire, the streamers were designed to approximate the direction of the prevailing winds that we jumpers would experience.

Parsons had tossed out the drift streamers over the jump spot, and he then directed the pilot to adjust the point of the actual jump location accordingly so that each jumper arrived at the approximate destination with a minimum of maneuvering. At least that is the way it is supposed to work. Later that same summer, I impressed a whole DC-3 load of jumpers as well as squad leaders and pilots by landing in the only tree standing in a perfectly clear jump zone next to a brush fire in Hell's Canyon.

The streamers floated colorfully to the ground five or six hundred yards to the east of the jump spot. That meant that Parsons would put us out about that same distance to the west so that we could float into the X . The trick, however, was that we always jumped two in the air at a time. In this particular instance, that meant that two jumpers had to use all their chute handling tricks to beat the other guy to the spot. Not only is it bad form and embarrassing to hang up on a practice jump, you were fined according to your distance from the spot, and a hang up would mean additional fines on top of the usual five or ten dollar penalty. All of the jump fines went into a fund that was used to pay for the end-of-the-season beer bust.

Parsons took us around a final time to explain that we had a pretty easy jump ahead of us and to remind us to be aware of a ground wind just above the tree tops. He asked if anyone had any questions and when nobody did, he started moving to allow the first two jumpers to hook up their static lines and take their positions in the door.

The fuselage of the Twin Beech is not large. Consequently, while one jumper was sitting on the floor of the plane with his foot resting on the jump step, his jump partner was standing just behind and above him with his hands holding onto the inside edge of the door. The feeling of standing in the door is a bit more precarious than sitting. You not only feel every bump and turn of the plane, you can see the ground and the jump spot coming up more clearly than the man on the step. Tension built before the jump. We practiced for hours to ensure a good exit from the plane on a "two man stick," and we had all heard the stories about jumpers missing the step or rolling through their lines by getting a bad exit. One of my favorite stories was told by one of the loft foremen who had become a jumper during World War II. As a member of one of the pacifist or "peace" churches during the draft, he was given a choice of doing alternate service as a smokejumper or acting as a guinea pig for chemical warfare experiments. He chose jumping. He related the experience of a jumper who was always complaining about his jump partner crowding him when he was the first in the door. Finally, his partner got so sick of the bitching that he booted this guy early in the jump pass, and the chronic complainer ended up hiking three extra miles up canyon to get to the fire. As I was recalling those stories, Anderton and Waldren made their exits and were corkscrewing their canopies into the trees and the jump spot.

Mike and I were next. I buttoned up, pulled the screen down over my face and slipped on my gloves. Mike was in the door with his left foot on the jump step. Looking over his shoulder, I could just barely glimpse the small orange X nestled in a big stand of pine trees two thousand feet below. I could see there was only room for one canopy to make it through, and I was determined that it would be mine. Parson's cheeks rippled in the prop blast as he grabbed Mike's boot and peered into the morning air looking for our exit point. The engine throttled back, and we smoothed into a level glide as the pitch of props dropped from their usual Pratt and Whitney roar to a calming hiss. Parsons brought up his knees and scooted back into the tail as Mike and I waited for him to smack Mike on the shoulder. Suddenly I heard the loud "thwack" of Parson's hands on Mike's jump suit and the door was open in front of me.

I slid my hands down the sides of the door, hit the step with my left foot, folded my hands over my reserve chute, and stepped into space. The rush of falling and the turbulence of the prop wash from the Beech tilted me over to the side like a ski jumper leaning into a stiff wind on a long jump. I straightened as the static line pulled the chute out of the backboard. In that instant I was suspended in the still air above the trees with only the sound of the wind in my ears. I heard Mike off to my left, laughing at me and realized that rather than simply sitting back to enjoy the ride, I had to get busy lining myself up for the spot.

Steering a parachute is somewhat like flying a helicopter. You have three dimensions affecting you at once: horizontal, vertical, and angle of descent, which is determined by the combination of wind, air temperature, and body weight. As I turned into the wind to gauge my forward movement toward the spot (judged by looking directly between my feet), I kept my eye on Mike, who was now just a couple of hundred feet below me and moving his own chute into the wind to stay upwind of the spot. I was moving too fast toward the spot and falling faster than Mike, and I could tell from this angle of descent I would either miss the spot or come too close to Mike's canopy. So I grabbed the risers— the metal links between my harness and my chute canopy—and did a chin-up. By pulling myself up to the risers and facing my chute into the wind, I created faster forward speed to stay upwind of the spot. This maneuver—called planing—is designed to provide more control over the chute. Unfortunately, Mike was using the same technique, and we were both headed for the same small opening in the trees. The Beech, with Parsons sitting in the door watching our battle for spot, continued to circle overhead.

Mike and I were separated by about 200 yards of air, drifting toward the same break in the trees. As our boss blathered away below us on his bullhorn, we turned our chutes to face each other directly in a final effort to make the spot. Mike was yelling at me to "turn right, turn right," the avoidance maneuver we are taught whenever two jumpers get too close in the air. We both decided at the last minute to make the maneuver rather than collide, and pulled our right guidelines sharply. This caused us to head directly into the tree canopy, and once I knew I was going to hang up, I headed directly into the biggest and brushiest crown I could find. It is embarrassing enough to hang up on a jump, but you are much safer if you hang up hard rather than soft because you will then have a platform from which you can safely let yourself down.

I felt the crack of limbs and the air going out of my chute and waited a minute to see how well I was hung up. I gently bounced a couple of times to test things and untied my leg pocket, took out my let-down rope, and tied off on the tight riser of my parachute harness.

Amid the catcalls and jeers from the other jumpers below, I began the standard series of knots required to rappel myself from my parachute to the ground using the nylon rope coiled in my leg pocket. I looked over at Mike to see how he was doing. He was on the other side of the clearing in a tree canopy about fifty yards from the one I had landed in. I was going to give him some shit in preparation for all the harassment we were going to take when we got down, but I could see something was wrong.

Mike was hanging very still, not moving at all, yet almost imperceptibly his parachute was sliding through the tree canopy. As he picked up speed, I yelled at him to pop his reserve, hoping that he could hang it over lower limbs or maybe even inflate it, given the hundred feet of bare trunk below him. Except for my yelling, all was quiet. My voice trailed off into the wind. The limbs cushioning Mike's fall gave way with muffled snaps. He said nothing at all. He just fell.

Below me people were screaming and yelling, and as soon as I dropped below the tree canopy I could see Mike's legs protruding

from the orange and white gores of the parachute. By the time I
slid to the ground, other jumpers were gathered around Mike,
who lay motionless at the base of the tree. He was breathing, but
blood covered his jumpsuit, and his legs angled oddly from the
rest of his body. McMullen was huddled over his head, trying to
keep him stable and making sure that his airway was clear.

McMullen radioed to the plane to send for an ambulance. Then
there was not much we could do but wait and try to keep Mike as
comfortable as possible. We waited for what seemed like hours.
For once, no one in the group said a damn thing. All we could
hear was the wind in trees over Mike's labored breathing.

The clarity of that moment is a frozen tableau in my memory.
Near misses in a car wreck by Mt. Shasta, the births of my two
sons, the flaming collapse of a row house roof that almost took me
with it, and a vicious riptide off the Oregon coast rest side by
side with Mike's broken body as defining moments in my life.
These moments do more than dramatize our slender hold on life;
they bring to the surface fears and power unrecognized until
the next event shakes us out of our complacency. Later, when I
quit jumping (this was to be my last season), my generation of
jumpers turned its attention to the war in Vietnam. A lot of the
guys I jumped with that day went to Vietnam because they saw it
as their responsibility, and others went for adventure. Many came
back hating and distrusting those of us who resisted. Some jumper
friends left the country, others became conscientious objectors,
and a few took off, never to be heard from again.

I have friends on both side of this issue. I never felt that I was
opposing those who went to Vietnam, but I was against the act of
war itself. My opposition to the war, I'm sure, affected its final
ending; I feel proud of those on both sides who acted on their
beliefs, yet I also acknowledge that those who went to Vietnam
came home to a reception that was unforgivable. Perhaps
recognizing this polarization can provide a meeting ground that
will heal what remains an open wound within my generation.
Recalling Mike lying on the ground surrounded by jumpers who

all took different paths to the war and remembering the impact it
had on their lives, the primacy of that moment is palpable. Mike's
fall mirrored our collective fall from innocence and invulnerability.
Later that summer, I traded most of my smokejumping brothers
for fellow antiwar activists. Other members of the crew joined the
military and traded the comparative simplicity of fighting fire for
the deadly reality of combat.

Mike was finally loaded into the ambulance. We found out later
he had broken his back and bitten off the end of his tongue. He
never jumped again. As I listened to the ambulance making its
way back down the highway to Sisters and Bend, I worried about
Mike and asked myself how much longer I wanted to risk my own
neck by jumping. This is a question all firefighters ask themselves,
and often we find the answer in the camaraderie of our trade—
the shared sense of responsibility born of work knowledge that
leads to trust and successful action. Even within a generation as
polarized as ours, when the bells hit, you can count on your
crewmembers to know what to do and how to do it without
question. Years later, when I was working with urban firefighters,
these same questions continued to be asked and answered by a
new generation from a variety of ethnic, gender, and minority
backgrounds. The fire service allows no ambiguity. You
either leave your differences with your street clothes and pull
your weight without question, or you never become a
member of the culture.

I pondered all this as I busied myself with the arduous task of
gearing up to climb the tree that held my chute. I grabbed the
nylon let-down rope and began to size up the six-foot trunk and
two-hundred-foot ponderosa that held my gear. As all jumpers do,
I gave the rope a hefty yank, hoping in spite of logic that all of
those tangled shroud lines would loosen their grip on the tree. To
my amazement and horror, the parachute canopy, harness, and
rope slid to my feet with an eerie clink of D-rings. McMullen and
the other jumpers in the clearing who were picking up Mike's gear
simply looked at me, looked up at the top of the tree, and walked
quietly up the road to our waiting truck.

Wild Places

Lois Melina

At Monumental Bar, we crossed the metal bridge over Big Creek and threw our packs on the ground. Then our bodies silently claimed the clearing as our home for the week. A light wind cooled our sweat-soaked backs and set a snag swaying back and forth, creaking like an abandoned old house.

"I think we should move," I told my family.

"That tree has probably been doing that for years," my husband said as he pushed himself off the ground and picked up his pack. The children followed us to the other side of the campsite. Minutes later the tree groaned one last time and toppled into the creek. Its tangled roots framed an old fire ring.

Wild places remind me that life is beautiful, unpredictable, and fragile. I go to wild places to learn how to be at peace with powers greater than I.

My husband and I wanted our children to grow up with regard for the simplicity as well as the complexity of wild places. Neither one of us had grown up in families that camped or hiked, but during our dating years in northeastern Ohio, we had found we both enjoyed outdoor activities in all kinds of weather: meandering through the woods along the Ashtabula River, kicking scarlet and orange maple leaves as we walked hand-in-hand; ice skating on a frozen pond by the light of a Coleman lantern. When we were ready to settle down, we headed west, to the open spaces of Idaho. Once there we took up skiing, hiking, and camping. When our children arrived, we shared our passion with them— perhaps too zealously at times.

Eager for our young kids to hike with us, we contrived various schemes to keep them interested on the trail. We stopped to look at every woolly worm inching its way across the dirt and pointed out how long needles circling a branch indicate a yellow pine tree. We promised M&Ms at the top of every hour. We thrust butterfly nets into their hands and sent them racing down the trail in pursuit of an orange-brown painted lady or a yellow and black-striped western tiger swallowtail. One afternoon as we packed up the car after tramping along the Selway River, we heard hikers describe the rattlesnakes they'd encountered on the same trail. After that, we didn't send the kids running ahead of us in pursuit of insects, but we didn't give up on family hikes.

We mounted our first family backpacking trip when our children were three and six. For insurance, we invited friends with children the same ages as ours. Still relatively new to Idaho then, we had not yet learned that the Fourth of July could still bring mountain snows or that when the guidebook says, "Moose can always be seen," it means, "Your campsite is in a swamp."

Our destination on that Independence Day weekend was Fish Lake in the Gospel Hump Wilderness of central Idaho—a two-mile trek to a lake where, we had been told, we'd surely see moose. ("When we get to the lake, we'll see some MOOSE!" we told the children.) We neared our campsite only to find the way blocked by a creek still fierce with spring run-off, a slippery fallen log the only bridge. Our friend D. successfully ferried three of the youngsters across the log but slipped with our son in his arms,

landing them both in the water. D. executed a quick Eskimo roll and
was holding our son above the water before I could even register the
ice-cold possibility of our son swept away by the rapid water.

The rain started not long after we made camp, then turned to wet
snow. None of us could walk through the boggy campsite without
soaking our feet, but because the four adults had carried all the
gear for eight people, we had not packed much spare clothing.
The few extras we had went to D. and our son after their spill in
the creek. After a nearly futile hunt for dry wood, I returned to
camp shivering, my wet jeans clinging to my knees and calves. My
husband quickly fed me a steaming mug of reconstituted chicken
noodle soup. I realized we needed a fire for survival, not just
comfort. D., a more experienced winter camper than we were,
volunteered to keep the first watch that night. We reassured each
other that we could carry the children up the trail in sleeping
bags, if necessary, while, oblivious to the risk of hypothermia and
freed from adult plans for hikes and fishing expeditions, the
children bounded from tent to tent, playing cards and making up
games. Although I was not on fire watch, I couldn't sleep that
night. My mind raced with imaginings—if we had not anticipated
perilous weather, what other dangers had we disregarded? My
pillow-soft sleeping bag felt like a tight band on my chest.

The next day we took advantage of a lull in the downpour and
dashed up the rocky trail awash with runoff, relieved to reach our
rigs unharmed.

Our friends never backpacked again.

We, however, continued our relentless efforts to instill in our children
a fondness for the outdoors. The following year, our family hiked
into a series of high mountain lakes that proved to be so mosquito-
ridden we had to pop the tent just to have a tolerable place to hold
the discussion of whether we would go or stay. We went.

It's not that we couldn't learn. We came to realize August held the
greatest likelihood of fair weather. We found we encountered

fewer mosquitoes when we camped near moving water. So it was that the August of 1991, when our children were eight and eleven years old, we decided to hike Big Creek in the Frank Church–River of No Return Wilderness, the largest wilderness area in the lower forty-eight states. We were drawn both by the splendor of the area and the isolation.

The trail along Big Creek begins at a remote Forest Service ranger station where we camped the night before beginning our hike. Once again, I slept poorly, imagining the disasters we might face. I had become prone to those Trailhead Anxiety Attacks—my own version of *Sophie's Choice*, in which I must decide what to do with the children when the tree falls on my husband miles from help. Will I leave them alone in the wilderness with their bleeding and comatose father, possibly setting them up for a lifetime of believing they could have done more to keep him alive but allowing me to dash for help? Or will I take my children with me, protecting them from a misplaced sense of responsibility but delaying emergency rescue?

My husband, had he not been sleeping soundly, would have said, "Everything seems worse at night," and it was true: the morning sun glinting on the door of our tent calmed my nerves. We ate a quick, cold breakfast of oatmeal trail bars, then hoisted our packs and set off.

Three miles from the trailhead we entered the boundary into the wilderness. Legally, that means no development—no roads, no designated campgrounds, not even outhouses. Fuel-driven machines, such as snowmobiles and chain saws are forbidden, too. However, parts of this 2.4-million-acre wilderness had been developed before Congress protected it in 1980, and any structures built before then were grandfathered in. We made camp at Monumental Bar, some five miles into the wilderness, but had we hiked farther, we would have seen pine cabins built by gold prospectors and even a few ranches accessible only by the trail we were on or by an airstrip farther down the river. We would have come to the Taylor Ranch, the University of Idaho's wilderness field station. Eventually, we would have seen Big Creek spill into the Middle Fork of the Salmon River. We take the wilderness designation seriously and wanted our children to, also. No battery-operated Gameboys accompany us. No tape players with headphones. We build a little kitchen out of whatever we can find and dismantle it when we leave. We dig a latrine, cover the waste, and burn the toilet paper. We release the trout we catch. We leave only footprints and occasionally a hole the children have dug part way to China.

Knowing the history of Big Creek, I was not surprised to find the metal bridge that led to our campsite. However, I was horrified to see that way out there, more than twenty-five miles from civilization (civilization in this case being the fifty people who live in the mining town of Yellow Pine), the bridge was covered with graffiti—names and dates of people who had camped there before us.

At home, I rise early. If the weather is cool, I belt on a wool robe, build a fire in the woodstove while the coffee drips, and enjoy the quiet of the house while my family sleeps. My routine in camp is much the same. Before anyone else is up, I slip out of the red fiberfill sleeping bag that I've owned since my first camping trip in 1977, pull a fleece sweater over my head, start a campfire, and pump up the stove to boil water to pour over filtered coffee grounds. I sit by the fire and adjust logs while I sip my drink, which will cool quickly in the still, crisp morning air. I take in the rich smells of coffee, wood smoke, and pine.

Sometimes in that early morning quiet, I see wildlife. At Big Creek, mule deer sauntered through our camp in the morning almost to the point of nuisance. Rather than being cautious around us, they seemed curious. Visiting the camp latrine one morning, I looked up to see a fawn just a few feet away, staring at me, his head cocked to one side.

Midway through our stay at Monumental Bar, I woke to a *thump-thump-thump-thump* that reminded me of the opening scene from the television series *M.A.S.H.* The wilderness is not as quiet as city dwellers might think. Lying in my bag at night I might hear a bull elk bugle or mistake a pica scurrying through camp for a bear. But these sounds are natural, not man-made. Even before I identified the noise as helicopters, I knew the sound did not belong in the woods. Emerging from the tent, I spotted the helicopters following the river, dangling buckets for carrying water. The aircraft disappeared over the ridge south of us. I looked for smoke, wondering how far away the forest was burning, but saw none. Later, the choppers returned, and the back-and-forth soon became a pattern, increasing in frequency. Just as traffic noises in the city become background sound, we became accustomed to the helicopters. But my husband caught me stealing glances at that southern ridge as we ate lunch and washed our stainless steel cups after dinner. Before retiring to the tent each night, I looked for a red glow illuminating the southern horizon, lifted my nose to the wind for a drift of smoke that might indicate the fire was turning our way. "Do you think we should head back?" I asked my husband. He reminded me that the wilderness covered hundreds of miles, the closest road ending at the ranger station eight miles away. The proximity of firefighters didn't mean the proximity of fire. "Let's wait and see," he said. I fell asleep each night mentally organizing a disciplined breakdown of the camp.

I would have packed up immediately had I known what would happen to the canyon nine years later, in August of 2000. During one of the worst forest fire seasons in Idaho history, hundreds of thousands of acres burned in the Frank Church–River of No Return Wilderness, including most of Big Creek canyon. The fire moved so fast that researchers at the Taylor Ranch fled downriver to a ranch on the Middle Fork of the Salmon. Fire caught up with them there, too, and some only survived by submerging themselves in the river as the blaze passed over them. They watched as the wind generated by the firestorm lifted the west end of a 270-foot suspension bridge, twisted it, and slammed it back into its footings.

When we camp, we reduce our activities to the most basic—keeping clean and warm, gathering fuel and water, preparing and eating food, sleeping. Each of those routine practices becomes more complicated in the wilderness, but we can devote ourselves fully to it, without distraction. I enjoy cooking in camp more than I do at home because I'm not simultaneously putting away groceries, opening mail, and taking phone messages off the answering machine.

Weeks before a camping trip, I plan menus, measure ingredients into small plastic bags, label them, then place all the ingredients for one meal into a large resealable bag and label it with the day of the week, the meal, and any cooking instructions. Over the years, we've experimented with different foods until coming up with a one-week plan that we all not only enjoy but have come to require. I make angel hair pasta with a sauce of canned anchovies fried in olive oil, black bean burritos with shredded cheddar cheese and tangy salsa, and a rice and lentil dish spiced with cumin. Dessert might be instant pudding shaken in a large-mouth drink bottle or melted chocolate and marshmallow s'mores—a throwback to my Girl Scout days, even though I had never camped as a Girl Scout.

After dinner, we linger around the campfire, drinking a carefully selected tea-of-the-day. The children poke the fire with sticks, and I read aloud by the light of a headlamp. Over the years we have progressed from Roald Dahl's *James and the Giant Peach* to John McPhee's *Encounters with the Archdruid,* our children cheering on the efforts of conservationist David Brower over the dam builders as they'd once rooted for James to triumph over his wicked aunts. As the fire dies to red embers, we watch the August sky for shooting stars. Camping reduces our existence to the basics: the light of the fire, the soothing warmth of chamomile, a good story, the awe of creation, the circle of family.

I spent my days at Monumental Bar hauling water, wandering down the stream until I found a shady place to read, or hiking along trails that I hoped would lead me to a surprise of huckleberry bushes. I kicked up a fine dust of dirt with each step, the late summer desiccation signaling the area's vulnerability and reminding me to drench the ashes in our fire ring before leaving camp or going to bed. Each time I crossed Big Creek the metal bridge vibrated and clanged. One day I stopped to read the names that had been scratched into the white enamel paint. What had at first looked like vandalism began to read like the guest book at a bed and breakfast. I couldn't help but notice STANLEY S., whose name appeared in sprawling block letters year after year, along with the names of his brother and sister. I noticed the visits had abruptly ended several years ago. But as I continued to scan the railing, I spotted the name again, this time neatly carved: STAN S. Below his, a new member of the family: THERESA S.. I traced the scrapings with my finger as I read the date of their visit: JULY 1990.

Around the campfire that night, I told my family about the boy I imagined had made the engravings. "I think he must have come here camping with his family when he was very young. Maybe he went fishing in the creek. Maybe he came back in the fall with his dad to hunt elk. Then he grew up and went to school, or maybe he left Idaho to find a job. And then he met a girl and told her about all the times he came to this campsite at Big Creek, and said, 'Oh, you have to see it. It's beautiful. I'll take you there one day.' Maybe they even came here on their honeymoon," I said, silently hoping my children would one day want to return to the places where we'd camped as a family, where both the joys and the dangers of living were simple and clear.

When we backpacked, our children were required to tote their own amusements. If they wanted to take three stuffed animals and four books, they could, but they carried them. If they found unusually shaped rocks that they felt they had to take home to their rooms, they had to carry them. Our son inevitably brought with him the ragged pink flannel bunny that accompanied him everywhere for many years. It didn't weigh much, but after a few days in camp I would have to turn my head when I saw my son snuggling with his lovey covered in dirt and ashes.

Because my husband wanted a fishing companion, he was willing to carry our daughter's fly rod, as well as his own. Each morning, while I prepared breakfast in camp—stewing dried peaches left to soak overnight, frying flaky currant scones, or browning canned corn beef hash that tasted like lobster in the cool morning at a campsite—and every evening while I prepared dinner, my husband and daughter fished. With her lean, muscular legs planted firmly in the icy water of Big Creek, our daughter patiently cast and reeled, cast and reeled. She caught and released the same cutthroat trout over and over again that week until she was familiar with every blush on its skin, as well as its playful morning personality and evening habits of resting under a particular rock.

Then, just as the meal was about to be served, she would race into camp, shivering, and screaming, "That water is freezing!" as though she'd just dipped in her toe when I knew she had been standing in the water for hours. She would pull on sweats and wool socks and warm herself by the campfire, first her front, then her back, turning the way we'd turn marshmallows on a stick over hot coals, evenly toasting each side.

Generally, however, our children entertained themselves in camp with what they found: sticks and rocks. They built forts with sticks, played checkers with rocks, and dug holes with both. They often excavated a pit just a few feet beyond the door to our tent. I was certain I would rise one night and head outside, half asleep, to go to the bathroom, only to step into the hole and sprain an ankle. I comforted myself with the thought that I would at least be conscious when my family headed off to get help for me. I didn't imagine extreme calamity, such as my impaired ankle preventing me from outrunning an approaching fire.

At the end of the week, we broke camp. As quickly as we'd adjusted to having each other as our only company and the importance of hanging our food from a tree each night, we allowed the memories of our usual life to seep into our consciousness. We stuffed our sleeping bags, crushed the air out of mattresses, and rolled the bright yellow dome tent into a matching yellow sack, all the while imagining the feel of clean sheets, fresh clothes, and hot water showers. As a final act, we doused the fire ring.

Once my husband has his pack balanced and strapped, he likes to keep moving. So I was surprised when, just minutes later as we crossed the bridge that led to the trail, my husband stopped, took off his pack, and leaned it against the metal railing. He reached into the front pocket of his dusty blue jeans for the Swiss army knife that had opened cans and cut fishing line all week. Releasing a blade, he offered the knife to the children. "Why don't you scratch your names there before we leave," he said, nodding toward the railing.

We hiked out quickly. We didn't need to encourage our children beyond conjuring up the taste of the greasy hamburgers and French fries we would order at the tavern in Yellow Pine. We stopped only for water, snacks, and to spy on a cinnamon bear picking huckleberries along the creek well below the trail. As we left the wilderness and made our way to the trailhead, my sense of sadness that I would soon be sharing my family with the world again was mixed with relief that we were out of the woods—both literally and figuratively.

The frenzy of activity that met us at the ranger station was both culture shock after a week in the wilderness and a reality check. The tranquil trailhead had been transformed into a staging ground for smokejumpers. Tents and a wall of port-a-potties lined

the camping area. Exhausted crews and a handful of politicians
who had come to assess Forest Service burn policies lined up
at the mess tent. The familiar helicopters as well as a twin engine
Islander were positioned in readiness on an airstrip not far
from where we had parked our Toyota hatchback. The fire was
big and dangerous.

No one looked more distraught than the ranger, who obviously
was unused to this much commotion at this remote outpost.
Nonetheless, I sought him out and questioned him about the
exact location of the fire. Even though we were unharmed
and the proximity of our camp to the blaze was moot, I wanted to
know—had we been foolish to stay? He verified that the fire was
quite a ways from Monumental Bar. But even knowing this, even
knowing the outcome, I knew we had taken a chance. People more
experienced with wildfires can misjudge their intensity, direction,
and speed. Wilderness residents, like those at the Taylor Ranch in
2000, get caught. Hotshots—elite wilderness firefighters—become
trapped. There is no such thing as a safe risk.

Nine years later, in August of 2000, I am driving through Idaho,
south on U.S. 95. At New Meadows I swing left onto Highway 55,
through McCall and past the turnoff for Yellow Pine. All day the
skies have corroborated news accounts of wildfires in the
backcountry. In some places the smoke settling on the highway
has been so thick I have had to slow down, take off my sunglasses,
turn on my headlights. Near McCall, I look east, to the Frank
Church–River of No Return Wilderness. Black smoke rises from
beyond the crest of the Salmon River Mountains as though an
entire community is warming their houses with woodstoves. But it
is ninety degrees outside and what few cabins might be in those
mountains are in danger of being consumed by the blaze I know is
outrunning firefighters in Big Creek Canyon.

In my mind I see the bridge at Monumental Bar where our
children had recorded their names on the roster of backcountry

visitors alongside those of Stan and Theresa S. I wonder if the bridge will survive the fire that is scorching the hillsides, consuming dead trees like the one that fell into Big Creek, the nesting cavities of boreal owls, and huckleberry bushes lush with fruit. But I know that even if the artifacts of early settlers and later campers are destroyed, the wilderness will rejuvenate. By the time my son and daughter have children old enough to hike into Monumental Bar, the canyon walls will be burgeoning with pinegrass and tender red osier dogwood. By the time Stan and Theresa have children ready to shoulder packs, shiny leaf ceanothus will have put forth shoots, the seeds of the shrub stimulated by the heat of the flames. I wonder who among those who carved out part of their childhood on Big Creek will guide their sons and daughters into wild places; who will consider the lessons to be learned there worth the risks.

Ignition

Lori Messenger

[T]hey're [dragons are] sacred animals. They're the sign of life, because fire is life, and they eat fire and spit out fire.
　　—Princess Seserakh in Ursula K. LeGuin, *The Other Wind*

The fire call came on July 19, 1997, at five o'clock, just as the heat of the high desert day faded. My crew—comprising twenty folks from the Lowman and Idaho City districts of the Boise National Forest—had been staged at the military barracks in Richfield, Utah, for three days. We threw on our bright yellow Nomex shirts and jumped into our fleet of four Forest Service trucks. An hour later we stood in line, listening to instructions, at the base of a mountain with smoke rising from a high flank. In two days, I would turn twenty-eight years old, and this was my first wildland fire; most on the crew were nearly a decade younger and had fought fire before. After three years at graduate school desks, I was eager for action and a new type of lessons.

The crew boss—followed by three Stihl-packing sawyers—led us up the first steep pitch, releasing mini avalanches of loose shale with each step. The rest of us carried fuel canisters, pulaskis, and shovels. Evening humidity intensified the smell of sage. As we gained altitude, the sun became a red ball dropping across the valley. Periodically squad leaders shouted encouragement down the line.

Gray dusk surrounded us when we pushed over the last boulders and reached the fire's edge. Small clumps of grass smoldered among rocks, producing smoke and not much else. Farther up the slope, we could see junipers outlined in flames, making pistol pop noises as the fire fed on their sap. We swallowed canteen water and set to work clearing and digging an eighteen-inch-wide path down to mineral soil that we hoped would stall the fire's progress. My shovel clanged against rocks. Hours passed in a haze of smoke. Occasionally, we took breaks, lowering our faces to the ground for a few breaths of cleaner air. We could hear the chain saws roaring ahead but caught sight of them only when a blade chewed into a burning trunk and spun a shower of embers around its operator.

By two in the morning we had built a trail around the seven-acre blaze. Next we circled the perimeter, spreading out to keep watch in pairs, directed to ensure that no fire escaped during the night's remaining hours. I leaned against my shovel and offered to take the first shift while my partner rested. He searched the ground for scorpions, moved some sharp rocks, and then rolled up burrito-style in the small tarp we all carried. I was glad when he slept and left me alone in this strange, new world. The flames had settled, but a few gnarled junipers continued to burn independently— their hairy trunks and limbs appearing to pirouette among flames and the shadows cast from the full moon. I felt like both witness and participant in a madcap, pagan celebration.

Growing up in Colorado and then central Idaho, I had never been far from fire. During winters, we heated our mountain homes with wood; during summers we congregated around campfires. Our family evenings around the fire offered pause from the rush of life-as-usual. We spoke of memories and hopes, played word games, roasted marshmallows, watched flames flicker through the blocks of pine or tamarack we had cut and hauled ourselves. We sang: "I love the mountains; I love the rolling hills; I love the campfire, when the lights are low . . ." and ". . . A million tomorrows may all pass away, ere I forget all the joy that is mine, today." Later, on those nights, I snuggled into bed or sleeping bag alongside my little brother and slept, content to know I belonged to this good world.

I vaguely understood that fires happened in the woods and that people tried to control them. When I applied for my first Forest Service job, I had anticipated that I would enjoy living outside and the excitement of pursuing a running blaze with a crew, but I had not imagined the way wildfire—fire free from borders of stone and brick—would bewitch and fulfill me.

The night of my first fire dispatch I never fell asleep. Dawn filtered over the mountain, accompanied by blush pink horizon. I kept sight of the moon until it finally faded. One by one, my squad members emerged from under their tarps, faces sleep-bruised and quiet. Our morning orders came over the radio: Cut down any trees and limbs within ten feet of the fire's edge. Those who had run saws the night before were worn out, and I grabbed the chance. It had been only a month since I had run my first chain saw, but we had been thinning ponderosa and lodgepole pine plantations daily on our home forest, and I felt ready to try burning trees.

I pulled the starter cord and approached a juniper. Flames glowed red through cracks in the bark. I held the bar against the trunk and gunned the trigger. The chain ripped into wood. Now it was me inside that spark shower. The world outside my earplugs and safety glasses grew muffled. I focused on tree shape and the geometry of angles to cut, moving from limb to limb, then to the main trunk: *face cut, back cut, "timber!" Breathe in, breathe out, stay steady.* It's possible that onlookers marveled momentarily that a woman ran that saw, I don't know, and at that moment I didn't care. The sound of tearing wood fiber ricocheted through the quiet morning and the snag fell. I moved to the next.

I don't remember much about finishing the job or sinking to the ground next to my crewmates, awaiting helicopter shuttle. Occasionally somebody spoke—a word or phrase, rarely a full sentence. Mostly, we were quiet. I remember that my fingers felt permanently cocked into the shape of the saw handle, that my boots had become a living part of my feet. I lay down against my backpack and let the earth hold me somewhere between wakefulness and sleep. The image of burning junipers licked about my consciousness. Perhaps this business could be more than a brief lark and a summer paycheck; perhaps I could be a smokejumper someday.

Now it is winter 2003, six fire seasons later, and I wonder if I've had enough, if I can give this profession up with any kind of grace, or if I need to. I am trying to get pregnant. Of course it's "we," not "I," but if conception occurs I will be the one who does not chase fire this summer. I have wanted to have a child ever since I became cognizant that such a thing was possible in my womanly future.

In June of 2000 I completed Missoula's smokejumper rookie training and in 2001 my husband followed. Each summer we leap from Sherpas and DC-3s, enjoy a three-minute ride through sky, and then take on the fires of the West's remote backcountry. Sometimes they escape and sometimes we catch them. In either case, we gather bruises, skills, and stories.

I like the idea of returning from a fire—tired, reeking of smoke, and happy—to share hugs and those tales with a daughter or son. My husband says that he could stay home a summer or two while I went out, or that possibly we could alternate dispatches. Our boss supports such tampering with tradition in order to keep experienced employees. He has the audacity to believe that people can be good firefighters and good parents, that the desire to care for public lands and the wish to nurture children can originate from a similar place, and that no one ought to die protecting trees. He will save a seat in the airplane for me, but I cannot know how I will feel about this exposure to risk when and if I am able to give birth. I know I will change, but I do not want to leave wilderness behind.

I recall watching birth videos in a college sociology class and remind myself that the process looked anything but tame—all that action happening inside the uterus and, then, at nine months with a lot of screaming, a final, slippery, bloody push brought a new person into the world. I wanted to do it right then. However, finding the man with whom to undertake the project had me stymied for a decade. I liked men; that wasn't the problem. But how was I to choose one among so many options?

Fire, finally, led me to him. During my second spring as a firefighter I arrived in La Grande, Oregon, eager to test myself with the Union Hotshot Crew. I became intrigued with a coworker who liked to draw. Evening darkness drew the two of us, like moths, to the bare light bulbs that usually hung in the chow tent. I filled journal pages, Scott sketched, and occasionally one or the other of us volunteered a frustration or pleasure from the day. Finally, a late August fire on the steep bluffs of the Salmon River fanned mutual interest into something with romantic possibilities.

During our first shift, while we were digging line across a high ridge spine, the main smoke column billowed up like a steroid-laden cauliflower head growing on time-lapse film. We took pictures. Then for the next twenty days the beast mostly behaved. We had to find other entertainment during tedious mop-up shifts along our assigned mile-long borderland. Alongside each other whenever possible, Scott and I hunted among roots and soil for heat. Then, on our final morning in Idaho, September 8, Scott and I arose at five, walked one hundred yards to the shore of the Salmon River, glowing silver in the dawn. We stripped salt-stiff, soot-stained clothes into a pile, dove, and swam into slow, deep current.

Nine days later our crew boss assigned me the position I had hoped for all summer, a chance to work with the saw squad. I wouldn't be running a chain saw, but would be right behind them, pulling the brush they cut out of the way for the diggers. Dead logs lay in a maze around standing trees on the forest floor. My partner and I threw the chopped-up fuel to the outside of the path we were clearing as fast as we could, barely noticing the pain of constantly banging knees and shins against rocks and smashing fingers between logs. We knew this could be our opportunity to

prove ourselves. The fire exhaled hot air and occasionally spat
embers over our backs. My eyes burned and snot dripped,
but I ignored it the way I had learned while working the hayfields
of my childhood. The diggers chopped and scraped a clear, dirt
trail behind us, and it pleased me to recall that Scott labored
among them.

The crew boss halted progress while a couple local managers
scouted ahead. He tossed me his can of Copenhagen. "Have a
chew, Lori, you're a sawyer now," he challenged. I caught it.

"Fuck you!" I retorted, and threw it back. "You'd lose a worker
because I'd be standing here puking."

"Yeah, but only the first time. Then you'd be addicted."

By 7:30 the temperature had dropped to fifty-one degrees and
showed no signs of stopping there. Our summer drew toward its
end. I monitored an area where several trees burned near the fire's
edge. Blue-edged triangles of red, orange, and yellow darted like
snake tongues from their combusting hearts. Happy crewmember
voices traveled up and down the line. I couldn't distinguish the
words, just the tone. My brush-pulling partner walked by. "Did
you hear?" he asked me. "The boss thought we did really good." I
smiled. A tall, skinny snag collapsed like a sideways capital Z,
releasing a firefly dusting of sparks.

The next day I felt brave and sat down close to Scott during lunch
break. If I could enjoy this man through the dirtiest of shifts and
the craziness that afflicts humans near the end of a fire season,
then perhaps we could build a life together.

December 1999, at Rosalie Sorrell's "An Imaginary Christmas in
Idaho" concert, Scott proposed with an antique watch inscribed,
Shall we stroll together? That winter in Boise we rented a house
with a woodstove and bought ourselves a chain saw we named

"Roaring Matrimony," or "Matty" for short. Each morning one of us crinkled newspaper, laid kindling on top, and touched a match to an edge of that week's ShopKo advertisements. Fir ignited and something inside me steadied.

The first of May 2001, Scott and I shoveled a lingering two feet of snow from the amphitheater on top of Bogus Basin's Shafer Butte in preparation for our wedding ceremony. This had not been part of the plan, but it was not going to quench our determination to marry outdoors, where our western horizon contained eastern Oregon's Eagle Cap Mountains and the Wallowa–Whitman Forest where we first worked together. On May 5, just before sunset, in the company of friends and family, Scott and I vowed to link our lives. A chill wind blew across our mountain perch, but tulips, daffodils, and dogwood blossoms festooned snow banks. The sun shone and afterward we danced ourselves warm.

Scott's sister had snapped a picture while my bridesmaids helped me into my wedding dress. My naked torso and shoulders appear corrugated, like a topographic map to my insides—muscles push flesh into forms it did not know five years ago. I love it. Somehow this is more tangible evidence of my devotion to this job than increasing jargon on my card of fire qualifications. What would that abdomen look like with a fetus growing inside? Fall 2001, Scott and I moved to Missoula and began discussing children as if they could be potentially real creatures. Spring 2002, we quit birth control and started studying ovulation.

Fireline motherhood is a controversial subject among my coworkers—on the rare occasions we discuss it. Some women made the decision twenty years ago that if they wanted an emergency response career they needed not to have children. Others felt the same way, got pregnant, and either found desk jobs in the organization or left. But I also know moms who picked up pulaskis again after weaning babies—summertime work providing income for winter free time. A Missoula squad leader began smokejumping when her two sons were already in late elementary school. Her husband ran a mechanic shop out of their home and was able to provide primary care. Now she is the head of our rookie physical training program. A picture of her three-year-old granddaughter, Phoenix, wearing a smokejumper helmet, sits on her desk. One time during a base tour a man asked this squad leader what was the hardest thing she had ever done, clearly looking for a gnarly story about firefighting. "Give birth," she answered.

I spent most of the 2002 season serving in my first squad leader position. Now it was my job to teach tool handling and basic fire strategy to a twenty-person crew of mostly beginners, as well as help sort out their conflicts. Most important, I was among those making the decisions to keep people alive out there. "You have to know what matters to you," coached a fellow squad leader. "You have to know what it is that you care about coming home to." He made this last statement while showing us a photo of his son.

Secrets don't last long on crews, and my coworkers soon knew my pregnancy hopes. Departing a stressful two weeks working a Wyoming fire, I lusted after a tub of Ben & Jerry's Cherry Garcia ice cream. My crew patiently explained to me that eating ice cream was not going to solve procreation. They began scheming on my behalf—if only a helicopter could deliver Scott to my tent when that egg popped through its ovarian wall! If only I knew when that happened.

I did see my husband once in July, and when early August and time for my period arrived with no blood, I was thrown into a tizzy of anticipation. Our crew was working twelve- to fourteen-hour days on Oregon's 87,000-acre Tool Box Fire. On the sixth day of waiting, I could stand it no longer and asked my colleague and crew boss to help me find a test. We knew there was no convenience store nearby, but he thought there was one we could reach in forty-five minutes, and he was game for the adventure.

We quietly left fire camp after shift that evening and drove to the Christmas Valley Store, arriving at 8:30 to a locked door. I stood in front of the glass panes, still in filthy work clothes and blackened face, and waved my arms to catch the attention of the woman I saw inside. She came to the entrance and stuck her head outside. "We're closed," she said, "but you can use the ATM if you want to."

"Do you have a pregnancy test?" I asked, trying to flash her a smile that showed both desperation and sweetness. She immediately understood the gravity of the situation and checked her shelves. All out. She called her sister-in-law who managed the local Chevron and asked her if she had any in stock. Bingo. I ran back to the truck, relayed the story to my bemused crew boss, and we followed the kind woman's instructions.

A group of farmers and ranchers lounged on the gas station porch, but I was glad to see only two women inside when I pushed through the door. "I'm Lori," I said to the one behind the counter. She pointed me to the correct shelf and asked if I was hoping for yes or no. "Yes!" I replied. "Can I use your bathroom to take the test?"

"You're welcome to, but you'd best do it in the morning. That's when the hormones are the most concentrated." Damn. I felt sheepish for never having done this before, but thanked her and left the store clutching my little sack. How was I going to manage this in the early morning dark of a fire camp port-a-potty? On the return trip I fantasized about my options for telling Scott if the results were positive. I decided I would send word through the dispatch center of the fire he was working on, and then they could announce the news to him over the radio.

My alarm beeped me awake at 5:30 the next morning. Before breakfast I snuck into the heated high-school gym—where the camp's logistical headquarters had been set up—with a Styrofoam cup and the box tucked inside my sweatshirt pocket. In a girls' locker room toilet stall I re-read the directions, dipped the tape into my urine cup, then waited. One purplish pink line emerged after only a few seconds. It couldn't be more clearly negative. I carried the stick with me in my pack that day, and checked it several times, just in case the line changed. It didn't. Two days later (while I still wondered if the test might have been wrong), my wayward period began.

Now it is winter and I listen to advice, eager as any rookie. I buy a basal body thermometer and the book *Taking Charge of Your Fertility*. A sister-in-law gives us two new brands of ovulation testing devices for Christmas. A friend of another in-law gives us her recipe: five to seven drops False Unicorn Root juice, one capsule cod-liver oil three times a day, one prenatal vitamin three times a day. My older sister calls to warn me that Scott should avoid hot tubs, tight underwear, and possibly even bicycle riding, to keep those millions of little swimmers alive and mobile. Another friend tells us she managed to coax sperm to egg by drawing her knees up under her stomach for an hour following intercourse. Although the books don't concur, I would stand on my head if I thought it would help.

In January, I traveled to Thomas Jefferson's Monticello to speak about smokejumping during a weekend symposium about the Lewis and Clark Expedition and what has happened to the land since they traveled through. I passed over the eager Boy Scouts in the front row and invited a teen-age girl at the back on to the stage. I coached her into a padded Kevlar jumpsuit, laid a parachute upon her back, and watched her become enthralled with this new idea of herself. During open questions at the end of my talk she asked me, "What happens if a smokejumper gets pregnant?"

I paused. Then laughed. No one had ever asked me this at the numerous presentations I've given. Finally I told her about the choices firefighting parents have made in the past, and the possibility for a future daycare program next to the Missoula base. I told how a West Yellowstone jumper recently delivered a son, and that while the pain was so intense that she puked several times during the final stages of her labor, she still said it was all worth it, and she wouldn't think twice about doing it again. Only later, when the young woman approached me in the parking lot, did I tell her about how I was preparing simultaneously to jump again in the spring or to be pregnant—how I live each day with these two potentials in front of me.

At home again, I fall back into patterns of daily runs with Scott and three times a week push my arms, torso, and legs through one exercise after another to refurbish muscle. If our baby-making endeavors fail over the next three months, I must be ready to pass the physical tests for another smokejumper season. Scott worries about being ready for the challenges of fatherhood. I fear the mistakes I will make as a mother. For the first time since I stood watch over gyrating junipers on a Utah hilltop, I do not know if I will see forest or grassland burning at night. I wonder instead what it might feel like when a newborn sucks milk from these breasts— which I have mostly covered with shapeless work clothes these past six years. Will I know the moment the fire of a new life ignites within me? Our Missoula home contains no woodstove, but we light a candle beside the bed and pursue creation.

Waiting

Diane Josephy Peavey

The possibility of fire looms large and terrifying in my life on our remote southern Idaho ranch where my summers are defined by days of drought and lightning strikes.

Perhaps I brought some fear with me from childhood. Then, on July 4, our town put on its heroic display of fireworks in the park across the street from our house. Although our family settled on blankets at the baseball diamond a block from home for a better view of the pyrotechnics, we were there to track flying sparks rather than to revel in the explosions. Our roof had caught fire during this annual celebration several years before we bought the place. We sat in dread of a repeat performance the entire evening, and when others moaned at the end of the evening's show, we cheered another year without incident.

Aside from this childhood memory, my experience with fire has been rather inconsequential. That is until I became a Westerner. It was here that fear of fire became a new and constant companion.

At first I became uneasy when, on several occasions, the Wood River community across the ridgeline from our ranch headquarters suffered angry summer fires that ravaged its hillsides, threatened homes, and charred the valley floor.

My anxiety increased when, one summer, fires in Yellowstone to the east and the Oregon mountains to the west reached such ferocity they turned daytime into darkness and sucked breathable air from the skies even at our ranch miles away from the conflagration. Our eyes and throats burned and familiar places became unrecognizable.

Later the knot of fear tightened again with terrifying stories from sheep ranching friends. The Soulens told of wildfires outside of McCall that sent bands of sheep scattering across mountain ridges, fleeing for their lives, and the Rich family whispered the story of fire in the Caribou National Forest that trapped and killed more than 1,500 helpless ewes and lambs, destruction and death that haunts them still.

Several years after I moved to this country, I had my own experience with uncontrolled fire. My husband and I saw a glimmer of flame in a pasture near the Last Chance corrals as we drove to Carey for the mail. In a moment, the small site was spinning thin flames into the air. We grabbed shovels and jackets from the pickup to smother the sparks. But the fire spread lightning fast and only after several ranch hands pulled up to help were we able to bring it under control.

I remember two things about this episode. First, the intense heat of the flames. I had to back off from time to time to breathe, and in its unpredictable fury I suddenly understood the terror of the word *inferno*. Second, I was stunned by the speed of the fire as it raced out of control and across the landscape. In an instant it was more than two of us could handle.

Certainly this experience only exacerbated any earlier misgivings I had about fire in this ranch country. But now my fear is palpable. I am alert, vigilant all summer. I never drive to town or return home without scanning the ridgelines that surround our headquarters and its large meadows. I search for the ominous dark clouds, thick and murky, the first signs of danger, knowing that within moments the sky will

turn black and red at once. It was this way with the fires in the
Wood River Valley.

There have been drought years so severe, the grasses and brush
so flammable, that I leave anything valuable, a silver serving spoon
or a set of gold earrings in town, fearing that in the dryness,
fire will sweep through our cabin and destroy everything in its
wake. And years, too, when I struggle with long lines of hose,
dragging them around the lawn and the surrounding fields of tall
wild grasses, moving them every twelve hours to keep the
land fully irrigated. At its worst, I have circled the house with
sprinklers, water sentinels to protect our home when we
must leave the ranch for several days at a time. It is a gesture
that should comfort me but somehow inspires even greater fear.

In this arid landscape, where years of drought are a regular
occurrence, we cannot fool ourselves about fire. Without
rain, fields and wild grasses dry and become brittle far too early
in summer. Over the years I have stood in our yard scanning
the skies for rain clouds to break the suffocating heat and relieve
the parched days. And yet I am torn, knowing that summer
moisture means thunderstorms with lightning that ultimately
brings fire. Worse, too, when it comes without the rains.

I have lain awake watching dry lightning defiantly crack through
the sky, ripping across the stars, spasmodically flooding the
darkness with light. I have crouched beside the open bedroom
window long after my husband is asleep, staring fearfully into
the tumult. I shrink from the sudden wind that stirs in the
stillness and cools the heat, and I wait for the putrid smell of
burning grasses, watch for an eerie orange glow out of the
blackness, somewhere. When these do not come, after a time I
return to bed but not to sleep, not until the sky is quiet, too.

When I wake in the morning it is to smell the air even before I
open my eyes. This is my summertime ritual, my first awareness of
each day. And it is not unfounded.

Several years ago, after a violent thunderstorm, I woke to the smell I feared. My husband was gone and in the kitchen I found a note that he was checking a blaze in a field. I followed him to the site he identified, all the while scanning the skies for smoke. It was not until I saw the two chartreuse Bureau of Land Management fire trucks, heard from the crew that the small blaze was out, that I took a full breath. "It's out," they informed me. "Your husband's across the canyon checking the cattle," they added.

We had avoided fire but not tragedy. That same night, lightning had struck and killed fifty-one of our ewes and two large bucks. When we found them, they were toppled on their sides by the force of nature, rigid, yet huddled together still as they must have been when they were standing. It was heartbreaking to see these animals crowding each other in their fear, seeking comfort in the bellicose storm. They were not in a high place or near trees but in a green alfalfa field. In their fear, they shared their death.

But now it seems odd that it was a cool October evening at dusk long after the dry season when I finally confronted fire at the ranch. I was returning from town with groceries when I saw the dreaded dark sky ahead of me. As the road swung east, south, southeast, then northeast, I tried to determine the location of the dark plume of smoke ahead of me, never taking my eyes off its blackness. Our son, Tom, with Jake, his five-year-old son, in the pickup next to him, had pulled up behind me, also trying to identify the fire location. Suddenly he sped up and shot past me, spraying rocks and dirt as he disappeared around the bend. I gripped the steering wheel tighter and raced to keep up. My heart had dropped to my stomach from what I seemed to be waiting for yet fearing all these years. This fire was at our ranch headquarters.

I drove the last two miles recklessly and turned into the gate. From there the road straightened, and I could see menacing red flames around the sheep corral; the thick grove of cottonwoods, aspens, and willow on the north side of Friedman Creek; and the brush around Tom's house. Trees looked like torches of fire and the flames leapt from one to another, sending sparks through dry grasses as darkness settled over the inferno.

I saw men in the shadows, hunters from nearby camps still dressed in camouflage suits, three or four in one group, two or three in another, all with shovels furiously trying to suffocate the flames. I drove past them across the bridge to our cabin to call for help. I shrieked into the phone when the operator told me she had not yet gotten a response from the Carey Fire Department. I was not the first to call in. "Well, then, call Wood River, Bellevue, Hailey, some other fire department," I pleaded, my heart racing faster than my words. "Our ranch is on fire!"

"Someone will be there," she tried to reassure me. "I'll get someone, I promise."

I felt my stomach heave as I grabbed the shovel from the woodshed and drove back to help the men at the corrals. I left the car parked on the side of the road, ready to head for town. It could be used as an escape vehicle if necessary.

The night was full of shouts and flashlights. Denny, our sheep manager, was calling out instructions. I held the light for him as he struggled to prime a small pump beside the creek. As soon as it kicked in, he attached hoses and the men began to stretch them down the road to the sheep corrals and into the woods beyond. I ran behind, unknotting the rubber lines, stomping out sparks that threatened to jump the road as a new and sudden wind kicked up around us.

"Water," the men shouted, frustrated by the light flow of low October creek water. "We need more hoses, more water." I watched the road, praying for the lights of the fire department trucks.

Suddenly, my husband, John, appeared from the edge of the woods. He quickly told me the story.

He had been at home with a visitor, a journalist doing an article about the ranch. They were the only ones there. It was about five in the afternoon and from the road they saw smoke coming from the direction of Tom's house. When they got there, flames surrounded the propane tank and were edging toward the house. The two men gathered tools to stop the fire and thought they had it under control, shoveling dirt and dumping water from five-gallon buckets on the flames. Then, suddenly, the propane tank vented and knocked out the electrical wires above it, killing the power and water supply from the house and shooting off sparks that spread the fire into the surrounding trees and brush.

Our cowgirl, Mary, arrived about then and went to let the sheep and several guard dogs out of the nearby corral in case the fire moved in that direction while John and his visitor ran from house to house connecting lines of hoses—close to 700 feet of it before they finished—and attaching them to the pump by the shop on the far side of the creek.

With only that much told, John rushed back into the thickest brush to tackle what now was the heart of the fire. Tom raced by me, disappearing into the dense woods behind his father as the rest of us watched aghast. I grabbed Jake standing at the edge of the corral with flashlight focused on the spot where his dad had disappeared. He seemed so small. I hugged him to me.

Then we all got back to the task at hand. There were flaming grasses around us, threatening the wooden panels of the sheep corral. In the dark, the fire was easy to track. Tree limbs reached shadowy red arms into the darkness and leaping sparks drew our attention here, there, in rapid succession. Around it all, burning aspen leaves gave off the sound of wind brushing through branches as they crisped.

Finally, I saw the lights of the Carey fire trucks coming down the road. I let the shovel drop and grabbed Jake again. We stood in soot and smoke and watched the firemen take over. They shouted and called into the eerie red darkness as they began spraying the woods with huge bursts of water, unlike anything we had been able to pull out of the creek.

Then, for the first time, I looked around me and realized that
even before the firemen arrived we had contained the fire,
saved the house and corrals, and stopped the flames from jumping
the road. The fire department with its heavy equipment could
handle the rest.

It was after 10:30 P.M. when we finally returned to our cabin, filthy,
sweaty, tired, and surprisingly hungry. I poured shots of whiskey
for all of us and tried to recapture the plans for dinner that had
seemed so simple four hours earlier.

The next morning, I confronted the smoldering damage and the
remains of my fears. At least five acres had burned but it
was a strategic five acres around our living quarters, and the fire
had come within several feet of our son's home. Now I could
claim I had faced fire and survived. But had I dispelled my fears
or only substantiated them?

What will summer bring? What does happen to fear? Will I cringe
by the window watching the sky again, fearful of nature's wrath?
Or will I turn over and sleep through it all. Perhaps I will know
only when I hear the first roll of thunder, see slashes of lightning
spread across summertime stillness. Or perhaps I already know
but am afraid to admit that this fear of fire is endemic to life
lived on the land. As long as there are wild, dry grasses and little
water, we live on the edge, waiting, the specter of fire a
constant companion.

All Wild Orange

Karen Seashore

FROG BOWLS

"If they find out, they'll send in the white coats again," my mother said to the room, a fake stage whisper that I could hear from the kitchen. I was stacking bowls, putting them back into the box from the Bon Marché. Is this why I drove down to my hometown in Utah to stay with my crazy mother, so I could run a retail race against her, returning the white couch, the Chinese vase with its lengthwise crack, a case of long fireplace matches, and these bowls with frogs painted on their broad scoops?

"These drapes should be taken out and shot," she said. She wanted to lure me in to look, but I knew what she was up to. She was unhooking the living room drapes, letting the heavy cloth drop in humps like dusky egg whites.

I placed a square of corrugated cardboard between each dish, nesting them in the box. When my sister, Christine, and I were in junior high, our mother took us to Dinosaur National Monument near Vernal. Maybe that was the beginning of her manic spells. Mother had seen a TV show about archeologists and the meticulous uncovering of bones. Over near the Utah–Colorado border, Vernal was practically in our backyard, wasn't it?

"We can watch it happening," she said. "We'll camp. Sleep under the Milky Way."

It was unlike her.

No. It was like her, but more so.

Mother drove Christine and me to Vernal in the green pickup. The first hour we were there, we spotted a diamondback rattlesnake. It lay stretched like a textured hose between two sagebrush clumps. After that, none of us dared to sleep on the ground, so we spread our bags in the bed of the truck, nesting together like three spoons. We listened to the coyotes and decided Mother was the soup spoon, I the teaspoon, and my sister the little spoon that Aunt Betty brought back from Sweden.

THE PORCH

Eleven years later, on the last day of December, we stood on the porch of my house in Sandpoint, Idaho—my mother in her gray wool coat, my brother in his leather jacket, me with hair still wet from the shower. Karl and Mother were heading back to Utah after spending Christmas with us in Idaho. In the driveway, my husband chipped ice off the windshield with a scraper. Our two kids stood inside, watching us through the window, barely tall enough to see over the sill.

I wasn't ready for this Christmas visit to be over. Things weren't finished.

It was too cold, too bitter cold. I felt my bangs freezing into stiff icicles on my forehead. The radio had dubbed the storm the Polar Express. Mother was way too skinny and she was constantly cold. She hated wind. At her house in Utah she sat under the electric blanket we had given her a few Christmases before. She watched TV or, more often, she sat and stared.

"Let's get Connie out of this wind," my husband, Tom, said. The porch was icy; the step was too high. The wind could have blown her over she was so light, so breakable. I helped her into the car and closed the door against the storm. I felt as though I should have carried her.

Tom knew I was scared to drive icy roads. He had taken the morning off work to drive us to Spokane's airport, eighty miles from Sandpoint. All morning, he'd been listening to the radio and reading the paper in the other room, coming into the kitchen to refill his coffee.

"It's nuts to go down there, Karl," he told my brother. "It's emergency travel only."

Karl's voice was faint. My opera-singing brother. He didn't seem to have enough energy to talk louder than a murmur. "I have to work tomorrow. I've already taken three extra days off."

Tom's voice was loud, as if that would urge Karl to speak up. "I seriously doubt any flights will go out."

My brother, who had been silent all week, unlaughing, untalkative, staring like our mother at the little fire in our woodstove's window, became insistent. "But we'll be in Spokane, ready to catch a flight out."

I didn't want anything to thwart my brother, to come up against him when there was so little of him there. Throughout that visit he had scared me. We were all used to it with Mother, but not Karl like this.

Mother and Karl's luggage was loaded in the back of the Suburban. We would sit in the car, all of us, Mother in the front near the heater, the kids in the very back with their pillows. There would be more time together and no distractions. Tom would help us talk, practical Tom. We could talk about the money.

The two men stood on the porch, both determined.

"They'll have the roads cleared by now," I said.

"That's not the point," Tom told me. "With this wind chill, if anything happens, it's serious."

"I have to go today," Karl said.

Tom looked at me, and I felt blamed for the trouble my family was causing. "You need to stay home with the kids," he said. "No point of us all dying."

Now, looking back, I would have braved the slick roads and driven them to Spokane. "You can stay here then," I would have told Tom.

I climbed into the back seat and reached for my mother, clumsy and stiff with the front seat between us. Her shoulder bones, I could feel them beneath the wool coat.

I said goodbye. I'm pretty sure I said I love you.

Here are her last words to me. "You know I hate living like this, Karen."

At the time, I thought I could write her a letter about Karl, about his depression, and how it had nothing to do with her and the money. They were so breakable, my two family members, twins in their depression. I wasn't done with them this visit and they were gone, but I'd been worried and nervous every minute of their visit. Walking back into our warm house, seeing the Christmas angel chimes on the table, and stooping down to hug the kids, my life felt lighter, as though a switch clicked back to normal.

When he got back home again, Tom told me they didn't talk all the way to the airport. He had listened to the radio and they'd been silent. Neither Karl nor Mother said a word. Tom was used to that by then.

ALL WILD ORANGE

Start with the flare. The explosion. Picture it from the street where my mother lived and where I had grown up, Sixth East. The second day of January just past midnight. So cold there are stars. The night quiet as the snow that covers the yards. Very few cars drive down Sixth East in that small Utah town so late on a winter night.

Start with a person I don't know. I haven't lived in Brigham City for thirty years. Still, the same neighbors are there. The Pearses, the Merrells, and our vet, Jim Simper. If it had been somebody we knew, that name would be in the story.

No, it was told that a person driving down Sixth East saw the sudden flash when our house blew up.

This is what happens when a building burns down: heat inside builds to an impossible point and then the windows blast. That's when you get flames. Until then, it's been a dirty secret, just smoke and heat smoldering like a cancer. Then *blammo*—all the panes in the front window, the two corner windows in the kitchen, the dining room window, and the wall of windows in the back. Glass blasts out under the porch roof and the awnings; a thousand shards slash the quiet blanket of snow.

It's all wild orange. A bonfire as big as that house where I grew up. A fiery rage.

When spring came, deep and muddy ruts showed in the front lawn where fire trucks had broken through the frozen ground. They crushed the underground sprinkling system my mother had finally put in that last summer of the house. I'm glad I didn't see it in the spring, the dark slashes in the greening grass and the wreck of the house. It was easier to see in January snow, cleaner, just black against white with a blue sky overhead.

After the fire, the night clouded over and new snow fell, a white shroud over the smoking rubble. By morning there were no tracks,

not even in the drive. But I can picture the ambulance in
our driveway like an ordinary visitor. Yellow-orange lights blinking
against the garage door. The firefighters found her in the back
hallway near the green cupboards where we stored the canned
peaches and dills, the pears, the bread and butter pickles,
and quart jars of applesauce. A gurney under the breezeway and
my mother so light, the men must have commented.

She's no heavier than a child, one might have said. It became part
of the story, how little she weighed.

No heavier than dust, she was thin bones and old skin. Her brown
eyes saw perfectly, her ears were keen as a fox's. We'd coaxed her
to eat, but she'd been living on milk.

"She wasn't burned up," my brother said. "Just singed." He said the
doctor assured him that smoke inhalation is nearly painless.

I think about the edges of pirate maps. I cannot put my mother
with that verb, *to singe*.

The late-night driver who called the alarm is a stranger. I think it
is a man, a person who works late and drove down our street on
his way home every night, admiring the quiet old house on the
corner of Beecher and Sixth.

My dad was smart after the fire. We thought he'd been diluted
like ice melt in the bottom of a glass, sloshed like half-full
bourbon bottles that rolled out from under the front seats of the
cars he drove over the years: the work trucks and station wagons,
the Oldsmobile and the El Camino. Someone called him with the
news that wild orange night, and he phoned Darryl and Norris
first thing the next morning. They had worked for Seashore's sheet
metal shop for more than twenty years.

"Can you get a crew to go board up the windows?" my dad asked
them. And he was right. The sheets of plywood made it dark in
that black house but it kept the neighbor kids away. It was like a

cave and bitter cold, but my brother and sister and I could work in there, feel private in our house that was now a grave.

How were we going to go on without her? The house was gone too, forever. Neither she nor the house there to take us in. She was crazy and we loved her. We were crazy with love for her.

It had been a house full of light. Morning sun flooded the TV-room windows, lacing its gleams through the weeping willow. That was the spot to be if you woke up early. I never did. I lay in my bed hating the sound of my little brother at the piano. He practiced before school, moving through the red, the purple, the black covers of the John Thompson piano books. From *Three Blind Mice* to *Lilac Serenade*, on up to Chopin's preludes. I couldn't stand how he forgot the same D flat, how he did it again and again. Four flats, I wanted to shout through the blue wall of my bedroom. B-E-A-D. Can't you read?

Daddy asked my brother to do something about the pipes that ran through the house's concrete slab, our enviable heating system, the warm floors we grew up on.

"You have to get those pipes drained," he told Karl after the fire. Our father had bought that house forty years before and moved out ten years before the fire.

In north Idaho, the Polar Express was still raging, dumping enough snow to shut down the airport. It was rush like hell to make reservations and get out of Sandpoint and then wait in Spokane. I called my brother from the tree of phones of Concourse B.

"All Eric can think about is the fucking pipes," my brother said.

"He rants about the furnace and Mother is dead."

"I'm trying to get there," I told him. I stared at empty coffee cups on the carpet. The airport was hot, with the smell of passengers marooned overnight. A barefoot man strummed his guitar. It was like a hootenanny or Woodstock, but our mother was dead.

I worried about the pipes, too, but I stayed quiet with my brother on the phone. All he could see was the fire, the house, our mother's body in the ER, and the nurse pulling off her ring, dropping it in his palm.

AFTER THE FIRE

I am wrapping the butterfly plates in pages of the *Salt Lake Tribune*. After my mother's dad died in 1947, my parents drove back to her family home in Kansas City and sold what they could of its furnishings. They shipped the things left over, these dainty plates among them, to Utah by train. The butterfly plates survived when the train derailed on the way. Now they have escaped a fire.

Everything stinks of water-soaked burn, a stench that never completely goes away. How can my mother be dead and this evidence of her everyday life be in my hands, her shaky *t*'s, *a*'s, and *g*'s that fill the tiny boxes of the crossword puzzles in newspapers I fold around the plates? My sister stands on a footstool, lifting eighty-year-old wine glasses down from the highest shelf. In a fire that destroyed the roof, torched the couch upholstery, and melted the telephone, the dishes inside the kitchen cupboards are browned but not broken. My brother wanders through the rooms, bending to look inside her purse that sits next to a chair. Its contents, even her pack of Kents, have withstood the flames.

Our frozen feet drive us out of the house and into my brother's car where we blast the heater and think we'll never be warm again. We want to stay inside this warm car and drive up the canyon away from the cold, burnt work we are doing. We want. We want it back the way it was. I have to pee; all the plumbing is frozen in our destroyed house. So we only drive as far as the Peach City Drive-In. The smell of char follows us in.

THE EPICENTER

Was it an accident? I see her in the chair in the dark room, hugging her knees to her chest with one arm. Maybe the backyard lights were on, and she watched the dance of snow through the bank of windows in the back of the house. Maybe there was only the glow of her cigarette. In the red wingback chair, the same chair where she had braided three endless strips of wool into a rug while we watched *I Love Lucy* and *Leave It to Beaver*, *Bonanza*, and *Laugh In*, she sat thinking, uncaring about her life.

Did the cigarette drop from her lethargy? Did she pretend she hadn't noticed; did she reach down for it; slide her hand between her hip and the chair's arm? Did she let her hand lie there, her pulse running through the forked blue veins?

The fire chief said it began in the chair. He called it the epicenter. Between two and four in the morning. She had been in her bedroom, probably in bed for the night, but she stepped out into the hallway and collapsed there.

I don't know how the firemen determined that red chair as the spot. . . . to me the ruin was the same through the TV room, the dining room, and the living room. My brother wanted it to be her electric blanket that shorted. He didn't want it written in that Mormon town's newspaper that smoking had killed her.

My sister wondered if it was a final, brave act to end a life our mother didn't consider worth living. I had thought about that too and discarded the idea of suicide because I knew she would never risk hurting another human with her act. We didn't mention our thoughts to Karl.

Did I kill her? I'd had the tools in my hand to help her and I didn't use them. I never got back to my mother after she asked me if Karl was brooding because the floundering business had to support her. Every time I started to talk to him, he scared me with his silence. When I finally asked, he said the retirement account was taking care of the alimony and it wasn't a problem. But I didn't get a chance to tell her. I thought my brother was the one I had to protect. I was looking the wrong way.

OUR ANSONIA

The clock still runs that my mother gave us, one of the wedding
presents she gathered that summer while on the longest road
trip of her mania. She picked it up at an antique shop in Palmyra,
New York, where she used to visit her cousins in the thirties.
An Ansonia with a tinny chime that I didn't like. That's how it
was. When she was up I distrusted all her instincts. The things she
bought annoyed me, the stories she never stopped telling, her
long caftans and the candles in wine bottles lined up across
the living room carpet. She never slept; she would never
stop talking.

Twenty-four years later, I love that pretty clock. Persnickety as the
princess and her pea, it won't run unless it's perfectly level. The
pendulum stalls even though it's sitting in the exact same position
on top of the piano. Maybe my husband rotated it a hair's width
when he wound it.

Now I like the chime, perky and light. Not heavy and somber,
damped like a grandfather. Now I love my mother's manic
poems, my incomplete memories of her stories, the pictures of her
gray hair grown long and pulled up into a French twist, her
manic idea of how she wanted to look. In this part of my life I
can love those times, know it was her spirit bursting out of
tiny holes, broken up like spray and flying out of her thick and
careful shell.

But she's gone, and I couldn't tell her the good parts even if she
were alive. Mentioning her manias was like slapping or striking
her. She was so ashamed.

VULTURES' WINGS

I feel the itchy push of vultures' wings trying to jut out of my shoulder blades. Why do I want to chronicle my mother's mysterious life, to open her up for strangers to look at? What is this fear of craziness, this way my palms are wet, my fingers slippery on the pen? I plumb her madness, investigate it with a warped magnifying glass. I am so much like her that I think the clues could lie inside myself.

The City Dump and the Truth about Fire

William Studebaker

The year is 1959. In the summer, the foothills around Salmon,
Idaho, are brown. The gray sagebrush gives way to the ripe
glow of Idaho fescue, crested wheat, and an array of short stocky
grasses. The patches of greasewood that grow along the edges
of crusted bentonite mounds are a black accent between the fields
of sage and the bentonite's milky turquoise. The chrysolite-green
prawns of the prickly pear cactus are slightly shriveled. The
animals are affected by summer's heat, too. The scorpion
has burrowed under an old board. The jackrabbit has retrofitted
a gopher hole. The coyote has scratched out a circle in a bit
of dust under a rock ledge, and the rattlesnake has stopped its
crawling to shade up under a thick sagebrush.

Northeast of Salmon, at the end of North St. Charles street, the
pavement ends and a dusty dirt road twists up and over a nearby
foothill. This is the Dump Road, decorated with the shimmer of
heat waves. At the end of the road, where it splays into a half-dozen
jeep tracks, the "city folk" dump their garbage in the dry ravine.

The loads and loads of debris are forming a slow-moving alluvial
of refuse. After decades, the gully would be full from top to
bottom if it were not for the constant smolder of a fire. No one
knows by whom or when the fire was set. It has always been there,

doing its work, slowly reducing a mountain of garbage to grimy slick soot. This strange brew of ash and malleable paste slumps from time to time, and the whole pile of tar paper, newspaper, tree limbs, lawn grass, cans, bottles, car seats, sofas, an assortment of dimensional lumber, and things hidden—hidden in gunny sacks, cardboard boxes, wooden crates, and wraps of canvas— shrinks, and the fire creeps up into new layers of fuel.

Flames are seldom seen. But on occasion, through a fissure formed around an old car body, the heat is so intense that flames sprout and spread across the surface. They lap up the easy stuff—the paper, the wood chips, the horsehair stuffing in the car seats and couches. If there's wind, the flowing fire is pushed along with a crackle. Once the light flammable fuel is consumed, the flames fade, and the black smoke of the smoldering fire humps into the air.

The city dump smoke can be seen throughout the valley. As one drives down State Highway 28 through the long finger of the high desert formed by Birch Creek and the Lemhi River, this column of smoke, aptly positioned just above the confluence of the Lemhi and the Salmon River, signals the location of Salmon and the turn north along the River of No Return.

The folks in Salmon don't worry about the dump. They worry about forest fires. Forest fires consume valuable pine and fir trees. They are the raw resources that feed the sawmills and locals' pockets with hard cash. Forest fires fill the valley with smoke. Sometimes the smoke is so thick folks can't see from one end of the six-block Main Street to the other. They worry about their sons practicing high-school football as they run and pound, taking those deep breaths the out-of-shape take at the beginning of the season. And they worry about their grandmas and grandpas. This smoke might be the death of them. They might asphyxiate, their old lungs too weak to sort oxygen from toxins.

The fires in the mountains are nothing to scoff at, so the U.S. Forest Service rallies all available men, eighteen years and older and a few seventeen year olds who can fake their age so they can

cash in on seasonal work. A few weeks on a forest fire will earn
them more money than they can make working several months at
the mill. Forest fires, in one sense eliminate wood and work, and
in another, create it. It's a paradox.

This was my world before I left Salmon at the age of eighteen. I
left to attend Idaho State University, the University of Idaho, and
a string of other colleges. By the time my enthusiasm for college
was extinguished, fire was no longer used as a cleansing agent at
the local dumps, and forest fires were being fought with the fury
of a professional army.

Now refuse disposal areas are huge pits lined with a nonabsorbent
sheet of miracle plastic. The pits are filled, and as they are, the
refuse is compacted and covered with a ten-foot layer of dirt.
Under the dirt, bacteria starts decay, and decay makes its own fire
as it digests the organic garbage. Residents are discouraged from
using burn barrels or igniting trash piles. Leaves and twigs are
hauled to compost heaps maintained by cities and counties. All
this activity is based on current wisdom: fire makes smoke, a
pollutant greater than a bacterial brew.

In the forests, fire signals a danger greater than the consumption
of a few mill logs. It is the message that Beauty is being destroyed.
Now the hills and mountains are not the harbors of endless
natural resources but the haven of Nature's crowning
glory: ponderosa, fir, and redwood. The army of firefighters
comes in platoons to extinguish the flames and mop up the last
ember. They are aided by airplanes. Bombers carry a slurry
of water and bentonite, and helicopters and cargo planes carry
Hotshot crews and smokejumpers. Nature's fires are Beauty's
enemy, and they will be contained and destroyed.

Such is my experience with local fire and fire control. It was and is
simple. Fire is an element that must be controlled. Like water,
wind, and earth, it *will* succumb to our will. So the popular

wisdom goes, but my education confused my certainty. During my studies in literature and mythology, fire took on the air of magic. It isn't so mundane any longer. I'm haunted and inspired by imagery of men and women being purified and tested through trials by fire.

After creating a perfect man, a man made purely of thought to carry on his work, the old magician stepped into a ring of fire and was not burned. It cleansed him. It transmuted him—body and soul—as a thought into thin air. This really happened . . . in Jorge Luis Borges' story "The Circular Ruins."

The power of fire fascinates. Its form mesmerizes, and hypnotic ribbons undulate up into the heavens conjuring smoke, the essence of the burned. Unlike Borges' new magician, mortals burn. Mortals have come to know fire's sobriety and its pleasure. It is one of the ancient elements manipulated by degree.

The famous library at Alexandria, Egypt, which had been founded by the Ptolemies, contained between 500,000 and 700,000 papyrus scrolls, the sum of the ancient world's scholarship, which the erudite came to scrutinize until, in 47 B.C., Julius Caesar set fire to the library and museum. More was lost by the flames of passion— his desire for Cleopatra. No matter, subsequent oppressors of Egypt shrewdly torched the remains of the voluminous collection until it was all ash. With the last ember, essentially all of the knowledge and art of Alexandria's library released its substantive knowledge, and the intellectual essence of the Occidental world went up in smoke. Ashes darkened the future, spread by the circular winds of transmutation, and Phoenix, the imagination, had to rebuild itself out of itself—a job that took more than the mythical 500 years. It took nearly 1,500 years.

Fire seduces the ignorant and the righteous power-mad warrior. But it is also the gift of the gods. It is the flaming sword of the Christian god. It is the energy by which Hephaestus worked his magic. It is the fire in the wind-road that fills the sails of a Viking's ship as he is transported to Valhalla. It is what led

Diogenes in his search for an honest man. It is Apollo's chariot pulled each morning by a team of wild, white horses across the sky. It is why Zeus could not defeat us. It is why Prometheus was bound. According to Anne M. Smith's collection of *Shoshone Tales*, it is what Coyote brought to the Shoshone people releasing them from a cold and dark world.

> *There were four animals and Coyote was the chief. There was Porcupine, Stink Bug, and Pack Rat. These four decided they would have a meeting and gather their people together and tell them that they were going south to get fire from the people down there who had fire. They said they were cold and needed fire in their land.*

These four tricksters take off on their journey, and when they find the people, the people are having a party, and the main attraction is the dance. Porcupine, Stink Bug, Pack Rat, and Coyote disguise themselves and mingle with the people, dancing with the young girls, who are very curious about them. By various shenanigans, Coyote gets near the fire and his hair is set ablaze. The four proceed to run off. The people chase them, and Porcupine, Stink Bug, and Coyote are killed. Before Coyote is killed, he passes an ember to Pack Rat.

> *Pack Rat carried the fire under his belly and kept on running. It was a charcoal he was carrying. He ran toward his nest. When he was almost there . . . he jumped up toward the cliff. He was going to divide up the fire. He put some fire in his nest and then he put fire in all the different directions—that is why all the wood burns. That is how they got fire to keep people warm.*
> [That is, the Shoshone people for whom the tricksters are totemic animals and shape shifters. In Shoshone tales, the Shoshone portray themselves as separate from all other people.]
> *From now on all wood will burn.*

Cleverly, the Shoshone credit themselves with spreading fire and for giving it to all people and for providing fuel to keep it burning. Also, the four adventurers become heroes (Stink Bug,

Porcupine, and Coyote come back to life.) They survive the first
trial by fire.

In the folk, mythical, and religious literature of the world, trials by
fire are commonplace. At the end of Aubrey Menen's version of
the *Ramayana*, when Rama's wife, Sita, is challenged to prove her
faithfulness to Rama, the warrior king, and Vishnu, the lord god,
the citizens want her put on a pyre of wood. If she burns, she is
unfaithful, and if she does not burn, it proves that she is faithful
to Rama. When Rama asks if this can be done, a magician, an
astrologist, says yes, by a fire called an Egyptian fire.

> *Sita was dressed in white and surrounded by weeping ladies-in-
> waiting. Bowing to Rama, she stood in prayer for a moment. Then
> she mounted the pyre amidst lower levels of the wood, which
> blazed instantly. Sita now began to walk slowly through the narrow
> corridor, and this burst into a furious flame and smoke of the most
> vivid colors. She was immediately lost to sight.*

> *Then, after a considerable interval, Sita emerged, soiled in places
> by soot, but otherwise unharmed. As the citizens caught their
> breath, white doves descended out of the sky and flew around Sita's
> head.*

I have college to blame for my appetite for mingling mysticism,
magic, and myth with experience and common sense. On one
hand, I see the fire beneath the heaps of garbage as cleansing, as
the transmutation of our excesses, and I see it as the light of
wisdom, the Golden Branch that leads us through darkness. On
the other hand, I see smoke as a pollutant rising up in ugly
toxic columns. And yes, fire destroys *our* wildernesses. It is the
torment in hell.

The long Lemhi valley is no longer distinguished by the smoke
signaling the confluence of two rivers and the northerly turn
toward the Continental Divide. Roads have been made farther
into the foothills, pits have been dug and lined, and garbage is
being compacted, made ready for the layer of earth. When the

smoke from a summer forest fire turns the valley air into a thick brown haze, the folks cheer on the convoy of buses carrying firefighters as they pass through town.

Sometimes in the bewitching heat of midsummer, I walk from Main to the end of North St. Charles and up the Dump Road to wander in the foothills above Salmon. As I amble along, I often recall my childhood and the smoldering alluvial of garbage. Is it charming because I knew no ecological laws and because I knew nothing of trial by fire? How could I have been so enchanted? Is it really this simple: fire is insight, the source of truth and goodness, and fire is ignorance, the source of destruction and evil, as it was at the city dump atop the black paste of flammability? All I can finally say is that contradiction governs fire in every degree.

Contributors

HOLLY A. AKENSON has lived at Taylor Ranch for fourteen years managing the University of Idaho's field station with her husband, Jim. In the heart of the Frank Church–River of No Return Wilderness and thirty-two miles from the nearest road in summer, Taylor Ranch Field Station is the most remote year-round residence in the lower forty-eight states. Holly and her husband were attracted to this backcountry lifestyle that gave them an opportunity to live close to nature while they worked to develop the research and education potential of the wilderness research station. Holly has a master's degree in wildlife biology from University of Idaho, and most recently has been studying the effects of wolf reintroduction on cougars and their prey—the elk, deer, bighorn sheep, and moose.

HORACE AXTELL AND MARGO ARAGON first met in 1992 when she interviewed him for her award-winning video documentary, *Nee-mee-poo: The Power of Our Dance.* Their collaborative book is entitled *A Little Bit of Wisdom: Conversations with a Nez Perce Elder.* Margo earned her undergraduate degree in English from Lewis-Clark State College and her M.F.A. in Creative Writing from Bennington College in Vermont. Both she and Horace are dedicated to the preservation of Nez Perce language and culture. In addition to studying the language, Margo hosts a bilingual television talk show. Horace lectures all over the world and has twice been one of the subjects of documentary films produced by the British Broadcasting Corporation. He teaches Nez Perce language at Lewis-Clark State College and assists with the Nez Perce Tribal Wolf Education and Research Center.

KIM BARNES is the author of two memoirs, *In the Wilderness* and *Hungry for the World*, as well as a novel, *Finding Caruso*. She co-edited *Circle of Women* with Mary Clearman Blew. She teaches creative writing at the University of Idaho and lives with her husband, the poet Robert Wrigley, and their children outside of Moscow, Idaho. "The Ashes of August" received a 2002 Pushcart Prize.

PETER CHILSON teaches creative writing at Washington State University. He is the author of *Riding the Demon: On the Road in West Africa*. His essays, journalism, and short stories have appeared in *The American Scholar, Ascent, The North American Review, Audubon Magazine, Gulf Coast, The Clackamas Review,* and *Best American Travel Writing*.

PAULA COOMER, a native of Kentucky, was raised in southern Indiana, emigrated to the Western United States in 1977, and is the mother of two college-age sons. Formerly a public health nurse and commissioned officer with the U.S. Public Health Service, from 1991–1996, she worked to develop public health programs on the Nez Perce and Coeur d'Alene Indian reservations of Idaho. She now teaches creative writing at Washington State University. Her fiction, poetry, and nonfiction have appeared in various journals and anthologies, most recently *Ascent, Voices on the Wind, Talking River Review,* and the upcoming anthology from Two Girls Press: *Northwest Edge II: Fictions of Mass Destruction*.

JENNY EMERY DAVIDSON was a member of a Bureau of Land Management wildland fire crew based out of Shoshone, Idaho, from 1992–1996. Since then, she has worked in journalism and pursued a doctorate degree in American studies from the University of Utah. Currently, she teaches composition at the College of Southern Idaho. She lives near Picabo, Idaho, with her husband, Mark.

CLAIRE DAVIS's work has been published in numerous literary journals, including the *Gettysburg Review, Southern Review,* and *Shenandoah.* Her short fiction has been included in the Pushcart Best of the Small Presses Anthology as well as Best American Short Stories. Her first novel, *Winter Range,* received the MPNA and PNBA awards for fiction. Her second novel, *Skin of the Snake,* and her collection of short stories *Labors of the Heart* are forthcoming. She lives in Lewiston, Idaho, where she teaches creative writing at Lewis-Clark State College.

PHIL DRUKER teaches writing at the University of Idaho and writes occasional columns for the *Lewiston Morning Tribune*'s Outdoor Page. An avid hiker, skier, and mountaineer, he usually spends his summers in the backcountry of the Northwest or Alaska, but because his wife is working in Bangladesh, he has spent recent summers in South Asia.

SUSAN GLAVE is an Idaho native. She is a graduate of Boise State University with a BA in English/Writing. She is a three-time recipient of the Wallace G. Kay Writing Award and the winner of Sigma Tau Delta's 2002 Best Personal Essay presented at a national convention. She has served as editorial assistant for the Boise State University Western Writers Series. Her work has appeared in *Cold Drill* and *Standing: Poetry by Idaho Women.* She lives on an acreage south of Boise with her husband, two geriatric Arabian horses, a tribe of terriers, and one outspoken cockatoo.

DIANNE IVERGLYNNE lives in Hagerman, Idaho. She earns her living making pottery, teaching primitive skills, and serving photographic archives throughout Idaho as a photographic conservation scientist. Phi Theta Kappa honored DiAnne with two International Hallmark Awards, Literature and Visual Arts, while she was a student attending the College of Southern Idaho in 1993. She holds a MFA in Fine Art Photography from Rochester Institute of Technology, in Rochester, New York, and is a graduate of the George Eastman House International Museum of Photography and Film in Photographic Preservation and Archive Practices.

ROBERT COKER JOHNSON lives and works in Lewiston. "What I Know of Fire" received *The Gettysburg Review* Award for Non, Fiction Prose in 1995.

WILLIAM JOHNSON teaches at Lewis-Clark State College in Lewiston, Idaho. The University of Idaho Press published his critical study, *What Thoreau Said*, in 1991, and Confluence Press has published two collections of his poetry, *At the Wilderness Boundary* (1996) and *Out of the Ruins*, which won the Idaho Book Award for 2000. Johnson has won fellowships from Fishtrap, the Environmental Writing Institute, the Idaho Humanities Council, and the Idaho Commission on the Arts. He served as Idaho Writer in Residence from 1998–2001.

JEFF P. JONES's writing has won several awards. He studies creative writing at the University of Idaho, where he is an editor of the literary journal *Fugue*.

STEVE KOEHLER is a computer lab and special education language instructor at Wendell Elementary School. He is a scholar for the Idaho Humanities Council Speakers Bureau who has published in *The Saturday Evening Post, Grit, Boys' Life*, and *Cicada*. An award-winning newspaper correspondent, fiction writer, photographer, and geologist, he lives in Wendell, Idaho.

ROBERT MCCARL literally grew up in firefighting cultures. At age sixteen he joined one of the earliest Hotshot crews in Oregon, spent a number of years running pumper crews in the Eugene area, and for four seasons was a smokejumper out of Redmond, Oregon. McCarl has continued to document and write about the world of urban and wildland firefighters both for professional and academic audiences. He currently is an associate professor of anthropology at Boise State University.

LOIS MELINA is the author of three books on adoption published by HarperCollins, including *Raising Adopted Children*. Her most recent book, *By a Fraction of a Second*, describes the experiences of elite swimmers training for the 2000 Olympics. She currently is working on a memoir exploring the impact of rock n' roll and the feminist movement on four middle-aged women. Melina lives on a domestic elk farm in Moscow, Idaho, with her husband.

LORI MESSENGER conceived twenty-three days after submitting this essay, and on November 12, 2003, gave birth to daughter Freya in their Missoula home. Lori and Scott continue to work for the U.S. Forest Service, and someday, when Lori sleeps more at night, she will make a decision about her future as a smokejumper. For a decade, Lori has been working on a nonfiction book about women wildland firefighters and hopes that someday you can read it.

DIANE JOSEPHY PEAVEY writes about the changing western landscape and her life on the family's southern Idaho sheep and cattle ranch. Her stories air weekly on Idaho Public Radio and appear in her book *Bitterbrush Country: Living on the Edge of the Land.* Her writings are also found in numerous magazines, journals, and anthologies. Among the latter are *Shadow Cat, Written on Water, Woven on the Wind,* and *A Road of Her Own: Women's Journeys in the West.* Diane was the literature director of the Idaho Commission on the Arts from 1992 to 1997 and is the founder of the nationally renowned October Trailing of the Sheep Festival. She lives with her husband, John, on their ranch north of Carey, Idaho.

KAREN SEASHORE'S work has appeared in *Barcelona Review, Fugue,* and *Black Canyon Quarterly.* She lives in Sandpoint, Idaho, with her husband, Tom, and a tortoiseshell cat named Ruby Tuesday.

WILLIAM STUDEBAKER grew up in Salmon, Idaho. He is the author of several collections of poetry. His most recent are *Passions We Desire* and *Travelers in an Antique Land. Short of a Good Promise* is a reminiscence about growing up in Idaho and watching his family's collective lives stall. A newspaper columnist and outdoor feature writer, he and his wife, Judy, live near Twin Falls, Idaho.